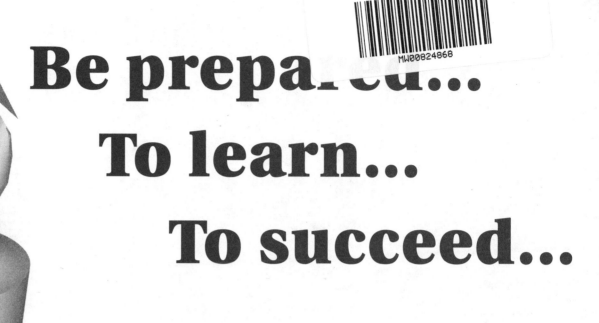

Be prepared...
To learn...
To succeed...

REA's preparation for the Florida Biology 1 EOC
is fully aligned with the Next Generation
Sunshine State Standards.

Visit us at ***www.rea.com***

Ready, Set, Go!®

FLORIDA
End-of-Course Assessment
Biology 1

John Allen

With a foreword by
Laurie P. Callihan, Ph.D.
University Fellow (2009)
Florida State University

 Research & Education Association

The benchmarks presented in this book were created and implemented by the Florida Department of Education (FLDOE). For further information, visit the FLDOE website at *http://fcat.fldoe.org.*

Research & Education Association
61 Ethel Road West
Piscataway, New Jersey 08854
E-mail: info@rea.com

***Ready, Set, Go!*®**
Florida Biology 1 End-of-Course Assessment

Library of Congress Control Number 2013930589

ISBN-13: 978-0-7386-1111-2
ISBN-10: 0-7386-1111-5

Contents

Practice Tests A & B are *also* available online at *www.rea.com/studycenter*

Foreword

The transition to end-of-course assessments (EOCs) in high school courses in Florida has meant a significant change in the way teachers need to prepare their course material.

The Next Generation Sunshine State Standards (NGSSS) form a real and explicit roadmap for the High School Biology course. The Florida Department of Education provides specific item specifications for preparation for the EOC exam. Still, the task of fully preparing students within the short school year for this high-stakes exam is daunting for teachers. In addition, the EOC asks students to do more than memorize information and learn concepts.

The test construction is based on the need for students to develop and demonstrate critical-thinking skills, mastering the ability to work with scientific information as it is presented in various complex ways through varying types of questions. Students need special preparation to deal with these challenges.

Even in the best Florida high school with the best Biology course that follows the NGSSS and the EOC item specifications, students and teachers will benefit greatly from John Allen's *Florida Biology 1 End-of-Course Assessment*. This book provides necessary summary and comprehensive review of the precise item-specification content explicitly marked for inclusion on the EOC. In addition, it provides practice in the type of assessment questions that will specifically prepare students in depth of knowledge and complexity to mirror what they can expect on the Biology EOC.

This book is of essential value for classroom use as an auxiliary preparatory resource and, quite frankly, to provide students an extra edge on test day. Moreover, I strongly recommend *Florida Biology 1 End-of-Course Assessment* as a resource companion to keep handy throughout the high school Biology course.

Laurie P. Callihan, Ph.D., Florida STEM Educator and Researcher

About Our Author

John Allen graduated from the University of Oklahoma. As a partner in BBE Associates, Ltd., he has worked in the educational publishing field for more than twenty-five years. He has authored or co-authored many books in the areas of science and mathematics.

About Our Technical Editor

Laurie P. Callihan, Ph.D., is a postdoctoral associate for the Promoting Science among English Language Learners (P-SELL) project in the Steinhardt School of Culture, Education, and Human Development at New York University. Her research areas within science education include policy, diversity, and teacher professional development. She was a 2009 University Fellow of Florida State University for the School of Teacher Education. She has fifteen years of classroom science teaching experience with expertise in diverse classroom settings. Her interests and experiences also include science teacher professional development and work with Florida Department of Education C-Palms (*flstandards.org*). Dr. Callihan has authored a variety of curricula, books, and academic materials in the K–20 science area.

About Research & Education Association

Founded in 1959, Research & Education Association (REA) is dedicated to publishing the finest and most effective educational materials—including study guides and test preps—for students in elementary school, middle school, high school, college, graduate school, and beyond.

Today, REA's wide-ranging catalog is a leading resource for teachers, students, and professionals. Visit *www.rea.com* for a complete listing of all our titles.

Acknowledgments

In addition to our author, we would like to thank Larry B. Kling, Vice President, Editorial, for his overall guidance, which brought this publication to completion; Pam Weston, Publisher, for setting the quality standards for production integrity and managing the publication to completion; Alice Leonard, Senior Editor, for project management; Diane Goldschmidt, Managing Editor, for preflight editorial review; and Kathy Caratozzolo of Caragraphics for typesetting the manuscript.

Introduction

Passing the Florida Biology 1 EOC Test

About This Book

This book, along with REA's true-to-format practice tests, provides you with the most up-to-date preparation for the Florida Biology 1 End-of-Course Assessment. Known simply as the Biology 1 EOC, this computer-based test measures your mastery of biology.

This test prep gives you all the review and practice you need to succeed on exam day. By studying the review and taking our practice tests (either in the book or online), you can pinpoint what you already know and focus on the areas where you need to spend more time studying.

Each of our eight review chapters covers one of the major Biology 1 EOC subject areas and shows you how each area will be tested. Easy-to-follow examples and a step-by-step approach help you build your knowledge and confidence as you study.

Our two full-length practice tests give you the most complete picture of your strengths and weaknesses. After you've finished reviewing with the book, take our practice exams online at the REA Study Center (*www.rea.com/studycenter*). Because the Biology EOC is computer-based, we recommend that you take the practice tests online to simulate test-day conditions. Each online test gives you instant score reports, diagnostic feedback, and on-screen detailed answer explanations.

If you're studying and don't have Internet access, you can take the printed tests in the book. These are the same tests offered at the REA Study Center, but without the added benefits of timed testing conditions and diagnostic score reports.

About the Test

The Florida EOC Assessments are part of Florida's Next Generation Strategic Plan, which is designed to increase student achievement and improve college and career readiness. EOC assessments are computer-based, criterion-referenced assessments that measure specific standards that have been developed for several courses, including Algebra I, Biology I, Geometry, and U.S. History.

How is this test given?

For the majority of students, the EOC assessments are computer-based. Exceptions are made for students with disabilities who need to take EOC assessments on paper.

What is the format of the test?

The Biology 1 EOC assessment is administered via a computer-based test (CBT) platform. Paper-based versions (print and Braille) will be provided for students with disabilities who require allowable accommodations, as specified in their Individual Educational Plans (IEPs) or Section 504 plans.

The Biology 1 EOC assessment is scheduled for a 160-minute session. However, any student not finished by the end of this period may continue working. Testing must be finished on the same school day.

There are multiple forms of the assessment, with a maximum of 66 items on each test form. About six to 10 of the items are experimental (field test) items, and are NOT included in student scores.

You will be provided with the following:

- A four-function calculator in the online TestNav platform

  If students take a practice test and decide they are not comfortable using the online calculator for testing, they may request the use of a hand-held FCAT four-function calculator.

- A Periodic Table of the Elements in the online TestNav platform

  If schools prefer, they may distribute hard copies of the periodic table to students.

- A four-page, hard-copy work folder to use as scratch paper

Who takes this test?

All students enrolled in and completing the following courses take the Biology I EOC:

- Biology 1

- Biology 1 Honors

- Pre-AICE Biology

- Biology Technology

- Biology 1 preIB

- IB Middle Years Program Biology Honors

- Integrated Science 3

- Integrated Science 3 Honors

Preparing for Computerized Testing

Official Practice Test

Prior to taking the Biology 1 EOC Assessment, students are required to participate in a practice-test session at their school in order to become familiar with the testing tools and platform. These are computer-based practice tests, called Electronic Practice Assessment Tools (ePATs). The online computerized practice tests included with this book will give you a valuable head start.

E-Tools for Exam Day

The tools and resources available to you on test day will vary slightly depending on the subject area assessed. All students taking a computer-based assessment will have access to the following e-tools in the computer-based platform:

- **Review:** Students use this e-tool to mark questions to be reviewed at a later time. Before exiting the assessment and submitting their responses, students are taken to a screen that identifies questions that are answered, unanswered, and marked for review.

- **Eliminate Choice:** Students use this tool to mark answer choices that they wish to eliminate.

- **Highlighter:** Students use this tool to highlight sections of the question or passage.

- **Eraser:** Students use the eraser to remove marks made by the highlighter or the eliminate-choice tool.

- **Help:** Students may click the Help icon to learn more about the e-tools. The Help text appears in a separate window.

- **Calculator:** Students are provided access to a scientific calculator, which appears in a pop-up window. They may request the use of a hand-held scientific calculator if they are uncomfortable with the online version.

- **Exhibit:** Students are provided a reference sheet of commonly used formulas and conversions to work the test questions. The reference sheet appears in a pop-up window under the exhibit icon.

- **Directions:** Students are also provided directions for completing fill-in response questions and a diagram and helpful hints for the appropriate calculator under the exhibit icon.

What to Do Before the Test

- **Pay attention in class.**

- **Carefully work through the chapters and problems in this book.** Mark any topics that you find difficult and review them.

- **Take the practice tests and become familiar with the format of the Biology 1 EOC Assessment.** Try to take these tests under simulated conditions — time yourself, stay calm, and pace yourself. Multiple-choice questions should each take about one minute. We make this easy with our online practice tests, which provide a timed, auto-scored experience. (*www.rea.com/studycenter*)

What to Do During the Test

- **Read the questions carefully to make sure you understand what is being asked.** Every word in the question gets you that much closer to the answer.

- **Read all of the possible answers.** Even if you think you have found the correct response, do not automatically assume that it is the best answer. Read through each answer choice to be sure you are not jumping to conclusions.

- **Use the process of elimination in multiple-choice questions.** This is one of the best techniques in answering these types of questions. Try to eliminate those choices that appear obviously incorrect. For each one you can eliminate, you've increased your odds dramatically of answering correctly. If you eliminate two choices, for example, you now have a 50% chance of answering the question correctly.

- **Work on the easier questions first.** If you find yourself working too long on one question, move on to the next question. When you've reached the end of the test, there will be a window on the computer that will pop up and tell you which questions were unanswered so you can go back to them.

- **Be aware of the correct units.** If the question asks for millimeters, make sure you're not selecting an answer choice that looks correct, but is in inches.

- **Answer all of the questions.** You will not be penalized for incorrect answers, so you'll increase your chances of improving your score by guessing. Even one good guess can increase your score by a point.

- *Relax.*

Good luck!

Standards for the Biology 1 EOC Assessment

The test is aligned with Florida's Next Generation Sunshine State Standards. These standards are presented below.

Next Generation Sunshine State Standards

Items for this grouping are placed in the appropriate reporting category based on the content of the item.

Standard 1	The Practice of Science
Molecular and Cellular Biology	
Standard 14	Organization and Development of Living Organisms
Standard 16	Heredity and Reproduction
Standard 18	Matter and Energy Transformations
Organisms, Populations, and Ecosystems	
Standard 14	Organization and Development of Living Organisms
Standard 16	Heredity and Reproduction
Standard 17	Interdependence

(continued)

Classification, Heredity, and Evolution	
Standard 15	Diversity and Evolution of Living Organisms
Standard 16	Heredity and Reproduction

Benchmarks

The following are the specific benchmarks of the Biology 1 EOC Assessment.

Strand A: (The Practice of Science)

SC.912.N.1.1   Define a problem based on a specific body of knowledge, for example: biology, chemistry, physics, and earth/space science, and do the following:

1. pose questions about the natural world;

2. conduct systematic observations;

3. examine books and other sources of information to see what is already known;

4. review what is known in light of empirical evidence;

5. plan investigations;

6. use tools to gather, analyze, and interpret data (this includes the use of measurement in metric and other systems, and also the generation and interpretation of graphical representations of data, including data tables and graphs);

7. pose answers, explanations, or descriptions of events;

8. generate explanations that explicate or describe natural phenomena (inferences);

9. use appropriate evidence and reasoning to justify these explanations to others;

10. communicate results of scientific investigations; and

11. evaluate the merits of the explanations produced by others.

SC.912.N.1.3   Recognize that the strength or usefulness of a scientific claim is evaluated through scientific argumentation, which depends on critical and logical thinking, and the active consideration of alternative scientific explanations to explain the data presented.

SC.912.N.1.4   Identify sources of information and assess their reliability according to the strict standards of scientific investigation.

SC.912.N.1.6   Describe how scientific inferences are drawn from scientific observations and provide examples from the content being studied.

SC.912.N.2.1   Identify what is science, what clearly is not science, and what superficially resembles science (but fails to meet the criteria for science).

SC.912.N.3.1   Explain that a scientific theory is the culmination of many scientific investigations drawing together all the current evidence concerning a substantial range of phenomena; thus, a scientific theory represents the most powerful explanation scientists have to offer.

SC.912.N.3.4   Recognize that theories do not become laws, nor do laws become theories; theories are well-supported explanations and laws are well-supported descriptions.

SC.912.L.14.4   Compare and contrast structure and function of various types of microscopes.

LA.910.2.2.3   The student will organize information to show understanding or relationships among facts, ideas, and events (e.g., representing key points within text through charting, mapping, paraphrasing, summarizing, comparing, contrasting, or outlining).

LA.910.4.2.2   The student will record information and ideas from primary and/or secondary sources accurately and coherently, noting the validity and reliability of these sources and attributing sources of information.

MA.912.S.1.2   Determine appropriate and consistent standards of measurement for the data to be collected in a survey or experiment.

MA.912.S.3.2   Collect, organize, and analyze data sets, determine the best format for the data, and present visual summaries from the following:

- bar graphs;

- line graphs;

- stem and leaf plots;

- circle graphs;

- histograms;

- box and whisker plots;

- scatter plots; and

- cumulative frequency (ogive) graphs.

Strand B: Molecular and Cellular Biology

SC.912.L.14.1   Describe the scientific theory of cells (cell theory) and relate the history of its discovery to the process of science.

SC.912.L.14.2   Relate structure to function for the components of plant and animal cells. Explain the role of cell membranes as a highly selective barrier (passive and active transport).

SC.912.L.14.3   Compare and contrast the general structures of plant and animal cells. Compare and contrast the general structures of prokaryotic and eukaryotic cells.

SC.912.L.16.3   Describe the basic process of DNA replication and how it relates to the transmission and conservation of the genetic information.

SC.912.L.16.4   Explain how mutations in the DNA sequence may or may not result in phenotypic change. Explain how mutations in gametes may result in phenotypic changes in offspring.

SC.912.L.16.5   Explain the basic processes of transcription and translation, and how they result in the expression of genes.

SC.912.L.16.8   Explain the relationship between mutation, cell cycle, and uncontrolled cell growth potentially resulting in cancer.

SC.912.L.16.9   Explain how and why the genetic code is universal and is common to almost all organisms.

SC.912.L.16.14   Describe the cell cycle, including the process of mitosis. Explain the role of mitosis in the formation of new cells and its importance in maintaining chromosome number during asexual reproduction.

SC.912.L.16.16   Describe the process of meiosis, including independent assortment and crossing over. Explain how reduction division results in the formation of haploid gametes or spores.

SC.912.L.16.17   Compare and contrast mitosis and meiosis and relate to the processes of sexual and asexual reproduction and their consequences for genetic variation.

SC.912.L.18.1   Describe the basic molecular structures and primary functions of the four major categories of biological macromolecules.

SC.912.L.18.7   Identify the reactants, products, and basic functions of photosynthesis.

SC.912.L.18.8   Identify the reactants, products, and basic functions of aerobic and anaerobic cellular respiration.

SC.912.L.18.9   Explain the interrelated nature of photosynthesis and cellular respiration.

SC.912.L.18.10   Connect the role of adenosine triphosphate (ATP) to energy transfers within a cell.

SC.912.L.18.11   Explain the role of enzymes as catalysts that lower the activation energy of biochemical reactions. Identify factors, such as pH and temperature, and their effect on enzyme activity.

SC.912.L.18.12   Discuss the special properties of water that contribute to Earth's suitability as an environment for life: cohesive behavior, ability to moderate temperature, expansion upon freezing, and versatility as a solvent.

Strand C: Organisms, Populations, and Ecosystems

SC.912.E.7.1   Analyze the movement of matter and energy through the different biogeochemical cycles, including water and carbon.

SC.912.L.14.7   Relate the structure of each of the major plant organs and tissues to physiological processes.

SC.912.L.14.26   Identify the major parts of the brain on diagrams or models.

SC.912.L.14.36   Describe the factors affecting blood flow through the cardiovascular system.

SC.912.L.14.52   Explain the basic functions of the human immune system, including specific and nonspecific immune response, vaccines, and antibiotics.

SC.912.L.14.6   Explain the significance of genetic factors, environmental factors, and pathogenic agents to health from the perspectives of both individual and public health.

SC.912.L.16.10   Evaluate the impact of biotechnology on the individual, society and the environment, including medical and ethical issues.

SC.912.L.16.13   Describe the basic anatomy and physiology of the human reproductive system. Describe the process of human development from fertilization to birth and major changes that occur in each trimester of pregnancy.

SC.912.L.17.2   Explain the general distribution of life in aquatic systems as a function of chemistry, geography, light, depth, salinity, and temperature.

SC.912.L.17.4   Describe changes in ecosystems resulting from seasonal variations, climate change, and succession.

SC.912.L.17.5   Analyze how population size is determined by births, deaths, immigration, emigration, and limiting factors (biotic and abiotic) that determine carrying capacity.

SC.912.L.17.8   Recognize the consequences of the losses of biodiversity due to catastrophic events, climate changes, human activity, and the introduction of invasive, non-native species.

SC.912.L.17.9   Use a food web to identify and distinguish producers, consumers, and decomposers. Explain the pathway of energy transfer through trophic levels and the reduction of available energy at successive trophic levels.

SC.912.L.17.11   Evaluate the costs and benefits of renewable and nonrenewable resources, such as water, energy, fossil fuels, wildlife, and forests.

SC.912.L.17.13   Discuss the need for adequate monitoring of environmental parameters when making policy decisions.

SC.912.L.17.20 Predict the impact of individuals on environmental systems and examine how human lifestyles affect sustainability.

HE.912.C.1.3 Evaluate how environment and personal health are interrelated.

HE.912.C.1.4 Analyze how heredity and family history can impact personal health.

HE.912.C.1.8 Analyze strategies for prevention, detection, and treatment of communicable and chronic diseases.

Strand D: Classification, Heredity, and Evolution

SC.912.L.15.1 Explain how the scientific theory of evolution is supported by the fossil record, comparative anatomy, comparative embryology, biogeography, molecular biology, and observed evolutionary change.

SC.912.L.15.4 Describe how and why organisms are hierarchically classified and based on evolutionary relationships.

SC.912.L.15.5 Explain the reasons for changes in how organisms are classified.

SC.912.L.15.6 Discuss distinguishing characteristics of the domains and kingdoms of living organisms.

SC.912.L.15.8 Describe the scientific explanations of the origin of life on Earth.

SC.912.L.15.10 Identify basic trends in hominid evolution from early ancestors six million years ago to modern humans, including brain size, jaw size, language, and manufacture of tools.

SC.912.L.15.13 Describe the conditions required for natural selection, including: overproduction of offspring, inherited variation, and the struggle to survive, which result in differential reproductive success.

SC.912.L.15.14 Discuss mechanisms of evolutionary change other than natural selection such as genetic drift and gene flow.

SC.912.L.15.15 Describe how mutation and genetic recombination increase genetic variation.

SC.912.L.16.1   Use Mendel's laws of segregation and independent assortment to analyze patterns of inheritance.

SC.912.L.16.2   Discuss observed inheritance patterns caused by various modes of inheritance, including dominant, recessive, codominant, sex-linked, polygenic, and multiple alleles.

Chapter 1

The Practice of Science

Your Goals for Chapter 1

1. You should be able to design and/or evaluate a scientific investigation using evidence of scientific thinking and/or problem solving.

2. You should be able to interpret and analyze data to make predictions and/or defend conclusions.

3. You should be able to compare and/or contrast the structure and function of the compound microscope, dissecting microscope, scanning electron microscope, and/or the transmission electron microscope.

4. You should be able to evaluate the merits of scientific explanations produced by others.

5. You should be able to assess the reliability of sources of information according to scientific standards.

6. You should be able to describe how scientific inferences are made from observations and identify examples from biology.

Standards

The following standards are assessed on the Florida Biology 1 End-of-Course Assessment either directly or indirectly:

SC.912.N.1.1   Define a problem based on a specific body of knowledge, for example: biology, chemistry, physics, and earth/space science, and do the following:

      1. pose questions about the natural world;

      2. conduct systematic observations;

3. examine books and other sources of information to see what is already known;

4. review what is known in light of empirical evidence;

5. plan investigations;

6. use tools to gather, analyze, and interpret data (this includes the use of measurement in metric and other systems, and also the generation and interpretation of graphical representations of data, including data tables and graphs);

7. pose answers, explanations, or descriptions of events;

8. generate explanations that explicate or describe natural phenomena (inferences);

9. use appropriate evidence and reasoning to justify these explanations to others;

10. communicate results of scientific investigations; and

11. evaluate the merits of the explanations produced by others.

SC.912.N.1.4 Identify sources of information and assess their reliability according to the strict standards of scientific investigation.

SC.912.N.1.6 Describe how scientific inferences are drawn from scientific observations and provide examples from the content being studied.

SC.912.L.14.4 Compare and contrast structure and function of various types of microscopes.

LA.910.2.2.3 The student will organize information to show understanding or relationships among facts, ideas, and events (e.g., representing key points within text through charting, mapping, paraphrasing, summarizing, comparing, contrasting, or outlining).

LA.910.4.2.2   The student will record information and ideas from primary and/or secondary sources accurately and coherently, noting the validity and reliability of these sources and attributing sources of information.

MA.912.S.1.2   Determine appropriate and consistent standards of measurement for the data to be collected in a survey or experiment.

MA.912.S.3.2   Collect, organize, and analyze data sets, determine the best format for the data, and present visual summaries from the following:

- bar graphs;

- line graphs;

- stem and leaf plots;

- circle graphs;

- histograms;

- box and whisker plots;

- scatter plots; and

- cumulative frequency (ogive) graphs.

Note to Students

The Nature of Science is a key foundational principle on the Florida Biology 1 EOC assessment. The benchmarks in this chapter are assessed as embedded within other benchmarks throughout the book. They serve as important information to be held in mind, and will be tested with other content. For example, Benchmark SC.912.L.15.6, "Discuss distinguishing characteristics of the domains and kingdoms of living organisms," also assesses SC.912.N.1.3, "Recognize that the strength or usefulness of a scientific claim is evaluated through scientific argumentation, which depends on critical and logical thinking, and the active consideration of alternative scientific explanations to explain the data presented" (from Chapter 2), and SC.912.N.1.6 "Describe how scientific inferences are drawn from scientific observations and provide examples from the content being studied" (from this chapter). So those last two benchmarks will actually be assessed in Chapter 5's section on classification. Think of the Nature of Science benchmarks as tools that are needed for scientific work of all kinds.

Conducting a Scientific Investigation

A **scientific investigation** is an experiment to test a hypothesis or solve a problem based on a body of scientific knowledge, such as biology, chemistry, or physics. You may be asked questions about planning or evaluating a scientific investigation.

A typical experiment includes the following steps.

1. **Pose a question about the natural world or an area of science.** The question or objective should be clearly worded, specific, and able to be answered with measurable results: "How is the rate of transpiration in a plant affected by conditions such as humidity, light, and wind?"

2. **Make observations related to the question.** Notice how indoor and outdoor plants are affected by water mist, sunlight or artificial light, and wind currents.

3. **Read in primary or secondary sources to see what is already known.** You should know the theory of transpirational pull—that for every molecule of water that evaporates from a leaf, another molecule of water is pulled into the plant through its roots.

4. **Review what is already known about the question.** Examine the empirical evidence, or direct observations, recorded by others. Many websites feature experiments about transpiration.

5. **Plan your investigation.** A classic experiment for transpiration is to insert four bean plant seedlings into four potometers and measure the amount of water use for each of the plants under four different conditions: humidity (misting the plant's leaves), light (shining a lightbulb on the plant), wind (training a fan on the plant), and control (no special conditions). The different conditions are the **independent variable** that is manipulated. The **dependent variable** is the change in the rate of transpiration. It is important for every experiment to have a control, in which the independent variable is set at some standard level. This allows you to determine that the changes are due to the different conditions and not to some other factor.

6. **Use tools to gather, analyze, and interpret data.** For example, you should measure the exact water level in each pipette for certain intervals of time. You might also use graph paper to trace the different-sized leaves and calculate their surface areas for better comparison of water loss.

7. **Describe the results in detail.** For this transpiration experiment, you should observe that increased light and wind also increase transpiration, while increased humidity reduces transpiration.

8. **Explain the results by making inferences.** Use evidence and reasoning to support your findings. Think about how your results translate to conditions in nature.

   - You might infer that when a leaf absorbs more light, a portion of the light energy changes to heat. With increased temperature, the transpiration rate increases.

   - Wind or air movement removes evaporated water from the leaf more quickly. As the air around the leaf becomes less humid and the water potential drops, the transpiration rate increases.

   - As the air around the leaf becomes more humid due to misting, the water potential increases and the transpiration rate decreases.

9. **Write a thorough description of the experiment and its results.** Make sure others can understand your procedures and conclusions.

10. **Compare your results and conclusions to those of others.** Be prepared to discuss the experiment in detail.

Using Microscopes

Experiments in biology often require the use of a microscope. Cells and their organelles cannot be seen at all without a microscope, and most living things are too small to be studied in detail without one. The main kinds of microscopes used today include the following.

- The **compound microscope** employs several lenses to achieve greater magnification. Like other light microscopes, it uses glass lenses to focus on a lighted specimen.

- The **dissecting microscope** (or stereomicroscope) is used to obtain a three-dimensional view of a specimen. It consists of two compound microscopes that are both focused on the same sample. The dissecting microscope also has a magnification limit about ten times lower than a compound microscope.

- The **transmission electron microscope** passes a beam of electrons through a thin specimen. The electrons are then focused to produce an image on a fluorescent screen or on film. This is the most common type of electron microscope, and it provides the best image resolution.

- The **scanning electron microscope** scans a narrow beam of electrons onto a specimen. This microscope collects the electrons that the surface of the specimen scatters and projects them onto a fluorescent screen. It has poorer resolution than the TEM but provides vivid three-dimensional surface images.

Standards of Scientific Information

When performing a scientific investigation, you must make sure that the sources you consult are accurate, valid, and reliable. Sources of scientific information can be divided into **primary sources** and **secondary sources**.

Primary Sources

- **Periodicals** such as journals, bulletins, and group proceedings form the bulk of primary source material for science and technology. These publications emphasize basic research and peer review.

- **Research reports** present the work of research scientists in laboratories sponsored by the government, universities, private foundations, or businesses. They often focus on ongoing research projects.

- **Trade magazines** feature scientific news and updates from various manufacturers, dealers, and trade organizations.

- **Trade books** on current topics in science and technology are written by experts in various fields and may be geared toward a wide popular audience. Books by amateurs and nonscientists, however, may not be reliable or current.

Secondary Sources

- **Encyclopedias** provide summaries of background knowledge in various fields of science and technology. Some focus on one particular area, such as the Encyclopedia of the Animal Kingdom. Online encyclopedias may be consulted, but are not always reliable. Information from online sources should be supplemented with respected print sources.

- **Dictionaries** provide concise definitions of technical terms and etymologies (word histories) that can be very helpful in scientific investigations.

- **Indexes** provide an alphabetical listing of topics, names, terms, and other items featured in a book or in periodicals, along with the page numbers where the items can be found. Indexes are a helpful shortcut to finding specific information in scientific publications.

- **Handbooks** are compact compilations of information from a specific field of study. They include data, tables, charts, diagrams, illustrations, and other information.

Standards of Measurement

Scientists use the International System of Measurement as the standard for experiments. This ensures that scientific findings can be tested by scientists anywhere in the world. The International System of Measurement is based on the metric system. It measures length in meters (m), mass in kilograms (g), temperature in kelvin (K), and time in seconds (s). Be sure to be consistent in using measurements in your own experiments. Don't begin by recording results in centimeters and then switch to inches. Also, be aware that every measurement is only accurate to a certain degree. Always think about the best way to minimize errors or uncertainty in measurements.

Charts and Graphs to Analyze Data

To analyze the results of a scientific investigation, you must be able to interpret the data presented in charts and graphs. These are visual summaries of the data gathered in experiments. Certain types of charts or graphs are better suited to present certain types of information. Graphic aids used to present data from experiments include the following.

- A **data table** is a table that contains the numerical results of an experiment, such as volumes, weights, and temperatures with their units of measurement. A data table is compiled before the data is used to make a chart or graph.

- A **line graph** presents data as connected points on a grid defined by a horizontal *x*-axis and a vertical *y*-axis. A graph shows the relationship between two variables. Points on the graph are connected to show trends in the data.

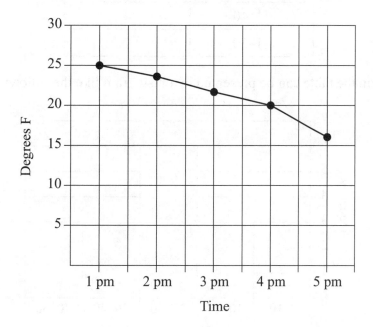

- A **bar graph** is used to compare quantitative data and qualitative data. For example, a bar graph might show the number of students in equal samples of four different hair colors.

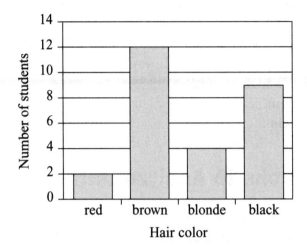

- A **histogram** is used to show a frequency distribution of data. Suppose an experiment yielded the following set of numerical results: {7, 12, 12, 18, 22, 24, 26, 27, 28, 29, 31, 36, 36, 39, 43, 47}. A table shows the data ranges and the frequency in each range.

Data Range	Frequency
0–10	1
11–20	3
21–30	6
31–40	4
41–50	2

The data in the table can be presented in a histogram like the following.

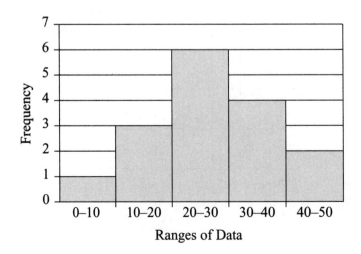

- A **stem and leaf plot** is another way to present a frequency distribution. Unlike a histogram, a stem and leaf plot allows you to present the actual data points. The tens digits are given on the "stem," or left-hand column. The ones digits are given on the "leaves," or right-hand column. Here is a stem and leaf plot using the same data set as for the histogram above.

Stem	Leaf
0	7
1	2 2 8
2	2 4 6 7 8 9
3	1 6 6 9
4	3 7

- A **circle graph** shows data as proportions of a whole. It is also called a "pie chart" because each piece of data is presented like a slice of a whole pie. Notice the percentages displayed in the circle graph below.

A Simple Pie Plot

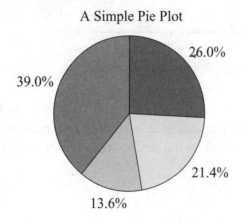

- A **box and whisker plot** divides data into five numbers on a number line. The median is the value that is exactly in the middle of an ordered set of numbers. The sub-median of the numbers to the left of the median is the lower quartile. The smallest number to the left of the median is the lower extreme. The sub-median of the numbers to the right of the median is the upper quartile. The largest number to the right of the median is the upper extreme. A rectangular box shows the interquartile range between the lower and upper quartiles. Whiskers, or horizontal lines, show the range from lower quartile to lower extreme and from upper quartile to upper extreme.

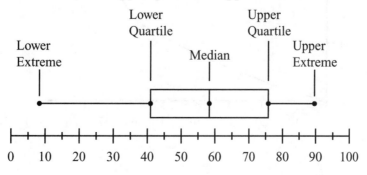

- A **scatter plot** shows data as a collection of many dots on a grid. If the pattern of dots slopes up from lower left to upper right, this shows a positive correlation between variable. If the pattern slopes down from upper left to lower right, this shows a negative correlation. Sometimes a "line of best fit" is drawn to show the trend of the dots in a scatter plot.

- A **cumulative frequency graph** plots the number of data scores that are less than or equal to a value *x*. For example, a cumulative frequency graph might show that 6 students scored 60 or less on a quiz, 10 students scored 70 or less, 15 students scored 80 or less, etc.

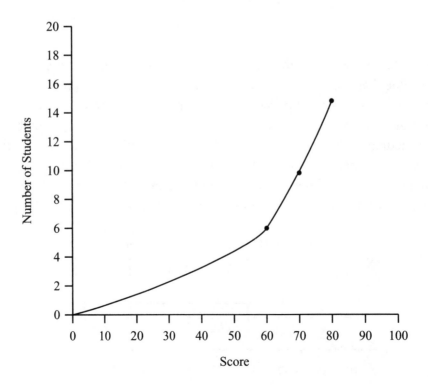

End-of-Chapter Quiz

1. **Which of the following is NOT a suitable question on which to base a scientific investigation into transpiration?**

   A. How does wind affect transpiration in bean plant seedlings?

   B. Which has a greater effect on transpiration in bean plant seedlings, humidity or light?

   C. What condition serves to increase the rate of transpiration in bean plant seedlings?

   D. Which is more beneficial to bean plant seedlings, photosynthesis or transpiration?

2. **When you look at the empirical evidence that relates to an experiment, what are you doing?**

   A. reviewing the direct observations on the subject recorded by others

   B. reviewing the various hypotheses on the subject

   C. predicting the results of the experiment

   D. planning the experiment so that the results will be meaningful

3. **A student wants to test whether temperature affects aerobic cellular respiration in organisms. The student places 3 crickets in a hot temperature environment (28°C) and 3 crickets in a cold temperature environment (15°C) and measures the rate of change in CO_2 levels for each cricket in 5-minute intervals. Which of the following would be the *best* improvement for this experiment?**

   A. an increase in the number of crickets tested

   B. the use of other organisms in addition to crickets

   C. the use of a control with 3 crickets in a room temperature environment (22°C)

   D. the use of a control with 3 crickets in a warm temperature environment (25°C)

4. A student conducts the following osmosis experiment. Nine discs cut from raw potatoes are used to represent cells with semipermeable membranes. The nine potato discs are first weighed and their masses recorded. Then the discs are grouped in threes and each group is soaked in a different concentration of salt water. The results are shown in the table below.

NaCl Concentration/M	Potato Disc Samples	Mass Before Soaking	Mass After Soaking	% Change in Mass
0.98	1A	1.93	1.42	−26.42
	2A	2.02	1.56	−22.77
	3A	1.88	1.31	−30.32
0.50	1B	2.00	1.45	−26.50
	2B	2.02	1.38	−31.68
	3B	2.00	1.47	−27.50
0.02	1C	1.98	2.17	+9.60
	2C	1.98	2.46	+24.24
	3C	2.04	2.48	+21.57

Based on the data in the table, which inference can be made about osmosis in cells with semipermeable membranes?

A. Water tends to leave the cell when the cell is in an environment of high water concentration.

B. Water tends to enter the cell when the cell is in an environment of medium solute concentration.

C. Water tends to enter the cell when the cell is in an environment of high solute concentration.

D. Water tends to enter the cell when the cell is in an environment of high water concentration.

5. Which of the following is NOT true of a dissecting microscope?

A. It passes a narrow beam of electrons through a thin specimen.

B. It has a magnification that is significantly lower than an ordinary compound microscope.

C. It is used to obtain a three-dimensional image of a specimen.

D. It is made up of two compound microscopes that are focused on the same sample.

6. **Most primary source material for information about science and technology is found in which form?**

   A. trade books

   B. periodicals

   C. encyclopedias

   D. research reports

7. **Which of the following sources would be the *least* likely to contain reliable and current information?**

   A. a research report on technology produced by a private foundation

   B. a peer-reviewed scientific journal from a major American university

   C. an online encyclopedia of science and technology

   D. an annual index of science and technology articles in periodicals

8. **The International System of Measurement is the standard for scientific work. What is it based upon?**

   A. the United States Customary System of Weights and Measures

   B. the metric system

   C. the British imperial system

   D. a combination of the United States system and the metric system

9. **A "line of best fit" is drawn on which kind of graph to emphasize a trend?**

   A. bar graph

   B. scatter plot

   C. box and whisker plot

   D. histogram

10. **A student wants to create a graph showing the four kingdoms (Protista, Fungi, Plantae, and Animalia) as fractions of all living things on Earth. Which kind of graph would be *most* appropriate?**

    A. bar graph

    B. histogram

    C. line graph

    D. circle graph

Answers to the Chapter Quiz

1. D

The idea of which process is more beneficial to bean plant seedlings is difficult to quantify and therefore to measure. The questions in answer choices A, B, and C can all be answered by measurable experiments.

2. A

Empirical evidence refers to information gathered by direct observation. You might look at empirical evidence to determine what others have found by doing similar experiments.

3. C

Every experiment should include a control condition in which the independent variable—in this case, the temperature of the environment—is at some standard value. Room temperature, neither hot nor cold, represents this standard value.

4. D

The table shows that the last three samples (1C, 2C, 3C) all gained mass after soaking in the low-solute or high-water concentration. This shows that water tends to enter the cell under conditions of high-water concentration.

5. A

A transmission electron microscope, not a dissecting microscope, passes a beam of electrons through a thin specimen in order to produce an image.

6. B

Most of the primary source material for science and technology is found in periodicals such as journals, bulletins, and group proceedings.

7. C

In general, the reliability of information in online sources is questionable. Such information should be checked against two or three other sources.

8. **B**

   The metric system employs base units, such as the meter and the kilogram, that are related to other larger and smaller units by powers of ten.

9. **B**

   The dots on a scatter plot often show concentrations that indicate a positive correlation or a negative correlation. A line of best fit can be drawn to emphasize the trend of the data.

10. **D**

    A circle graph shows the relationship of portions or fractions to a whole.

Chapter 2

Cellular Biology

Your Goals for Chapter 2

1. You should be able to describe and/or explain the cell theory.

2. You should be able to describe how continuous investigations and/or new scientific information influenced the development of the cell theory.

3. You should be able to identify ways in which a scientific claim is evaluated (e.g., through scientific argumentation, critical and logical thinking, and consideration of alternative explanations).

4. You should be able to explain the development of a theory.

5. You should be able to compare and/or contrast the structures found in plant cells and animal cells.

6. You should be able to compare and/or contrast the structures found in prokaryotic cells and in eukaryotic cells.

7. You should be able to describe how structures in cells are directly related to their function in the cell.

8. You should be able to describe the role of the cell membrane during active and passive transport.

Standards

The following standards are assessed on the Florida Biology 1 End-of-Course Assessment either directly or indirectly:

SC.912.L.14.1   Describe the scientific theory of cells (cell theory) and relate the history of its discovery to the process of science.

SC.912.L.14.2   Relate structure to function for the components of plant and animal cells. Explain the role of cell membranes as a highly selective barrier (passive and active transport).

SC.912.L.14.3   Compare and contrast the general structures of plant and animal cells. Compare and contrast the general structures of prokaryotic and eukaryotic cells.

SC.912.N.1.3   Recognize that the strength or usefulness of a scientific claim is evaluated through scientific argumentation, which depends on critical and logical thinking, and the active consideration of alternative scientific explanations to explain the data presented.

SC.912.N.2.1   Identify what is science, what clearly is not science, and what superficially resembles science (but fails to meet the criteria for science).

SC.912.N.3.1   Explain that a scientific theory is the culmination of many scientific investigations drawing together all the current evidence concerning a substantial range of phenomena; thus, a scientific theory represents the most powerful explanation scientists have to offer.

SC.912.N.3.4   Recognize that theories do not become laws, nor do laws become theories; theories are well-supported explanations and laws are well-supported descriptions.

Cell Theory

Modern **cell theory** includes three principles:

1. All living organisms are composed of one or more cells.

2. The cell is the basic unit of structure and function for all organisms.

3. New cells are formed only by division of a preexisting cell.

Generally, cells are microscopic in size. For this reason, they were not discovered until the invention of the microscope in the 1600s. The first to examine cells was Robert Hooke in 1665. He called the shapes he observed in cork *cellulae,* which is Latin for "small rooms." Anton van Leeuwenhoek, "the father of microscopy," was the first scientist to study live cells, or microorganisms. From these discoveries, it took 150 years for biologists to see the full importance of cells. In 1838, a botanist named Matthias Schleiden observed that all plants are composed of cells — the first statement of the cell theory. One year later, Theodor Schwann made the same observation about animals. In 1855, Rudolf Carl Virchow proposed that all cells must come from already existing cells. These ideas form the basis of modern cell theory.

Virchow's theory clashed with the views of most scientists of the time. They believed that living cells could appear from nonliving matter in a process called "spontaneous generation." Louis Pasteur disproved this concept with a classic experiment. First, he boiled equal amounts of broth in two beakers to kill any living matter in the broth. The liquids were left in the beakers at room temperature and in open air. One beaker had a long straight neck, the other had a long neck curved in an S-shape. Several weeks later, the broth in the straight-neck beaker was discolored and cloudy from germs in the air that fell straight down. The broth in the other beaker was unchanged; no germs had reached it because of its curved neck. Pasteur concluded that if spontaneous generation were real, the broth in the curved-neck beaker would also have been contaminated with germs. Pasteur's experiment bolstered cell theory and helped establish the scientific method.

Prokaryotes and Eukaryotes

There are two main types of cells, and they are distinctly different. **Prokaryotes** are cells that are very small and simple, and include all bacteria. They have no nucleus or interior compartments. **Eukaryotes** are much more complex, with a nucleus and internal membranes. Eukaryotes are the cells of protists, fungi, plants, and animals, including humans. Comparing a prokaryotic cell to a eukaryotic cell is like comparing a one-room cabin to an office building or luxury hotel. Also, prokaryotic cells are more ancient.

Prokaryotic Cells	Eukaryotic Cells
No nucleus, internal membranes, mitochondria, vacuoles, or other organelles	Contain distinct organelles
Single naked DNA molecule	DNA wrapped with proteins into chromosomes
Ribosomes are very small	Ribosomes are larger
Metabolism: anaerobic or aerobic	Metabolism: aerobic
No cytoskeleton	Cytoskeleton
Chiefly unicellular	Chiefly multicellular
Very small	Larger

Structures and Functions of Cells

An important rule in biology is that function determines form and vice versa. Cells with different functions look different. A nerve cell is long and spiky, the better to send electric impulses. A fat-storing cell is large and rounded.

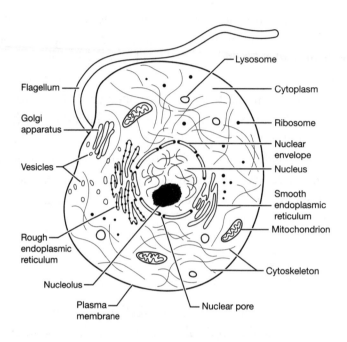

Figure 2.1. Animal Cell

Different cell types may look different but they all contain the same organelles, or specialized parts. A typical animal cell (Figure 2.1) has the following features.

- **Nucleus:** The nucleus contains chromosomes, or rod-shaped bodies wrapped with proteins to form a network called **chromatin**. This is the DNA information of the cell. The nucleus is surrounded by a **nuclear membrane or envelope** with **nuclear pores** for the transport of molecules. The membrane is selectively permeable, meaning that only certain substances go through it.

- **Nucleolus:** In the cell's nucleus is the nucleolus, a concentration of DNA where the components of ribosomes are produced. More than one nucleolus are called **nucleoli**.

- **Ribosomes:** The ribosomes are where **protein synthesis** occurs in the cell. The RNA molecules and proteins that make up ribosomes travel through the nuclear envelope and into the cytoplasm.

- **Cytoplasm:** The cytoplasm is made up of a gelatin-like aqueous fluid, or **cytosol,** outside the nucleus of a cell. It contains organelles such as mitochrondria.

- **Endoplasmic Reticulum:** The endoplasmic reticulum (ER) consists of a system of flattened sacs and mazelike channels that crisscross the cytoplasm. There are two kinds of ER. **Rough ER,** which has ribosomes, is the site of protein synthesis. **Smooth ER,** with no ribosomes, has several functions, including the synthesis of lipids and hormones.

- **Golgi Apparatus:** The Golgi apparatus is a group of flattened sacs stacked liked bowls and lying near the nucleus. The sacs package proteins and lipids into vesicles.

- **Vesicles:** The many small, spherical sacs that store substances and move them within the cell. The vesicles often migrate to the plasma membrane and secrete their contents to the outside of the cell.

- **Vacuoles:** Membrane-surrounded sacs for storing substances in cells are called vacuoles. Vesicles are very small vacuoles.

- **Lysosomes:** Vesicles from a Golgi apparatus that contain digestive enzymes are called lysosomes. Their function in the cell is to break down food, debris, and invading bacteria. This allows the cell to renew itself continually.

- **Mitochondria:** Cellular respiration, in which energy in the form of ATP is produced from carbohydrates, is carried out in the mitochondria. An active cell may contain more than 2,000 mitochondria. They consist of an outer double membrane and an inner series of folded membranes called **cristae**.

- **Cytoskeleton:** The cytoskeleton consists of a network of protein filaments that forms the internal structure of the cytoplasm. In decreasing diameter, these filaments are **microtubules, intermediate filaments,** and **microfilaments**. These give shape to a cell, allow it to move, and attach organelles to its plasma membrane.

- **Flagella and Cilia:** These are structures that extend from the cell membrane and consist of microtubules. Flagella are long and few; cilia are short and numerous. A single flagellum may propel sperm. Cilia in the respiratory tract clear away debris. The microtubules of both flagella and cilia have a **9 + 2 configuration**: 9 pairs of microtubules (or doublets) around 2 singlet microtubules.

A typical plant cell is larger than a typical animal cell. It also has unique parts and is organized differently. A plant cell (Figure 2.2) has the following structures that an animal cell doesn't have:

- Rigid **cell walls** made of the polymer, cellulose

- **Chloroplasts** where photosynthesis is carried out

- A large central **vacuole**

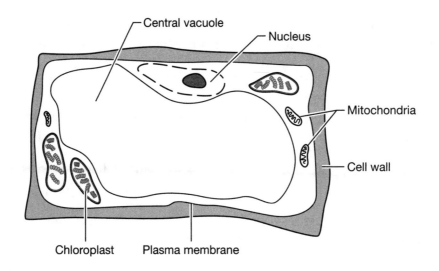

Figure 2.2. Plant Cell

The following chart will help you compare cell features and organelles in prokaryotic cells and eukaryotic cells and in plant and animal cells.

Feature	Structure	Function
Common to All Cells (Prokaryotes and Eukaryotes)		
Plasma membrane	Lipid bilayer containing proteins for transport and other functions	A barrier; controls the entrance and exit of substances into and out of the cell
Cytoplasm	Gelatin-like aqueous fluid (cytosol) with dissolved substances and organelles	The site of many biological reactions, such as synthesis of protein and glycolysis
Common to Plant and Animal Cells (Eukaryotes)		
Mitochondrion (plural: mitochondria)	Small organelle with two membranes; inner membranes called *cristae* are folded to increase surface area for electron transport	Site of aerobic respiration
Ribosome(s)	Tiny organelles; no membrane; contain rRNA and protein; bound to the ER or float free in the cytoplasm	Sites of protein synthesis

Feature	Structure	Function
Endoplasmic reticulum (ER)	Rows of flattened, membranous sacs with ribosomes attached (rough ER) or without ribosomes attached (smooth ER)	Sites of protein and membrane synthesis
Golgi apparatus	Rows of flattened, membranous sacs	Modifies and transports proteins, etc., for export from the cell
Vesicle(s)	Small, spherical, numerous; surrounded by one membrane	Move substances from the ER to the Golgi apparatus and from there to the plasma membrane
Lysosome(s)	Small, spherical; surrounded by one membrane	Contains hydrolytic enzymes that digest macromolecules, pathogens, and old organelles
Cytoskeleton	Network of microfilaments and microtubules throughout the cytoplasm	Controls cell shape; causes movement of chromosomes and organelles within the cell
Cilia and flagella (singular: flagellum)	Hairlike; cilia are short and flagella are longer; 9 + 2 arrangement of microtubules	Locomotion of cells; movement of fluid surrounding a cell
Nucleus	Large, round; surrounded by nuclear membrane consisting of two membranes studded with pores	Site of chromosome (DNA) storage and RNA synthesis (transcription)
Nucleolus	Dense, spherical area within the nucleus	Site of rRNA synthesis and ribosome production
Plant Cells Only		
Cell wall	Rigid; contains cellulose	Provides support and protection for cells
Vacuole(s)	Small or large; surrounded by single membrane	Provides turgor pressure for gross plant support; storage of substances
Plastid(s) (chloroplasts, etc.)	Various membrane-bound organelles; chloroplast has double membrane plus thylakoids shaped like stacked coins to increase surface area	Chloroplasts are the site of photosynthesis; other plastids store starches or fats

The Plasma Membrane

The **cell membrane** or **plasma membrane** protects a cell from its immediate environment. It is also **selectively permeable,** meaning that it allows some substances to pass through it but not others. In other words, it regulates the traffic entering and leaving the cell.

Figure 2.3 shows the structure of the plasma membrane. The plasma membrane consists mainly of a **phospholipid bilayer** with **proteins** embedded in the layers. A phospholipid is **amphipathic**. This means it has a hydrophobic (water-fearing) tail and a hydrophilic (water-loving) head. The cytosol inside the cell and the fluid outside the cell are both aqueous (watery) environments. That is why phospholipids form a **bilayer**, or a membrane with two molecular layers. The hydrophilic heads associate with the cytoplasm and the extracellular fluid, while the hydrophobic tails associate with each other.

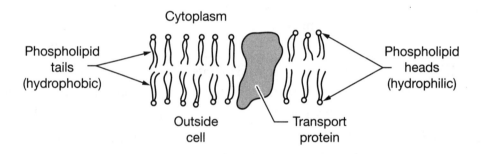

Figure 2.3. Plasma Membrane Structure

Cellular Transport

The movement of substances into and out of a cell is called **cellular transport**. There is **active transport** and **passive transport**. Active transport requires energy (usually ATP), while passive transport does not.

Two main types of passive transport are **diffusion** and **osmosis**.

- **Diffusion** (Figure 2.4) is the net movement of substances from an area of higher concentration to an area of lower concentration. (This is also called moving down the concentration gradient.) The movement is the result of constant and random motion characteristic of all molecules. The substances transported are small, uncharged molecules such as carbon dioxide and oxygen. In diffusion, they move directly across the lipid bilayer to a state of equilibrium, or uniform distribution.

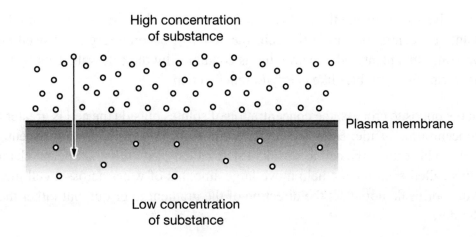

High concentration
of substance

Plasma membrane

Low concentration
of substance

Figure 2.4. Diffusion

- **Facilitated diffusion** (Figure 2.5) is the movement of charged molecules (e.g., potassium ions) and larger molecules (e.g., glucose) into and out of the cell. Like simple diffusion, facilitated diffusion moves a substance down its concentration gradient from an area of higher to an area of lower concentration without the use of ATP. Unlike in diffusion, however, the substance moves with the aid of carrier proteins or through a channel protein.

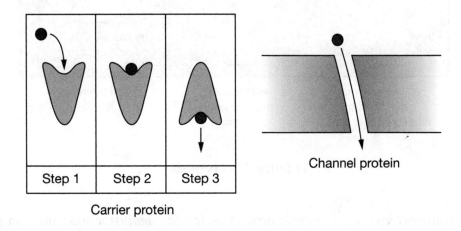

| Step 1 | Step 2 | Step 3 |

Carrier protein

Channel protein

Figure 2.5. Facilitated Diffusion

- **Osmosis** (Figure 2.6) is the movement of water molecules across the selectively permeable plasma membrane. The molecules move from a **hypotonic solution** to a **hypertonic solution**. A hypotonic solution has a lower concentration of solutes (dissolved substances) than a hypertonic solution. When water flows into the higher solute concentration inside the cell, the cell will become turgid, or swell almost to bursting. In a plant cell, the swelling is contained by the cell wall. This **turgor pressure** causes vegetables like celery to remain crisp.

In the opposite process, the concentration of solutes outside the cell is greater than the concentration inside. Here, water flows out of the cell to the lower concentration of water. This causes the cell to shrink, a state called **plasmolysis**. Special channel proteins called **aquaporins** help move large amounts of water across a cell membrane. Aquaporins do not affect the direction of the gradient in or out, but rather the rate of the flow.

Two solutions that have equal concentrations of solutes are called **isotonic**. In this situation (also called dynamic equilibrium), there is no net movement of molecules across the plasma membrane.

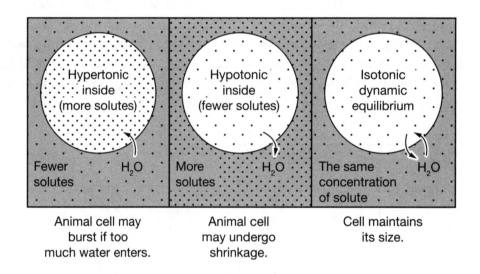

Figure 2.6. Osmosis

Active transport involves the movement of molecules *against* a concentration gradient. This movement requires the cell to use energy, usually ATP. In active transport, pumps or carriers move substances across the plasma membrane.

The **sodium-potassium pump** (Figure 2.7) is a type of carrier protein called a cell membrane pump. This pump uses energy to move substances (in this case, sodium ions: Na^+ and potassium ions: K^+) against their concentration gradient from areas of low concentration to areas of high concentration. In animal cells, the sodium potassium pump is important in maintaining a difference in charge across the plasma membrane. The sodium-potassium pump moves 3 Na⁺ ions out of the cell for every 2 K⁺ ions it moves into the cell. As shown in Figure 2.7, the sodium-potassium pump picks up 3 Na⁺ ions on the inside of the cell and changes shape, causing it to deposit the ions outside the cell after ATP adds a phosphate to the pump. By a similar shape change, the pump moves 2 K⁺ ions in the opposite direction as the phosphates leave the pump protein.

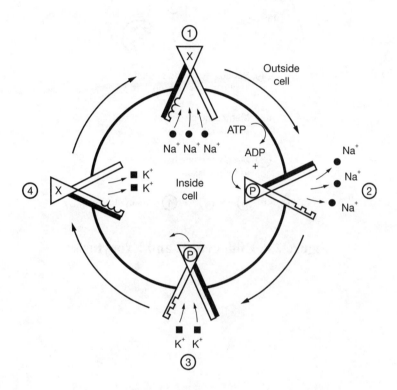

Figure 2.7. The Sodium-Potassium Pump

Vesicular transport is a form of active transport that uses vesicles or other organs in the cytoplasm to move large molecules and food particles across the plasma membrane, again with the use of ATP. There are two main types of vesicular transport (Figure 2.8).

- **Exocytosis** is the process whereby vesicles fuse with the plasma membrane and release their contents to the outside of the cell. The contents in the vesicles are newly synthesized proteins and other molecules that have been transported from the ER and Golgi apparatus to the plasma membrane.

- **Endocytosis** is basically the opposite process of exocytosis. In it, substances outside the cell are captured by an in-folding of the plasma membrane, enclosed in a vesicle, and moved into the cytoplasm. In **pinocytosis,** or "cellular drinking," dissolved substances enter the cell as a liquid. In **phagocytosis,** or "cellular eating," undissolved or solid substances enter the cell.

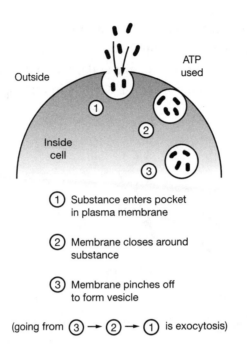

(1) Substance enters pocket in plasma membrane

(2) Membrane closes around substance

(3) Membrane pinches off to form vesicle

(going from (3) → (2) → (1) is exocytosis)

Figure 2.8. Endocytosis and Exocytosis

End-of-Chapter Quiz

1.   **Which of the following is NOT a principle included in the modern cell theory?**

   A.   New cells are formed only by division of a preexisting cell.

   B.   The cell is the basic unit of structure and function for all organisms.

   C.   Living cells appear spontaneously from nonliving matter.

   D.   All living things are composed of one or more cells.

2.   **The development of the cell theory was the result of which of the following?**

   A.   the work of a series of scientists over many years

   B.   the invention of the microscope

   C.   the discovery that all plants are composed of cells

   D.   Virchow's idea that all cells must come from already existing cells

3.   **Which of the following *best* describes a prokaryotic cell?**

   A.   small and simple

   B.   large and complex

   C.   mainly multicellular

   D.   composed of distinct organelles

4.   **In comparing prokaryotic and eukaryotic cells, which of the following is found in both?**

   A.   lysosomes

   B.   ribosomes

   C.   vacuoles

   D.   mitochondria

5.   **With regard to the form and function of cells, which of the following is true?**

   A.   All cells look the same, but they have very different functions.

   B.   Cells have a variety of shapes, but they all perform the same functions.

   C.   Cells with different functions have different forms.

   D.   The form of a cell has nothing to do with its function.

6. **Which of the following describes a key difference between plant and animal cells?**

    A. Only animal cells have a nucleus.

    B. Only animal cells have mitochondria.

    C. Only plant cells have a plasma membrane.

    D. Only plant cells have cell walls.

7. **Which of the following is the organelle where sacs package proteins and lipids into vesicles?**

    A. endoplasmic reticulum

    B. Golgi apparatus

    C. nucleolus

    D. mitochondria

8. **Which of the following describes the function of lysosomes in a cell?**

    A. produce and distribute proteins

    B. produce fats

    C. break down or digest food, debris, and invading bacteria

    D. carry out detoxification of alcohol

9. **Which of the following parts of a cell is the site of protein synthesis?**

    A. ribosomes

    B. peroxisomes

    C. smooth ER

    D. mitochondria

10. **Cellular respiration takes place in which part of a cell?**

    A. nucleus

    B. peroxisomes

    C. Golgi apparatus

    D. mitochondria

11. Which of the following is the *best* description of vesicles?

    A. very large microtubules

    B. very large vacuoles

    C. very small vacuoles

    D. very small nucleoli

12. The "9 + 2 configuration" refers to which of the following?

    A. microtubules in flagella

    B. microtubules in flagella and cilia

    C. protein filaments in the cytoskeleton

    D. nuclear pores in the nuclear membrane

13. Which of the following is the *best* description of the plasma membrane's basic structure?

    A. a hydrophilic head and a hydrophobic tail

    B. a phospholipid layer and a protein layer

    C. a protein bilayer with phospholipids embedded in the layers

    D. a phospholipid bilayer with proteins embedded in the layers

14. What is the name for the net movement of small, uncharged molecules from an area of higher concentration to an area of lower concentration?

    A. osmosis

    B. turgor pressure

    C. diffusion

    D. facilitated diffusion

15. Which of the following is NOT an example of passive transport?

    A. diffusion

    B. facilitated diffusion

    C. osmosis

    D. endocytosis

16. **Which of the following is an important difference between active transport and passive transport?**

    A.   active transport requires proteins for energy

    B.   active transport moves molecules down the concentration gradient

    C.   passive transport requires proteins for energy

    D.   passive transport employs pumps or carriers to move substances

17. **Which of the following describes one of the main functions of the sodium-potassium pump?**

    A.   maintain an equilibrium of charge across the plasma membrane of animal cells

    B.   maintain a difference in charge across the plasma membrane of animal cells

    C.   exchange all potassium ions for sodium ions

    D.   use energy to move sodium and potassium ions from areas of high concentration to areas of low concentration

18. **"Dynamic equilibrium" is a situation associated with which of the following?**

    A.   hypotonic solutions

    B.   hypertonic solutions

    C.   vesicular transport

    D.   isotonic solutions

19. **Which of the following *best* describes the process called endocytosis?**

    A.   Solutes flow out of a cell to a lower water concentration.

    B.   Substances inside the cell are released to the outside via a vesicle.

    C.   Substances outside the cell are moved into the cytoplasm via a vesicle.

    D.   The cell shrinks due to a diminishing level of water in the cell.

20. **"Cellular eating" is another name for which of the following?**

    A.   exocytosis

    B.   plasmolysis

    C.   phagocytosis

    D.   pinocytosis

Answers to the Chapter Quiz

1. C

The idea that living cells could appear from nonliving matter in a process called "spontaneous generation" was disproved by Pasteur.

2. A

The development of the cell theory is an example of the scientific process, in which a series of scientific investigations leads to a theory to explain a range of phenomena. Answers B, C, and D were all steps in this process.

3. A

Prokaryotes are cells that are very small and simple. They are mainly unicellular and have no nucleus or other organelles.

4. B

Prokaryotic cells are very small and simple and do not have lysosomes, vacuoles, or mitochondria. They do have small ribosomes, as opposed to the larger ribosomes of eukaryotic cells.

5. C

An important rule in biology is that function determines form and form determines function. Thus, cells with different functions have different forms.

6. D

Only plant cells have a rigid cell wall. Both animal cells and plant cells have a nucleus, mitochondria, and a plasma membrane.

7. B

The Golgi apparatus lies near the nucleus and consists of flattened sacs that package proteins and lipids for secretion through vesicles.

8. C

Lysosomes are digestive enzymes that break down food and debris in the cell.

9. **A**

Protein synthesis is carried out in the ribosomes, which is made up of RNA molecules and proteins that move through the nuclear envelope and into the cytoplasm. Answer C is incorrect because smooth ER, unlike rough ER, has no ribosomes and so is not the site of protein synthesis.

10. **D**

Cellular respiration, in which energy in the form of ATP is produced from carbohydrates, is carried out in the mitochondria.

11. **C**

Vesicles are actually very small vacuoles, or membrane-surrounded sacs for storing substances.

12. **B**

The 9 + 2 configuration refers to the arrangement of microtubules in both flagella and cilia.

13. **D**

The plasma membrane consists mainly of a phospholipid bilayer with proteins embedded in the layers. The hydrophobic tail and hydrophilic head are part of a phospholipid.

14. **C**

This net movement of substances from an area of higher concentration to an area of lower concentration is also called moving down the concentration gradient.

15. **D**

Endocytosis is a form of active transport.

16. **A**

Since active transport moves molecules against a concentration gradient, it requires the cell to use energy, usually the proteins of ATP.

17. B

The sodium-potassium pump moves 3 sodium ions out of the cell for every 2 potassium ions it moves into the cell, thus maintaining a difference in charge across the plasma membrane.

18. D

Two solutions that have equal concentrations of solutes are called isotonic and are said to be in dynamic equilibrium because there is no net movement of molecules across the plasma membrane.

19. C

Endocytosis is basically the reverse process of exocytosis, and moves substances that have been captured by an in-folding of the membrane into the cell's cytoplasm.

20. C

In phagocytosis, or "cellular eating," undissolved or solid substances enter the cell.

Chapter 3

Plants

Your Goal for Chapter 3

1. You should be able to explain how the structures of plant tissues and organs are directly related to their roles in physiological processes.

Standards

The following standard is directly assessed on the Florida Biology 1 End-of-Course Assessment:

SC.912.L.14.7: Relate the structure of each of the major plant organs and tissues to physiological processes.

Plant Tissues

A plant has four distinct types of tissue. Each type has a specific function.

- **Ground tissue** is the most common type of plant tissue. There are three basic kinds of ground tissue cells that differ according to their cell walls.

  — **Parenchyma cells** are the most common cell type in plants. They have thin and flexible cell walls. Their functions include storage, photosynthesis, and secretion.

  — **Collenchymal cells** have thick but flexible cell walls. They serve as mechanical support for the growing stem of the plant.

  — **Sclerenchyma cells** have very thick cell walls and also function as support.

- **Dermal tissue** provides cover and protection for plants. **Epidermis cells** cover the surface of plant parts. **Guard cells** surround stomata. Other specialized dermal cells include hair cells, stinging cells, and glandular cells. Epidermis cells secrete a waxy substance called the **cuticle** that also protects the plant.

- **Vascular tissue** includes two major types of tissues, xylem and phloem. Together, these tissues form **vascular bundles**.

  — **Xylem** conducts water and minerals and provides support for the plant. Xylem cells have both a primary cell wall and a secondary cell wall for extra strength. Water passes from one xylem cell to another through **pits,** or areas where there is no secondary wall. At maturity, xylem is mainly dead cells made up of only cell walls and transported material. There are two kinds of xylem cells: tracheids and vessel elements. **Tracheids** are long, thin, overlapping cells with tapered ends. **Vessel members** are wider and shorter, with thinner cell walls and less tapered ends. Wood consists of xylem cells.

  — **Phloem** conducts sugars by active transport from photosynthesizing leaves to the rest of the plant. Phloem consists of chains of cells called **sieve-tube members** (or sieve-tube elements). These chains form conducting tubes called **sieve tubes**. **Sieve plates** in the end walls of sieve-tube members help fluid flow from one cell to another. Unlike xylem cells, sieve-tube members are still living at maturity, although without nuclei and other cell parts. Each sieve-tube member has at least one adjacent **companion cell** with a full set of organelles (nuclei, vacuoles, etc.) for physiological support.

- **Meristematic tissue** is the plant's growth tissue. It is where most cell division occurs. It is also called undifferentiated tissue, because meristematic cells will eventually develop into ground, dermal, or vascular tissue. The meristematic tissue at the tips of roots and stems is called the **apical meristem**. This is where the plant's primary growth takes place. Secondary growth, or lateral growth, occurs in the two **lateral meristems**: vascular cambium and cork cambium. Secondary growth is when trees and shrubs grow thicker in girth.

Plant Organs

Plant organs can be divided into two groups: reproductive organs and vegetative organs. The **reproductive organs** vary in different kinds of plants.

Two types of seed plants are angiosperms and gymnosperms. **Angiosperms** are seed plants that reproduce with structures called flowers and fruits. Brightly colored and heavily scented flowers attract animals that transport their pollen over long distances to other plants. Colorful, sweet fruits tempt animals to eat the fleshy substance, resulting in the fruit's seeds passing through the digestive tract and being scattered with the animals' fertilizing feces. Angiosperms can also pollinate through wind-borne seeds and clinging burrs. **Gymnosperms**, or conifers, are seed plants with naked seeds that are not enclosed inside a fruit. To adapt to a dry environment, they have modified leaves that form cones and needle-shaped leaves with a protective cuticle. Gymnosperms rely on wind-borne pollination, and include pines, redwoods, and junipers.

The Seed

The **seed** consists of an **embryo**, a protective **seed coat**, and the **endosperm** or **cotyledon**, which stores food for the embryo. The **embryo** is made up of several parts. The top portion is the **epicotyl,** which becomes the shoot tip. Below the epicotyl is the **hypocotl**, which is attached to the cotyledon. The hypocotl develops into the young shoot. In many embryos, a **radicle** emerges as the first organ from the germinating seed. The radicle becomes the root.

Once a seed is mature, it remains dormant until certain environmental cues are met, the most important of which is water. Other possible environmental cues include specific temperatures, light, or something that causes damage to the seed coat. Some seeds remain dormant for a certain period regardless of outside factors.

Germination starts with absorption of water, which triggers enzyme activity. This in turn sets off chemical processes such as respiration. The absorbed water swells the seed and causes the seed coat to crack. Roots growing from the radicle anchor the seedling in the soil. Then the hypocotl elongates to produce a young shoot.

The **flower** is the reproductive organ of angiosperms. It includes the **pistil** (the collective term for the carpels), which is the female organ of reproduction. It also includes the **stamens**, which are the male reproductive organs. Male reproductive cells, called **pollen**, fertilize the female reproductive cells, called **ovules**.

The **vegetative organs** maintain the structure and functions of the plant. They include the following.

- Roots have three main functions: absorb nutrients, anchor the plant, and store food. To carry out these specialized tasks, roots have the following tissues and structures.

Roots

Roots have three main functions: absorb nutrients, anchor the plant, and store food. To carry out these specialized tasks, roots have the following tissues and structures.

- The **epidermis** covers the outside surface of the root. Epidermal cells have **root hairs** that increase the surface area for absorption of water. These root hairs die as the zone of maturation ages. New epidermal cells from the zone of elongation in turn become the new zone of maturation, and these cells form additional root hairs. Roots must always be growing to produce new root hairs for water absorption.

- The **cortex**, which makes up most of the root, has the main function of storing starch in parenchymal cells.

- The **endodermis** is a tightly packed ring of cells at the innermost center of the cortex. A band of waxy material called **suberin** encircles each endodermal cell in a water-impenetrable barrier called the **Casparian strip**. The result is that all water passes through endodermal cells and not between them, which controls the movement of water and minerals into the vascular tissues at the root's center.

- The **stele**, or **vascular cylinder**, is made up of vascular tissues (xylem and phloem) covered by one or more layers of tissue called the **pericycle**. The pericycle is where lateral roots are produced.

The root's growth can be broken down into areas based on the activity of its cells (Fig. 3.1). The tip of the root, or **root cap**, protects the apical meristem where primary growth occurs. Cells of the apical meristem divide to form the **zone of cell division**. The new cells absorb water and elongate to form the **zone of elongation**. Above this zone is the **zone of maturation** (or the zone of differentiation) where cells mature and differentiate into xylem, phloem, parenchyma, or epidermis.

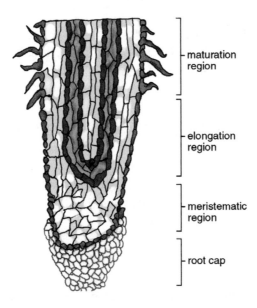

Figure 3.1. The Root's Areas of Growth

Stems support a plant's leaves and flowers and move water and food within the plant. Stems have **primary structures** and **secondary structures**, which correspond to primary growth and secondary growth.

Stems

Stems have **primary structures** and **secondary structures**, which correspond to primary growth and secondary growth.

- **Primary growth.** Primary tissues are much like those in the root. The **epidermis** is made of cells covered with a waxy substance, **cutin**. The cutin creates a protective layer known as the **cuticle**. The **cortex** is the layer of various tissues lying between the epidermis and the **vascular cylinder**. The vascular cylinder runs the length of the stem. It is made up of xylem, phloem, and pith in arrangements called **vascular bundles**. In monocots, these bundles are scattered through the stem, while in conifers and dicots they form a ring around the stem's edge. Primary growth in the seedling proceeds at the **apical meristems**, which are the tips of the roots and shoots. These tips have **meristematic cells** that divide actively. This causes the plant to grow in length.

- **Secondary growth.** While primary growth lengthens plant parts, secondary growth widens their girth. Woody plants have both kinds of growth. The secondary growth takes place at the **vascular cambium** and the **cork cambium**. These two **lateral meristems** have cells that divide and create new cells during periods of growth. When a tree alternates growing seasons with dormant periods, the growth can be seen as tree rings. These also serve to record the tree's age and the amount of seasonal rainfall in the area. Tissues arising from the vascular cambium are called the **secondary xylem** (wood) and the **secondary phloem**. **Periderm** (such as bark), the protective outside covering of woody plants, comes from the cork cambium.

Leaves

Leaves maximize a plant's food production through photosynthesis and minimize water loss through water collection and transpiration. Leaves also protect the plant's stem and root system with shade and shelter.

Like the stem, a leaf is protected by the **epidermis** and **waxy cuticle**. In the leaf, this waxy **cutin** reduces the loss of water by evaporation. Modified epidermal cells called **guard cells** are photosynthetic and also open and close the stomata. The inner leaf contains the **palisade mesophyll** and the **spongy mesophyll**, which are parenchyma cells that are specialized for photosynthesis. These cells are tightly packed in the upper part of the palisade layer and more loosely arranged below in the spongy layer. **Vascular bundles**, or leaf veins, contain xylem and phloem tissues. The xylem carries water and nutrients from the soil to the leaf for photosynthesis. The phloem transports the sugars produced by photosynthesis to other plant areas. To protect vascular tissues from air bubbles that could impede water movement in the leaf, specialized cells called **bundle sheath cells** cover the vascular bundles.

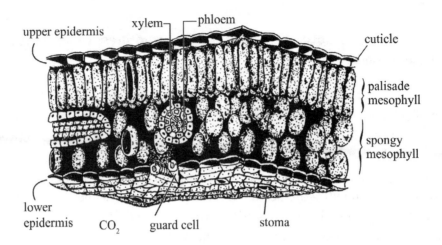

Figure 3.2. The Structure of a Leaf

Stomata

Stomata (plural for stoma) are pores that make up about 1 percent of the leaf's surface. Each stoma is controlled by two **guard cells**. When the guard cells become turgid with absorbed water, the stoma opens. When the guard cells become flaccid from losing water, the stoma closes. When open, the stoma allows CO_2 to enter the leaf. When closed, CO_2 cannot enter. Thus, the activity of guard cells in opening and closing stomata helps produce a state of balance in the leaf that maximizes photosynthesis and minimizes transpiration. Most of the water that a plant loses escapes through the stomata. Stomata tend to open when CO_2 leaf concentrations are low, resulting in active photosynthesis. They tend to close in higher temperatures, which preserves water but prevents photosynthesis.

Physiological Processes of Plants

The key physiological processes of plants are transpiration, photosynthesis, cellular respiration, and reproduction.

- **Transpiration** is the process of evaporation of water from leaves. Water is *pushed up* through the xylem tissue by **root pressure**. This pressure is created when water moves from the soil to the stele of the plant's root and into the xylem. Root pressure results in small droplets of sap forming on the tips of leaves and small herbs in the early morning — a process called **guttation**. Water also can be *pulled up* through the xylem tissue by **transpirational pull**. The **cohesion** of water, which is caused by a strong attraction between water molecules, results in a negative pressure or tension throughout the xylem tissue, from roots to leaves. As water evaporates on leaf surfaces, more water is pulled up through the xylem to replace it.

The **rate of transpiration** slows in high humidity and accelerates in low humidity. Wind increases the rate of transpiration by lowering humidity around the stomata. More intense light increases the rate of transpiration by increasing photosynthesis and production of water vapor. When stomata close, transpiration ceases.

- **Photosynthesis** is the process of using sunlight energy to make carbon compounds such as glucose. Photosynthesis consists of two main processes that only occur in the presence of light. The **light reactions** use energy from light to produce ATP. This ATP in turn powers the **light-independent reactions**, which include the **Calvin cycle** and its process of **carbon fixation**, or the production of sugar. The chloroplast contains **grana,** which consists of layers of membranes called **thylakoids** and is the site of light reactions. The chloroplast also contains **stroma**, where the light-independent reactions take place.

Photosynthesis begins with photosynthetic pigments in the leaf that absorb light energy. Different pigments absorb different wavelengths of light. The main groups of pigments are **chlorophylls** and **carotenoids**. Energy from the absorbed light is converted to ATP and an energy-rich molecule, NADPH. These are the light reactions, a process also called **photophosphorylation**. Then the Calvin cycle uses ATP and NADPH to fix the carbon of CO_2 that enters from the atmosphere into a glucose molecule, or sugar. These are the light-independent reactions. The gases for photosynthesis are thus exchanged through the surface of the leaf.

For photosynthesis to occur, the stomata (leaf pores) in the surface of the leaf must be open to enable CO_2 to enter. When stomata are open, water can escape. Thus, plants in hot, dry climates move CO_2 to bundle sheath cells surrounded by tightly packed mesophyll cells with very little extra space for oxygen. This allows for more efficient fixing of carbon and more efficient photosynthesis overall. The stomata are open for much less time and as a result the cells lose much less water.

- **Cellular respiration** is a process that generates ATP within cells by extracting energy from the carbon compound glucose. With oxygen present, cellular respiration is called **aerobic respiration** and consists of three steps: glycolysis, the Krebs cycle, and oxidative phosphorylation. **Glycolysis** is the process of decomposing glucose to **pyruvate**. It is the first step of both aerobic and anaerobic respiration. The **Krebs cycle** (or the citric acid cycle) is a series of reactions that take place in the **matrix** of the mitochondria and are catalyzed by enzymes. The Krebs cycle requires pyruvate, the end product of glycolysis. For each glucose molecule, the Krebs cycle produces 2 ATP, a small amount. **Oxidative phosphorylation** is the process of pulling ATP from the co-enzymes NADH and FADH$_2$. This occurs as electrons from NADH and FADH$_2$ pass along an **electron transport chain**, or a collection of molecules fixed in the convoluted **cristae membrane** of the mitochondrion. Through a process called **chemiosmosis**, H$^+$ ions from the co-enzymes move down a concentration gradient across the inner membrane of the mitochondria and into the matrix. They travel through the **ATP synthase channels**, which results in the catalysis of ATP. For each step of the chain, electrons from NADH produce about 3 ATP and electrons from FADH$_2$ produce about 2 ATP. (Photosynthesis and cellular respiration will be covered more thoroughly in Chapter 8.)

- **Reproduction** in plants can be asexual or sexual. **Asexual reproduction** is when a piece of a plant, such as the root, stem, or leaf, produces a new plant that is identical genetically to the original plant. **Sexual reproduction** in flowering plants includes pollination, germination, and fertilization. The process begins with the **flower**, which is the plant's sexual organ. The first step occurs when a single grain of pollen alights on the flower's sticky **stigma**. This is **pollination**. The pollen grain absorbs water and sprouts a pollen tube that extends down into the **ovary**. This is **germination**. The two **sperm nuclei** in the pollen grain travel down the tube into the ovary, where they enter the **ovule** to perform a process called **double fertilization**. One sperm nucleus fertilizes the egg and becomes the **embryo,** and the other fertilizes two polar bodies and becomes the **triploid endosperm**, the growing embryo's source of food. Once fertilization occurs, the ovule turns into the seed and the ovary becomes the fruit.

End-of-Chapter Quiz

1. **Which is the *most* common type of plant tissue?**

   A. dermal tissue

   B. xylem

   C. vascular tissue

   D. ground tissue

2. **Dermal tissue includes which of the following?**

   A. parenchyma cells

   B. guard cells

   C. chains of cells called sieve-tube members

   D. vascular bundles

3. **Xylem and phloem combine to form which of the following?**

   A. epidermis cells.

   B. vessel members.

   C. guard cells.

   D. vascular bundles.

4. **Which part of a seed's embryo becomes the root?**

   A. radicle

   B. endosperm

   C. hypocotl

   D. epicotyl

5. Plant cells differentiate into cell types such as parenchyma or epidermis in which area of the root?

    A. root cap

    B. zone of cell division

    C. zone of elongation

    D. zone of maturation

6. Which of the following is NOT true about the vascular cambium?

    A. It produces secondary xylem.

    B. It is one of the lateral meristems.

    C. It creates a protective layer for the root.

    D. It increases the girth of a plant.

7. The palisade mesophyll and the spongy mesophyll are parenchyma cells in the inner leaf that are specialized for what natural process?

    A. transpiration

    B. photosynthesis

    C. reproduction

    D. cell respiration

8. Which of the following is a correct description of guard cell activity with regard to stoma?

    A. When the guard cells become turgid with absorbed water, the stoma closes and CO_2 cannot enter.

    B. When the guard cells become flaccid from losing water, the stoma opens.

    C. The activity of guard cells in opening and closing each stoma helps maintain a state of balance in the leaf that maximizes photosynthesis and minimizes transpiration.

    D. Each stoma is controlled by a single guard cell, which absorbs water to open the stoma and loses water to close the stoma.

9. Most of the growth in shoots and root tips occurs in which area?

   A. meristematic cells

   B. the zone of cell division

   C. the zone of maturation

   D. the zone of elongation

10. The Casparian strip performs what function in the root?

    A. stores starch in parenchymal cells

    B. forms a water-tight barrier around endodermal cells

    C. increases the surface area for absorption of water

    D. produces lateral roots

11. Which of the following is the *most* important environmental cue in changing a seed from being dormant to active growth?

    A. water

    B. light

    C. temperature

    D. damage to the seed coat

12. Which of the following is NOT one of the main functions of roots?

    A. absorb nutrients

    B. store food

    C. carry out reproduction

    D. anchor the plant

13. Which is the end product of glycolysis and a requirement for the Krebs cycle?

    A. glucose

    B. pyruvate

    C. ATP

    D. CO_2

14. Which of the following *best* explains how the surface of the leaf is used in a plant's natural processes?

    A. Cellular reproduction begins with pollination on the sticky surface of a leaf.

    B. Complex chemical reactions occur at the leaf's surface for cellular respiration.

    C. Water enters a plant through the leaf's surface in transpiration.

    D. Photosynthetic processes exchange gases through the leaf's surface.

15. A pollen grain, having absorbed water, sprouts a tube that extends down into the ovary. What is the name of this particular process?

    A. pollination

    B. germination

    C. sexual reproduction

    D. fertilization

16. Which of the following is the *best* description of the electron transport chain?

    A. a chemical process in plants that requires proteins for energy

    B. a chain of molecules that move down a concentration gradient from the matrix to the inner membrane of the mitochondria

    C. a chain of molecules embedded in the convolutions of the cristae membrane located in the mitochondrion

    D. a process in which H^+ ions travel through the ATP synthase channels to burn large amounts of ATP

17. What are chlorophylls and carotenoids?

    A. photosynthetic pigments in the leaf that absorb light energy

    B. layers of membranes involved in light reactions

    C. energy-rich molecules produced by the chemical reactions in photosynthesis

    D. tightly packed cells that surround bundle sheath cells and allow for more efficient fixing of carbon and more efficient photosynthesis

18. **Carbon fixation is the process that takes place during which of the following?**

    A.   the Krebs cycle

    B.   the Calvin cycle

    C.   photophosphorylation

    D.   oxidative phosphorylation

19. **Which of the following is NOT necessary for the photosynthesis process?**

    A. O_2

    B. CO_2

    C.   NADPH

    D.   ATP

20. **Which is the *best* explanation for the small droplets of sap that form on the tips of leaves in the early morning?**

    A.   low rate of transpiration

    B.   high humidity

    C.   transpirational pull

    D.   root pressure

Answers to the Chapter Quiz

1.   **D**

     Ground tissue, which functions in support, storage, and photosynthesis, is the most common type of plant tissue.

2.   **B**

     Among the cells that make up dermal tissue are guard cells that surround stomata.

3. **D**

   Vascular bundles are combinations of the vascular tissues xylem and phloem. Epidermis cells and guard cells are dermal tissues, not vascular tissues. Vessel members are a kind of xylem cell.

4. **A**

   The radicle, which is the first organ from a germinating seed to emerge in many plants, becomes the plant's root. The endosperm stores food for the embryo. The hypocotl becomes the young shoot of the embryo, and the epicotyl becomes the shoot tip.

5. **D**

   In the zone of maturation (or zone of differentiation), cells mature and differentiate into xylem, phloem, parenchyma, or epidermis.

6. **C**

   The vascular cambium does not create a protective layer for the root. That is a waxy substance called cutin that is part of the primary tissues. The vascular cambium is part of the secondary tissues involved in secondary growth.

7. **B**

   The palisade mesophyll and spongy mesophyll are parenchyma cells specialized for photosynthesis. They are tightly packed in the upper part of the palisade layer and more loosely arranged in the spongy layer.

8. **C**

   The role of the guard cells in allowing the stoma to open and close, thus allowing CO_2 to enter or keeping it out, helps keep the CO_2 concentrations in the leaf at levels that result in more active photosynthesis and less loss of water by transpiration.

9. **D**

   New cells absorb water and elongate in the zone of elongation, the area behind the shoots and root tips. The expansion of cells due to water absorption accounts for cell growth. Meristematic cells and the zone of cell division are areas where cell division occurs, but the new cells do not grow until they absorb water and expand.

10. B

Each endoderm cell is enclosed within the Casparian strip, which is made of a band of waxy suberin that creates a barrier between cells that is water-impermeable, causing water and minerals to pass through endoderm cells and not between them.

11. A

The most important environmental factor in initiating germination in a seed is the absorption of water.

12. C

The root may be used in asexual reproduction to produce a new plant through cuttings or graftings, but its three main functions are to absorb nutrients, anchor the plant, and store food for the plant.

13. B

Glycolysis is the process in which glucose is decomposed to pyruvate. The Krebs cycle needs pyruvate to begin its series of enzyme-catalyzed reactions.

14. D

In photosynthesis, the stomata on the leaf's surface open to allow CO_2 to enter the leaf and water vapor to escape.

15. B

The particular step in the sexual reproduction of a plant in which the pollen grain sends a tube down into the ovary is called germination. It occurs after pollination and before double fertilization.

16. C

The electron transport chain is a chain of molecules found in the convoluted cristae membrane of the mitochondrion. Describing it as a chemical process in plants that requires proteins for energy is insufficiently detailed. It is a chain of molecules that move down a concentration gradient and into the matrix, not out of the matrix. The process in which H^+ ions travel through ATP synthase channels is called chemiosmosis, not the electron transport chain.

17. A

Chlorophylls and carotenoids are the main groups of light-absorbing pigments involved in photosynthesis. Answer B, "layers of membranes involved in light reactions," describes thylakoids. Answer C, "energy-rich molecules produced by the chemical reactions in photosynthesis," describes products such as ATP and NADPH. Answer D, "tightly packed cells that surround bundle sheath cells and allow for more efficient fixing of carbon and more efficient photosynthesis," describes mesophyll cells.

18. B

The Calvin cycle and its process of fixing carbon or producing sugar molecules is the main step of the light-independent reactions in photosynthesis.

19. A

Oxygen (O_2) is a released by-product of photosynthesis, but is not necessary for the photosynthetic process to occur.

20. D

Root pressure is created when water moves from the soil to the root's stele and into the xylem. Root pressure pushes water up through the xylem tissue.

Chapter 4

The Human Organism

Your Goals for Chapter 4

1. You should be able to identify the major parts of the brain on diagrams.

3. You should be able to identify factors that affect blood flow and/or describe how these factors affect blood flow through the cardiovascular system.

4. You should be able to identify and/or explain the basic functions of the human immune system, including specific and nonspecific immune responses.

5. You should be able to describe how the human immune system responds to vaccines and/or antibiotics.

6. You should be able to explain the significance of genetic factors, environmental factors, and pathogenic agents to health from the perspective of both individual and public health.

Standards

The following standards are assessed on the Florida Biology 1 End-of-Course Assessment either directly or indirectly:

SC.912.L.14.26 Identify the major parts of the brain on diagrams or models.

SC.912.L.14.36 Describe the factors affecting blood flow through the cardiovascular system.

SC.912.L.14.52 Explain the basic functions of the human immune system, including specific and nonspecific immune response, vaccines, and antibiotics.

SC.912.L.14.6 Explain the significance of genetic factors, environmental factors, and pathogenic agents to health from the perspectives of both individual and public health.

HE.912.C.1.4   Analyze how heredity and family history can impact personal health.

HE.912.C.1.8   Analyze strategies for prevention, detection, and treatment of communicable and chronic diseases.

Major Parts of the Brain

Look at the following diagram of the human brain. On the Biology 1 End-of-Course Assessment, you should be able to identify the labeled parts of the brain. You will NOT be asked about the functions of the various parts. Notice that this diagram shows the right hemisphere of the brain. The cerebrum, the largest part of the brain, consists of both left and right hemispheres.

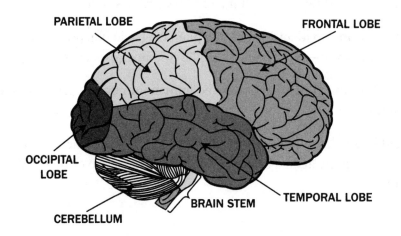

Figure 1. The Human Brain

The Cardiovascular System

In the **cardiovascular system** of the human body, the heart pumps blood into the **arteries**, which branch into an arterial "tree" that extends to the microscopic **arterioles**. Blood from the arterioles enters a complex latticework of narrow, thin-walled tubes called **capillaries**. In the network of capillaries, blood reaches all the organs and tissues, which is where materials such as oxygen and nutrients are exchanged for carbon dioxide and other waste products. From the capillaries, blood collects into microscopic **venules** that connect to larger **veins**. Blood returns to the heart through the veins.

Blood pressure is the pressure that drives the flow of blood through the body's system of arteries, capillaries, and veins. As the ventricles of the heart contract, pressure is created and transferred to the arteries. The rhythmic pulse you can feel in your wrist or neck comes from changes in pressure caused by the expansion and contraction of arteries. Doctors measure blood pressure to check on a person's **cardiovascular health**. Many factors can cause an increase or decrease in blood pressure, sometimes to a dangerous degree.

Doctors use a device called a spygmomanometer to measure blood pressure. The upper arm is wrapped with a cuff that is then inflated to tighten it, thus stopping blood flow to the lower arm. As the cuff deflates and loosens, blood resumes its pulsation in the artery. A stethoscope or an electronic meter is used to "read" the pulsation. The beginning of the pulsing sound indicates the **systolic pressure**, or the peak blood pressure during the contracting of the ventricles. Further loosening of the cuff allows the pulsing sound to stop. This indicates the **diastolic pressure**, or the point of least pressure between heartbeats when ventricles relax. A **blood pressure reading** is a ratio of systolic pressure over diastolic pressure. Generally, a healthy young person has a blood pressure of 120/75 (which is measured in mm Hg, or millimeters of mercury). **Hypertension**, or high blood pressure, is a condition in which a person's systolic pressure is greater than 150 mm Hg or diastolic pressure is greater than 90 mm Hg.

Blood flow in the cardiovascular system is determined by how constricted the arteries are and how much they resist healthy flow. It is also affected by the **viscosity** of blood, for thinner blood is less resistant to flow. Here are some factors and conditions that affect blood flow in the human body.

- **Atherosclerosis** is a condition in which plaques such as fatty materials, cholesterol, or other cellular debris accumulates in the arteries, thus constricting the arterial pathway and obstructing blood flow. **Cholesterol** is found in two forms: low-density lipoproteins (LDL) and high-density lipoproteins (HDL). HDL is often labeled "good cholesterol" because it is able to send cholesterol to the liver for elimination, while LDL is "bad cholesterol" because it carries cholesterol to all the body's cells. Some people have naturally high levels of serum cholesterol, while others reach high levels through diet. Atherosclerosis itself can be due to genetic inheritance, hypertension, inactivity, and smoking. It can cause a **heart attack**, or myocardial infarction, in which an insufficient flow of blood to the heart results in the death of one or more parts of the heart muscle. **Angina pectoris**, or chest pain, is a less lethal indicator of faulty blood flow to the heart.

- **Arteriosclerosis** is also called hardening of the arteries. It results when calcium deposits build up on arterial walls, and often is found with severe atherosclerosis (buildup of fats and cholesterol). Hardened arteries not only have restricted blood flow, they also have a reduced ability to expand normally, forcing the heart to work much harder and raising blood pressure.

- **Blood clots** are blockages in an artery that interrupt blood flow. The presence of a blood clot in a cerebral artery can interfere with blood flow to the brain and cause a stroke. Another cause of stroke is when a blood vessel bursts in the brain.

- **Diabetes** is a condition in which the blood contains elevated levels of sugar. The body converts this glucose to fatty **triglycerides**, which mix with blood and cause it to have greater viscosity, or thickness, thus decreasing its flow.

- **Exercise** burns energy, making the heart work harder to deliver glucose and oxygen through the bloodstream. This results in slightly widened blood vessels and an increase in blood flow. Regular exercise also improves the body's levels of cholesterol and fat and keeps blood vessels open and flexible.

- **Raynaud's disease** is a condition that issues in short periods of **vasosperm**, or narrowing of the arteries. Raynaud's disease constricts blood flow to fingers and toes, and during attacks of the condition the sufferer's skin may turn white and then blue.

- **Caffeine use**, when excessive, can reduce a body's ability to increase blood flow to the heart.

- **Cold temperatures** cause blood vessels to constrict and muscles to contract, thus reducing blood flow. In extreme cold, fingers and toes can suffer **frostbite**, which is the freezing and eventual death of skin tissues.

- **Hyperventilation** can affect levels of carbon dioxide in the blood, causing the blood to become alkaline, or have a higher blood pH value. This in turn causes blood vessels to constrict and reduces blood flow. This accounts for the lightheadedness and fainting associated with hyperventilation.

- **Vasodilators** are medications for high blood pressure that help to open blood vessels by relaxing muscles in vessel walls. This in turn causes blood pressure to go down and blood flow to increase. **Vasoconstrictors**, such as antihistamines and decongestants, constrict blood vessels, raise blood pressure, and reduce blood flow.

It is important to remember that the Florida Biology 1 End-of-Course Assessment will include items on describing the factors that affect blood flow.

The Human Immune System

Living, as we do, surrounded by germs, our bodies must rely on three interlocking lines of defense to ward off threats of disease. On the Florida Biology 1 End-of-Course Assessment, you must demonstrate knowledge of the **human immune system**, including specific and nonspecific immune responses. You should also be able to describe the purpose of vaccines and antibiotics. You may also be asked about genetic factors, environmental factors, and pathogenic agents.

Nonspecific Defense Mechanisms: First Line of Defense

The body's first line of defense against disease-causing agents, or **pathogens**, is a protective barrier that keeps things out. This first line includes the following.

- **Skin**, the largest organ in the body, forms an overall barrier and has oil and sweat glands on its surface that inhibit growth of unwanted microorganisms.

- **Mucous membranes** release a layer of mucus that traps microorganisms and then is swept away to eliminate them. These mucous membrane surfaces protect the digestive tract, the respiratory tract, and the urogenital tract, each of which is open to external factors.

- **Stomach acid and saliva** kill microbes and other harmful agents in food.

- **Cilia** line bronchial passages and sweep mucus out of the lungs and into the digestive system.

Nonspecific Defense Mechanisms: Second Line of Defense

When injury such as a cut or scrape breaks the skin, the second line of defense employs cellular and chemical resources to repel the invading pathogens. This is also called **innate immunity** and includes the following.

- The **inflammatory response** begins when infected or injured cells release **histamine** as a sort of alarm system. (Histamine is also associated with cold symptoms such as coughing, sneezing, runny nose, itchy eyes, etc.) The histamine sets off **vasodilation** (enlarging blood vessels), which rapidly increases blood flow to the area and makes it red and warm (the key sign of inflammation). Certain chemicals also increase permeability of capillaries, which results in **edema**, or the swelling of tissue — another sign of infection. This swelling of tissue pressures nerve endings in the area, causing pain and problems with function.

- Greater capillary permeability helps bring in **phagocytes** that "eat" invading microbes. Phagocytes include **neutrophils**, which die in a few days, and **monocytes**, which transform into **macrophages** and continue to ingest large numbers of microbes for a long period. Pus, which occurs with some infections, is a mixture of neutrophils, tissue cells, and pathogens that are dead or dying.

- An **acute-phase response** occurs with the inflammatory response and causes body temperature to increase several degrees above normal. This temperature increase, or **fever**, stimulates phagocyte activity.

- The **complement system** is a chemical defense made up of 30 different proteins moving freely in the blood plasma and available during an inflammatory response. These proteins attack pathogens' membranes, fill them with fluid, and cause them to burst. This is also called a **membrane attack complex**.

- **Interferons** are another class of proteins that come to the body's defense. They protect healthy cells from becoming infected by neighboring infected cells.

Specific Defense Mechanisms: Third Line of Defense

The third line of defense against invading pathogens is **specific** — that is, it attacks and eliminates any invading microorganisms or viruses that managed to survive the various components of the nonspecific immune system. The specific defense mechanism is triggered by **antigens,** or molecules that set off an immune response or the production of antibodies. **Lymphocytes** with receptor proteins recognize certain parts of antigens called **epitopes**. The specific immune system includes the following lymphocytes, which circulate in the blood, lymph fluid, and lymphatic tissues such as lymph nodes, spleen, tonsils, and adenoids.

- **B lymphocytes**, or B cells, migrate to the bone marrow where they mature into disease-fighting cells. The B cells produce proteins called **antibodies** at the rate of 2,000 per second. These antibodies rush through the bloodstream to the area of infection, where they bind to the antigens and "tag" the toxic bacteria, enabling phagocytes to recognize it and engulf it. This process is called **humoral immunity**.

- **T lymphocytes**, or T cells, mature after traveling from the bone marrow to the thymus gland. T cells do not produce antibodies, but instead they bolster the immune response of other cells or attack diseased cells directly. When meeting with antigens, T cells are stimulated to divide and differentiate into two kinds of specialized T cells: **cytotoxic T cells** and **helper T cells**. Cytotoxic T cells kill virus-infected cells or tumor cells. Helper T cells secrete proteins called **cytokines** that bind to specific receptors on other cells' membranes. This binding serves to initiate signals in these cells, thus alerting the immune system that foreign antigens are present in the body. Both kinds of T cells also divide into **plasma cells** and **memory cells** in a mechanism called **clonal selection**. Short-lived plasma cells fight antigens for about two weeks in the **primary immune response**. Memory cells live much longer, remaining in the bloodstream for a lifetime and having the ability to reactivate immediately should the same antigen reappear. This response, which takes only a week or less, is the **secondary immune response**. The ability of the human immune system to "remember" past immune responses is why a person cannot get a viral infection such as chicken pox more than once. T cells are also the primary cells that tend to reject transplanted organs. Overall, the T cells make up what is called **cell-mediated immunity**.

Diseases of the Immune System

In **autoimmune diseases** such as lupus or multiple sclerosis, the immune system fails to distinguish between **self** and **nonself tissues**. The system mistakes healthy structures in the body as invading substances and attacks them. For example, in multiple sclerosis the immune system attacks the protective sheath around certain nerves in the central nervous system. Another disease of the immune system is **AIDS**, which stands for Acquired Immune Deficiency Syndrome. This disease weakens the body's immune system, rendering it unable to repel other illnesses, infections, and cancers. A retrovirus called **HIV** (human immunodeficiency virus) attacks mainly helper T cells in the body and causes AIDS.

Vaccines and Antibiotics

A **vaccine** is a preparation that improves a person's immunity to a certain disease. It contains weakened or dead forms of the virus, its toxins, or enough of its surface proteins to stimulate a full immune response. The body then "remembers" the virus for lifelong immunity. When a child is **vaccinated** for a disease such as chicken pox, he or she receives an agent that contains a killed form of the chicken pox microorganism. Of course, a person makes his or her own antibodies following an episode of viral illness. This kind of permanent immunization is called **active immunity**.

Antibodies can also be transferred from one person to another. For example, a mother passes antibodies to a growing fetus through the placenta, or to a baby via breast milk. A person may receive a boost to a weak immune system through an injection of gamma globulin, which contains antibodies from many people. This kind of temporary immunization is called **passive immunity**.

While vaccines protect against future infections, **antibiotics** are given to people who are already sick. Antibiotics, or antibacterials, are medicines that kill bacteria or inhibit their growth. Some antibiotics also kill fungi. There is concern today that overuse of certain antibiotics may result in bacteria becoming resistant to the drugs.

Heredity and Family History

The genes passed from your parents to you not only determine such traits as your height, build, and eye and hair color, but also aspects of your health. Each person receives two copies of each gene, one from the person's father and one from the person's mother. **Mutations** or abnormalities in genes can be inherited just like other traits, and can increase a person's likelihood of developing certain diseases. Some conditions are entirely determined by genes, while others result from a genetic predisposition that is triggered by lifestyle choices or environmental factors. For example, a person whose father had a stroke as a result of cardiovascular disease may also be somewhat predisposed to these conditions. However, if that person also smokes or has an unhealthy diet, the chances of developing cardiovascular problems greatly increase.

Types of genetic inheritance include the following.

- In **autosomal dominant inheritance**, only a single copy of the abnormal gene needs to be passed on to a child for the disorder to appear. A parent with an autosomal dominant condition has a 50 percent chance of passing it to each of his or her children.

- With **autosomal recessive inheritance**, both parents carry the mutated gene. In this situation, the parents don't have the disease or condition but by passing on two copies of the defective gene they give their child a 25 percent chance of getting it and a 50 percent chance of also being an unaffected carrier. Sickle cell anemia and cystic fibrosis are examples of autosomal recessive conditions.

- In **X-linked inheritance**, the problem gene is found on the X chromosome. Since women have two copies of the X chromosome and men have one X and one Y, this condition is more likely to affect men.

- In **mitochondrial inheritance**, diseases come from mutations in the mitochondrion of the mother's egg. These diseases mostly affect tissues, such as muscles, the brain, and the liver, that consume a great deal of energy.

Environmental Factors That Affect Health

Environmental factors can affect health in both positive and negative ways. Positive environmental factors are often promoted as part of **preventive medicine**. For example, infectious diseases such as typhoid and cholera have been greatly reduced as public health problems due to clean water and improvements in sanitation.

Positive factors include:

- clean water

- efficient waste sanitation

- plentiful sources of nutrition

- clean air quality

- space for exercise

Negative factors include:

- invasive microbes such as viruses and bacteria

- poor water quality

- poor air quality

- poor management of wastes (solid, gases, liquids)

- environmental disruptions, such as floods, droughts, fires, earthquakes, volcanoes

Aside from these general influences, environmental factors can affect an individual's health on the molecular level. Recent research has identified a gene that plays a key role in cancer prevention. It is called the **p53 gene**, and its product, the **p53 protein**, monitors for DNA errors. If the p53 protein detects damaged DNA, it stops cell division and acts to stimulate special enzymes to repair the damaged cells. If the DNA is successfully repaired, p53 enables cell division to proceed. If the DNA is damaged beyond repair, p53 causes the cell to destroy itself. With its role in halting the division of damaged or mutated cells, p53 was described as a cancer-fighting gene.

However, certain environmental influences can cause mutations in the p53 gene and disrupt its role in cellular repair. These environmental influences might include radiation, viruses, or toxins in the blood. And indeed scientists have discovered that p53 is missing or too damaged to function properly in the great majority of cancer cells. With no p53 to suppress them, cancer cells can proliferate. Thus, environmental factors can prevent the body from deploying its own cancer-fighting resources.

Pathogenic Agents and Infectious Disease

As we have seen, **pathogenic agents** are microorganisms that cause disease in otherwise healthy persons. These pathogens can be transmitted in many ways. Respiratory illnesses and a spinal condition called meningitis are contracted by contact with airborne droplets spread by sneezing, coughing, or even talking. Gastrointestinal diseases are transmitted from eating food or drinking water that is contaminated. Sexually transmitted diseases are contracted from sexual contact and bodily fluids. Blood-borne diseases such as malaria and West Nile Virus can be spread by insect bites. If a disease kills its host rapidly, the pathogen may not spread to other hosts. However, slower-acting pathogens may result in numerous widespread infections, a situation called an **epidemic**. Preventive measures include frequent washing of hands, use of disinfectants and antibacterial soaps, pest control (insects, rats, and mice), and quarantining, or preventing contact between infected people and those who are uninfected.

End-of-Chapter Quiz

Use the illustration of the human brain below to answer questions 1–2.

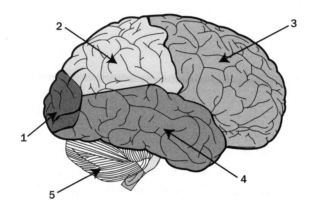

1. **Labels 1–4 designate the lobes of the human brain. What lobe corresponds to label 1?**

    A.   parietal

    B.   occipital

    C.   frontal

    D.   temporal

2. **What part of the human brain is designated by label 5?**

    A.   medula oblongata

    B.   brain stem

    C.   pons

    D.   cerebellum

3. **In the cardiovascular system, materials such as oxygen and nutrients are exchanged for carbon dioxide and other waste products through the extensive branches of which of the following?**

    A.   arteries

    B.   arterioles

    C.   capillaries

    D.   veins

4. **Which of the following creates blood pressure?**

   A. stoppage of blood flow to the lower arm

   B. narrowing of the arteries

   C. contraction of the heart's ventricles

   D. relaxing of the heart's ventricles

5. **With regard to blood viscosity, which of the following is true?**

   A. Thinner blood is less resistant to healthy flow.

   B. Thicker blood is healthier because it contains more nutrients.

   C. Thicker blood requires narrower vessels for healthy flow.

   D. The viscosity of blood has nothing to do with blood flow.

6. **A man aged 43 has a blood pressure reading of 142/85. Which of the following best describes this reading?**

   A. low blood pressure

   B. normal blood pressure

   C. elevated blood pressure but not hypertension levels

   D. blood pressure at hypertension levels

7. **Why are high-density lipoproteins (HDL) often called "good cholesterol"?**

   A. They tend to carry cholesterol to all the body's cells.

   B. They are the result of lifestyle choices rather than genetic inheritance.

   C. They are the result of genetic inheritance rather than lifestyle choices.

   D. They tend to transport cholesterol to the liver where it is eliminated.

8. **A person has a severely reduced flow of blood to the heart, resulting in the death of part of the heart muscle. What is the common name for this condition?**

   A. Arteriosclerosis

   B. heart attack

   C. stroke

   D. angina pectoris

9. A person has large deposits of calcium built up on arterial walls, which reduce
    the ability of the arteries to expand properly and also restrict blood flow. What
    is the name for this condition?

    A. Arteriosclerosis

    B. Atherosclerosis

    C. diabetes

    D. blood clots

10. Which of the following tends to increase blood flow temporarily?

    A. Raynaud's disease

    B. drinking caffeinated beverages

    C. exposure to cold temperatures

    D. vigorous exercise

11. The reactions associated with hyperventilation such as a feeling of lighthead-
    edness or loss of consciousness are due to what condition?

    A. blood clot in a cerebral artery

    B. elevated levels of sugar

    C. high blood pH value

    D. low blood viscosity

12. A patient who is prescribed a vasodilator probably has what condition?

    A. low blood pressure

    B. high blood pressure

    C. a throat infection

    D. diabetes

13. Which is NOT part of the immune system's nonspecific first line of defense?

    A. skin

    B. mucous membranes

    C. phagocytes

    D. cilia

14. In the inflammatory immune response, a certain agent is released that causes blood vessels to enlarge and rapidly increases blood flow to the infected area. What is the name of this agent?

   A. histamine

   B. interferon protein

   C. monocytes

   D. phagocytes

15. Which is the *best* description of monocytes?

   A. Monocytes are a chemical defense made up of 30 different proteins that move freely in the blood plasma and are available during an inflammatory response.

   B. Monocytes are a type of phagocyte that eat microbes for a very short period of time.

   C. Monocytes are a type of phagocyte that change into macrophages and ingest large numbers of microbes over a long period of time.

   D. Monocytes are a separate class of proteins that come to the body's defense by protecting healthy cells from being infected by neighboring infected cells.

16. Proteins that attack the membranes' of pathogens, fill them with fluid, and cause to them to burst apart are components of which of the following?

   A. cell-mediated immunity

   B. the complement system

   C. acute-phase response

   D. interferons

17. The third line of specific immune defense relies primarily on which of the following?

   A. plasma cells

   B. B lymphocytes

   C. T lymphocytes

   D. B lymphocytes and T lymphocytes

18. **A person who has had the measles as a child is unlikely to suffer a recurrence of the disease later in life. This phenomenon is primarily due to which of the following?**

    A. B cells that produce antibodies

    B. clonal selection

    C. T cells called memory cells

    D. T cells called plasma cells

19. **A person contracts certain blood toxins that cause somatic mutations in the p53 gene. The person later develops thyroid cancer. Which of the following statements best describes this situation?**

    A. Increased levels of blood toxins, caused by the presence of the p53 gene, caused the person to develop thyroid cancer.

    B. Environmental influence in the form of toxins caused mutations that weakened the cancer-fighting properties of the p53 gene and enabled the thyroid cancer to develop.

    C. Increased levels of the p53 gene, and thus of p53 proteins, often causes certain cancers such as thyroid cancer.

    D. Neither blood toxins nor the mutation of the p53 gene ultimately has any great effect on the development of cancer cells.

20. **Pathogens in the form of airborne droplets are most likely to cause which of the following illnesses?**

    A. throat infection

    B. stomach flu

    C. AIDS

    D. malaria

Answers to the Chapter Quiz

1. **B**

   Label 1 designates the occipital lobe of the brain.

2. **D**

   Label 5 designates the part of the brain called the cerebellum.

3. **C**

   The complex branching network of capillaries carries out the exchange of materials with organs and tissues.

4. **C**

   As the heart's ventricles contract, they generate pressure that drives the flow of blood through the arteries. Stopping blood flow to the lower arm (A) is a technique for measuring blood pressure. Narrowing of the arteries (B) can result in higher blood pressure, but does not initiate blood pressure.

5. **A**

   Thinner blood generally flows more easily through arteries and other blood vessels.

6. **C**

   Normal blood pressure for a healthy young person is 120/75. Hypertension levels begin at a systolic pressure greater than 150 and a diastolic pressure greater than 90. Thus, a reading of 142/85 is high for both systolic and diastolic pressure, but does not reach hypertension levels.

7. **D**

   High-density lipoproteins are able to remove cholesterol from arteries and transport it back to the liver, where it can be eliminated or reused. People with higher levels of HDL tend to have fewer problems with cardiovascular disease.

8. **B**

   A severe reduction or interruption of blood flow to the heart that results in the death of heart cells is an occurrence that is called a heart attack.

9. **A**

   A buildup of calcium deposits on arterial walls that reduces the arteries' ability to expand properly and also restricts blood flow is called hardening of the arteries, or arteriosclerosis.

10. **D**

    Vigorous exercise increases cardiac output and blood flow due to an increase in heart rate and stronger contractions of the heart ventricles. Raynaud's disease (A), drinking caffeinated beverages (B), and exposure to cold temperatures (C) all tend to restrict blood flow.

11. **C**

    During hyperventilation, a person breathes faster or deeper than normal, thus expelling more carbon dioxide and causing arterial levels of carbon dioxide to fall rapidly. This causes the blood to become alkaline, or have a higher than normal pH value.

12. **B**

    Vasodilators are medications that help to open blood vessels by relaxing muscles in vessel walls. They are used to treat high blood pressure because they increase blood flow and reduce blood pressure.

13. **C**

    Phagocytes are part of the immune system's nonspecific second line of defense, which includes the inflammatory response. Phagocytes "eat" invading microbes. The other answer choices all are part of the protective barrier that forms the first line of immune system defense.

14. **A**

    In the inflammatory response, injured or infected cells release histamine, which in turn sets off vasodilation, or enlarging of the blood vessels.

15. C

The description in answer choice C is the best description of monocytes. Answer A describes the complement system. Answer B describes neutrophils. Answer D describes interferons.

16. B

The complement system is a chemical defense made up of 30 different proteins that are available during an inflammatory response and that attack and burst the membranes of pathogens.

17. D

Both B lymphocytes and T lymphocytes originate in the bone marrow and form the immune system's third line of specific defense.

18. C

Memory cells are long-lived T cells that remain in a person's bloodstream for a lifetime and "remember" past viruses in order to reactivate at once should one of the viruses reappear in the body. B cells that produce antibodies are not memory cells. Clonal selection is the mechanism by which T cells divide into plasma cells and memory cells.

19. B

Contracting blood toxins would be an example of an environmental influence. Should such toxins cause somatic mutations in the p53 gene, the gene's ability to fight cancer by repairing damaged cells or destroying cells that are beyond repair would be compromised. This would help cancer cells to spread in the thyroid.

20. A

A respiratory illness such as a throat infection is most likely to be caused by pathogens in airborne droplets spread by sneezing or coughing.

Chapter 5

Evolution

Your Goals for Chapter 5

1. You should be able to identify evidence and/or explain how the scientific theory of evolution is supported by the fossil record, comparative anatomy, comparative embryology, biogeography, molecular biology, and observable evolutionary change.

2. You should be able to identify examples of and basic trends in hominid evolution from early ancestors to modern humans.

3. You should be able to identify ways in which a scientific claim is evaluated (e.g., through scientific argumentation, critical and logical thinking, and consideration of alternative explanations).

4. You should be able to classify organisms based on the distinguishing characteristics of the domains and/or kingdoms of living organisms.

5. You should be able to identify and/or describe how and/or why organisms are hierarchically classified based on evolutionary relationships.

6. You should be able to identify and/or explain the reasons for changes in how organisms are classified.

7. You should be able to describe scientific explanations of the origin of life on Earth.

8. You should be able to identify situations or conditions contributing to the origin of life on Earth.

9. You should be able to explain and/or describe the conditions required for natural selection that result in differential reproductive success.

10. You should be able to explain and/or describe the scientific mechanisms, such as genetic drift, gene flow, and nonrandom mating, resulting in evolutionary change.

11. You should be able to use Mendel's laws of segregation and independent assortment to analyze patterns of inheritance.

12. You should be able to identify, analyze, and/or predict inheritance patterns caused by various modes of inheritance.

Standards

The following standards are assessed on the Florida Biology 1 End-of-Course Assessment either directly or indirectly:

SC.912.L.15.1: Explain how the scientific theory of evolution is supported by the fossil record, comparative anatomy, comparative embryology, biogeography, molecular biology, and observed evolutionary change.

SC.912.L.15.10: Identify basic trends in hominid evolution from early ancestors six million years ago to modern humans, including brain size, jaw size, language, and manufacture of tools.

SC.912.L.15.4: Describe how and why organisms are hierarchically classified and based on evolutionary relationships.

SC.912.L.15.5: Explain the reasons for changes in how organisms are classified.

SC.912.L.15.6: Discuss distinguishing characteristics of the domains and kingdoms of living organisms.

SC.912.L.15.8: Describe the scientific explanations of the origin of life on Earth.

SC.912.L.15.13: Describe the conditions required for natural selection, including: overproduction of offspring, inherited variation, and the struggle to survive, which result in differential reproductive success.

SC.912.L.15.14: Discuss mechanisms of evolutionary change other than natural selection such as genetic drift and gene flow.

SC.912.L.15.15: Describe how mutation and genetic recombination increase genetic variation.

SC.912.L.16.1: Use Mendel's laws of segregation and independent assortment to analyze patterns of inheritance.

SC.912.L.16.2: Discuss observed inheritance patterns caused by various modes of inheritance, including dominant, recessive, codominant, sex-linked, polygenic, and multiple alleles.

SC.912.N.1.3: Recognize that the strength or usefulness of a scientific claim is evaluated through scientific argumentation, which depends on critical and logical thinking, and the active consideration of alternative scientific explanations to explain the data presented.

SC.912.N.1.4: Identify sources of information and assess their reliability according to the strict standards of scientific investigation.

SC.912.N.1.6: Describe how scientific inferences are drawn from scientific observations and provide examples from the content being studied.

SC.912.N.2.1: Identify what is science, what clearly is not science, and what superficially resembles science (but fails to meet the criteria for science).

SC.912.N.3.1: Explain that a scientific theory is the culmination of many scientific investigations drawing together all the current evidence concerning a substantial range of phenomena; thus, a scientific theory represents the most powerful explanation scientists have to offer.

SC.912.N.3.4: Recognize that theories do not become laws, nor do laws become theories; theories are well-supported explanations and laws are well-supported descriptions.

The Scientific Theory of Evolution

Evolution is the scientific theory that accounts for genetic changes in populations, species, and groups of species over time. There are two main areas of evolution study. **Microevolution** examines changes in a single gene pool from generation to generation. **Macroevolution** looks at patterns of changes in genetically related species over long periods of time. These patterns reveal **phylogeny**, or how species and groups of species are related through evolution. Over time, a species may replace another species or it may branch out from a parent species.

The theory of evolution is an ideal example of how a scientific theory develops through the contributions of many different scientists, each building on past knowledge and adding discoveries of his or her own. Key figures in the development of evolutionary theory include the following.

- Swedish botanist **Carl von Linné** (also called Linnaeus, 1707–1778) invented a system for naming, ranking, and classifying organisms. His system is still the basis for classifying species today.

- British economist **Thomas Malthus** (1766–1834) studied how populations of organisms would tend to grow geometrically until reaching an inevitable limit on their size.

- British geologist **Charles Lyell** (1797–1875) described the slow, continuous activity that results in geological change. He believed the Earth to be much older than the 6,000-year figure advanced by religious thinkers.

- Austrian monk **Gregor Mendel** (1822–1884) experimented on plants to develop a theory of genetics, or how hereditary traits are transferred from parents to children. Mendel published his ideas in 1866, but scientists did not realize until the 1900s that Mendel's principles were essentially correct.

- French scientist **Jean-Baptiste de Lamarck** (1744–1829) published his own theory of evolution in 1809, the year of Charles Darwin's birth. Lamarck believed that more complex organisms evolved from prior, less complex ones. His ideas included "use and disuse," which described how frequently-used body parts can develop while unused parts grow weak, and "inheritance of acquired characteristics," which attempted to explain how, for example, giraffes developed long necks due to stretching to reach leaves in taller trees. Lamarck was correct about organisms changing over time, but incorrect as to the mechanism.

- British naturalist **Charles Darwin** (1809–1882) developed the modern concept of evolution in his 1859 book *On the Origin of Species*. Darwin established that all species descend over time from common ancestors due to a process he called **natural selection** — which has often been restated as "survival of the fittest." (Darwin never actually used the term "evolution" in his famous book.) By the middle of the 20th century, Darwin's theory, with some modifications, had become widely accepted as the best explanation for the broad diversity of life.

- British biologist **Alfred Russel Wallace** (1823–1913) also produced a theory of natural selection that caused Darwin to publish his own theory. Through his extensive fieldwork on species, Wallace came to the same conclusions as Darwin, and can be seen as the co-developer of the theory of evolution. Wallace was an expert on the geographical distribution of animal species and made several contributions to evolutionary theory. Among these is the idea of "warning coloration" in which the bright or unusual coloring of individuals in a species protects them by warning away predators.

Evidence That Supports the Theory of Evolution

The theory of evolution, like other scientific theories, is the culmination of many scientific investigations drawing together all the current evidence from many different fields of knowledge. It represents the most powerful current explanation for the genetic development of life on Earth that scientists have to offer. The following are five major areas of science that provide support for the scientific theory of evolution.

1. **Paleontology**, which includes the study of the fossil record, reveals that now-extinct species existed in prehistoric times. It is the best direct evidence for evolution. Fossilized deposits are usually discovered in layers of sediment, with the oldest fossils buried deepest. Scientists can use fossils to track changes in species, mass extinctions of species (such as dinosaurs), and the emergence of new species.

2. **Biogeography**, or the study of how species are distributed geographically, reveals that unrelated species in widely separated regions of the world nevertheless resemble each other when living in similar environments. In other words, species evolve in similar ways when they react to similar surroundings.

3. **Comparative anatomy**, or the study of similarities and differences in the structures of organisms, reveals how evolution has brought about anatomical changes in species.

    • Body parts in different species that look similar because they have evolved from a common ancestor are called **homologous structures**. For example, a bat's wing, a whale's fin, and the human arm, while they have different functions, all have a very similar bone structure. This is due to their evolution from the same ancestral mammal.

    • Body parts in different species that look similar because they have adapted to similar environments are called **analogous structures**. For example, dolphins, sharks and seals all have similar fins and overall shapes that are adapted for swimming.

4. **Comparative embryology**, or the study of embryos in different species, reveals that species that are closely related have similar stages of development, called **ontogeny**. These similarities indicate similar adaptive or evolutionary changes, a pattern of relationships called **phylogeny**. For example, the embryos of humans, pigs, fish, and chickens all have rudimentary gills and tails.

5. **Molecular biology** studies and compares the amino acid and nucleotide sequences in the DNA of different species. The more closely related two species are, the higher the percentage of these sequences that they share. For example, humans and chimpanzees

share more than 98 percent of nucleotide sequences. This supports the idea that different species evolved through changes in some shared ancestral genetic code.

Examples of Hominid Evolution

Hominids, which include humans and their direct ancestors, are thought to have diverged from gorillas and chimpanzees about 4–6 million years ago. The most basic adaptation that distinguished hominids was **bipedalism**, or walking upright. The following are some of the most important stages of hominid evolution.

- The first true human—a member of the genus *Homo*—was **Homo habilis**, or "handy man," who evolved from *Australopithecus afarensis* about 2.3 million years ago. Stone tools scattered around hominid fossil remains indicate this species could manufacture tools. It is thought that *Homo habilis* had a brain volume of about 650 cc, significantly larger than that of *Australopithecus*.

- **Homo erectus** replaced *Homo habilis* about 1.8 million years ago. Homo erectus was about 1.5 meters in height and had a much larger brain, about 1,000 cc. Like modern humans, it had a rounded jaw, although one that protruded with very large molars. Its thick skeleton implies greater strength than modern humans. It seems to have used fire and was able to make more sophisticated tools than its predecessors. This species survived longer than any other species of human—more than a million years.

- **Early Homo sapiens** first appeared in archaic forms about 500,000 years ago. Branching off from this ancestral line were Neanderthals and Cro-Magnons. The **Neanderthal**—our cousin rather than ancestor—had a slightly larger brain than modern humans, was short and powerfully built, and had a protruding jaw and receding forehead. It made tools such as spearheads and scrapers and buried these implements with the bodies of the dead. Neanderthals probably came to Europe from Africa about 150,000 years ago. **Cro-Magnons** were another *Homo sapien* group whose earliest remains have been dated to 43,000 years ago. Cro-Magnons seem to have abruptly replaced Neanderthals about 35,000 years ago. Cro-Magnons were generally heavy and solidly built. Their foreheads were more vertical than the sloping foreheads of Neanderthals, and their brow ridges protruded only slightly. Their jawbones provided them with prominent chins. The Cro-Magnons had social organization and the ability to speak. They fashioned tools with decorations, carved ivory images of humans and animals, and left striking cave paintings of animals that are found throughout Europe. Our true ancestors, the Cro-Magnons are sometimes designated as European Early Modern Humans.

- **Modern Homo sapiens** *(Homo sapien* meaning "wise man") are the only surviving hominid species, and have continued the long trend towards less robust skeletons, smaller molars, high and short braincases, and vertical foreheads with smaller brow ridges. Brain size is about 1550 cc. This progressive increase in brain size has enabled *Homo sapiens* to distinguish themselves from other species in countless ways. Modern humans' ability to make and use tools, employ symbolic language to transmit ideas, and think conceptually makes our species dominant in the animal kingdom.

Classifying Organisms

The system for classifying organisms is called **taxonomy**. The biologist Linnaeus invented the system in the 1700s, and it is still in use today. Each **species** is assigned a name that consists of two parts: a species name and a **genus** name. As you have seen, a human is *Homo* (genus) *sapien* (species). A domesticated dog is *Canis familiaris*. Species that are closely related are placed in the same genus. For example, a wolf is *Canis lupus*. Species are also grouped in broader classifications; in order from specific to more general, these are **species, genus, family, order, class, phylum, kingdom**, and **domain**.

On the Florida Biology 1 End-of-Course Assessment, you will be tested only on certain domains and kingdoms. You are not required to have specific knowledge about organisms that are classified in any particular domain or kingdom. Instead, you should be able to describe what characteristics organisms in a certain classification share, and how evolution is used as the basis for classifying organisms.

The twentieth century saw changes in the system of classifying organisms. The original taxonomic system developed by Linnaeus had two kingdoms, **Plantae** and **Animalia**. In the 1960s, it became apparent to scientists that some organisms had characteristics of both plants and animals. The classification system changed to reflect a deeper understanding of evolution's effects on major groups of organisms. Three kingdoms were added to make a five-kingdom system: **Monera, Protista, Fungi**, Plantae, and Animalia. Around 1990, a sixth kingdom was added—**Archaebacteria**, made up of microorganisms that seemed to differ significantly from bacteria. Today, scientists use the **three-domain system**, which is based on differences in DNA structure or **evolutionary relationships** (phylogeny). In this system, life forms are classified into three domains: **Bacteria, Archaea**, and **Eukarya**. Domain Eukarya includes four of the original kingdoms: Protista, Fungi, Plantae, and Animalia. *(Note: Your study should focus on the three domains and the four kingdoms that make up Domain Eukarya.)* This most recent change in classification resulted from research into DNA and **genetic sequencing**. Taxonomy today is gradually being replaced by **systematics**, an area of study that includes taxonomy but focuses on evolutionary outcomes and tracing the ancestors of organisms. In general, organisms are classified **hierarchically** (arranged in levels from lower to higher) to show the degree of relatedness between and among living things.

Overall, classification of living things begins with two kinds of cells and the major methods that organisms employ to get energy. **Prokaryotes** are cells that are small, very simple in structure, and very numerous. **Eukaryotes** are more complex cells, and they are also larger and less numerous than prokaryotes. **Autotrophs** are organisms that make their own organic molecules, either by using light energy (photosynthesis) or by using energy from inorganic substances (chemosynthesis). **Heterotrophs** are organisms that get energy by consuming the organic material made by autotrophs. Heterotrophs include **parasites**, which get energy from living tissues, and **saprobes**, which get energy from matter that is dead and decaying.

Now you are ready to look more closely at how organisms are classified.

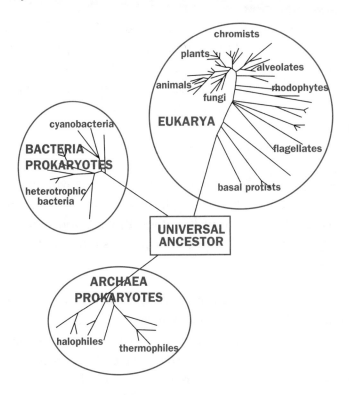

Figure 5.1: The Three-Domain Classification System

The Three Domains

The characteristics of each of the three domains are presented below.

Domain Bacteria

- All are single-celled prokaryotes.

- Cell walls of most are thick and rigid, and made of a polymer called peptidoglycan.

- Able to grow and reproduce very rapidly.

- Activity of the ribosome is inhibited by the antibiotics streptomycin and chloramphenicol.

- Many are disease-causing pathogens.

- Play an important role in the decomposition of dead organic matter.

- Are classified by such features as shape, cell wall, mode of movement, and mode of nutrition or metabolizing food.

- Include such organisms as *E. coli* that live in the human intestine, *Leptospira* that causes serious livestock disease, disease-causing bacteria such as *Streptococcus*, and nitrogen-fixing bacteria on certain plant roots.

Domain Archaea

- All are single-celled prokaryotes.

- Contain various polysaccharides in cell walls, but no peptidoglycan, cellulose, or chitin.

- Like eukaryotes, have DNA with histone proteins.

- Activity of the ribosome not inhibited by the antibiotics streptomycin and chloramphenicol.

- Includes major groups such as **methanogens**, which are methane-producing organisms living in swamps, mud, and intestines; and **extremophiles**, which are organisms living in extreme environmental conditions. For example, **Halophiles**, or "salt lovers," live in high-salt surroundings such as the Great Salt Lake. **Thermophiles**, or "heat lovers," exist in extremely warm environments such as geysers or hot springs.

Domain Eukarya

- All are eukaryotes, either single-celled or multicellular.

- No peptidoglycan in cells.

- Have DNA with histone proteins.

- Activity of the ribosome not inhibited by the antibiotics streptomycin and chloramphenicol.

Domain Eukarya is essentially a superkingdom that includes the kingdoms Protista, Fungi, Plantae, and Animalia.

Kingdom Protista

This kingdom consists of a wide variety of organisms: fungus-like, algae-like or plant-like, and animal-like. They can be either single-celled or primitively multi-celled, and include both heterotrophs and autotrophs. Some carry out a form of sexual reproduction called conjugation. These tiny aquatic organisms exchange gases and eliminate wastes through simple diffusion. Evolutionary relationships among these groups of organisms are often weak and/or poorly understood. Shared features seem due to **convergent evolution**, in which similar traits arise independently. Thus Kingdom Protista is more a grouping of convenience for organisms such as slime molds and seaweed that don't fit into the plant or fungi kingdoms. Protists are defined chiefly by what they are not: they are not bacteria, fungi, plants, or animals. It is uncertain how many species there are in this grouping, but estimates range as high as 200,000.

The **fungus-like protists** form either filaments or stalks bearing spores that are similar to those in fungi. The **algaelike protists** are autotrophs, manufacturing energy by photosynthesis, and are categorized by their chlorophylls, cell-wall makeup, and number of flagella. The **animal-like protists**, or **protozoa**, are heterotrophs that obtain energy by consuming other living cells or dead organic matter. All higher forms of animal life derive from protozoa. Many protozoa cause diseases such as amoebic dysentery.

Kingdom Fungi

This kingdom consists of heterotrophic organisms that recycle dead organic matter into nutrients that are useful to plants and other organisms. Some fungi are parasites that sap energy from living things. Fungi grow as threadlike filaments called **hyphae** and serve the ecosystem as decomposers that absorb and pass on nutrients. They digest food outside their bodies by releasing into the surrounding area enzymes that break down organic matter into products the fungi can absorb by diffusion. Plants in a symbiotic relationship with fungi benefit by taking in the nutrients from fungi growing among their roots. Fungi reproduce asexually by several means. One way is by releasing spores from its fruit, called a mushroom. The spores, carried by the wind, produce the organism's next generation. The cell walls of fungi are made of **chitin**, not cellulose. Among the organisms in this kingdom are mushrooms, truffles, bread mold, yeast, mildews, and "athlete's foot" fungus.

Kingdom Plantae

This kingdom consists of all land plants. These autotrophic organisms evolved to survive the transition from water to land. They adapted in ways that helped them obtain water and avoid losing it by drying out, or **desiccation**. The upper parts of plants have a waxy outer covering called the cuticle, which reduces the plants' tendency to dry out. A vascular system to distribute water throughout the plant also developed. This made plants less dependent upon being near water for replenishing cells and allowed plant tissues to grow more specialized for separate tasks. Thus plants developed leaves for photosynthesis, stems for framework, and roots for obtaining water and anchoring each plant in the soil. Plants further adapted to meet the challenges of seasonal differences in sunlight and water. For example, to minimize loss of water during dormant seasons when growth slows, **deciduous** trees shed their leaves. Kingdom Plantae includes a huge variety of plants, from ferns and mosses to conifers and flowering plants. More information on plants is available in Chapter 3.

Kingdom Animalia

This kingdom consists of all animals, which are multi-celled heterotrophic organisms. Members of this kingdom have cells organized into tissues that are specialized for particular functions. Most reproduce sexually, with a small, flagellated (having tiny organs of motion) sperm fertilizing a larger, nonmoving egg. Most animal embryos undergo a period of development in which three layers of tissues (called **germ layers**) form. The outer layer, or **ectoderm**, becomes the skin and nervous system. The middle layer, or **mesoderm**, becomes the blood and bones. The inner layer, or **endoderm**, becomes the digestive system. During the development of the embryo, a fluid-filled cavity called a **coelom** forms to protect the organs and allow them to expand and contract. More sophisticated animals have **bilateral symmetry**, meaning that the body is formed along an axis of longitude that divides it into left and right sides that mirror each other. As these organisms increase in complexity, they have progressively more nerve tissue for brains with associated sensory organs. This development of the anterior end is called **cephalization**. Reproductive, digestive, and excretory parts are located at the posterior end.

Figure 5.2: Animal Development from Primitive to Complex

From Primitive Animals . . .	. . . To More Complex Animals
Lives in water	Adapted to live on land
Two cell layers: ectoderm and endoderm	Three cell layers: ectoderm, mesoderm, and endoderm
No cephalization	Cephalization, with brain and complex sensory organs
No bilateral or radial symmetry	Bilateral symmetry, with a well-developed anterior end and posterior end
No coelem	Coelem forms in the developing embryo
Unspecialized aggregations of cells	Cells in specialized groups called tissues, organs, and organ systems
Basically immobile	Mobile

Scientific Explanations of the Origin of Life on Earth

Related to the study of evolution is the study of how life began on Earth. **Chemical evolution** is a widely accepted scientific theory about the conditions and the overall process that scientists believe led to the first living things. The basic steps in the process include the following.

- **Formation of the Earth and atmosphere:** The ancient atmosphere formed when the Earth's molten interior released (through volcanoes) a variety of inorganic molecules but no free oxygen.

- **Formation of primordial seas:** Cooling of the Earth led to condensation of gases that produced seas of water and minerals. (*Primordial* means "existing from the beginning of time.")

- **Synthesis of complex molecules:** Energy caused the formation of increasingly complex organic molecules from inorganic molecules. The organic molecules were created in a sort of **"primordial soup"** filled with compounds that reacted with energy. The sources of energy were mostly ultraviolet light, lightning, and heat. The new organic molecules, which included amino acids, remained stable due to the absence of oxygen to degrade them. It was these organic molecules that ultimately became the building blocks of life. In the 1920s, the Russian scientist A. I. Oparin and the British geneticist J. B. S. Haldane each separately theorized about this process, which became known as the **Oparin-Haldane hypothesis**. In the 1950s American scientists Stanley Miller and Harold Urey confirmed this hypothesis by synthesizing organic molecules from simple gases using ultraviolet light and electricity to mimic the conditions of the early atmosphere. This is known as the **Miller-Urey experiment**. More recently, Sidney Fox performed experiments that demonstrated how organic molecules could have produced cell-like proteins with membranes.

- **Concentration of organic molecules:** Organic molecules became concentrated into **protobionts**, which were the precursors of cells. These pre-cells could carry out some chemical reactions and exchange some materials but could not reproduce.

- **Formation of heterotrophic prokaryotes: Prokaryotes** such as bacteria were the first cells on Earth. They were **heterotrophs** that consumed organic matter from the primordial soup. As they reproduced, natural selection favored the prokaryotes best able to obtain food.

- **Mutation into autotrophic prokaryotes:** Some prokaryotes mutated into **autotrophs** able to produce their own food. They manufactured organic compounds by light energy (photosynthesis) or by getting energy from inorganic materials (chemosynthesis).

- **Release of oxygen and formation of ozone layer:** With photosynthesis occurring, oxygen was released into the atmosphere. The oxygen reacted with ultraviolet light to produce the ozone layer, which began to absorb UV light and ended the source for abiotic synthesis of primitive cells.

- **Formation of eukaryotes:** Various kinds of prokaryotes, such as mitochondria, chloroplasts, and other organelles began living inside larger prokaryotic cells. According to the **theory of endosymbiosis**, this was a mutually beneficial symbiotic relationship that became permanent. The result was the formation of the more complex **eukaryotes**. Evidence for this theory includes the observations that (1) mitochondria and chloroplasts have their own DNA; (2) this DNA resembles the DNA of prokaryotes more than the DNA of eukaryotes; (3) and mitochondria and chloroplasts have double membranes, indicating the process of a smaller, separate cell becoming enclosed by a larger cell.

Studies based on radiocarbon dating indicate that the earth is about 4.5 billion years old. Prokaryotes began to evolve about 3.5 billion years ago, with eukaryotes appearing about 2 billion years ago.

Natural Selection

Darwin's theory of natural selection, or **"descent with modification,"** as he called it, explains one important mechanism of evolution. Certain individuals in a population have inherited characteristics that allow them to survive and produce more offspring than individuals who lack these characteristics. In more technical terms, they have **alleles** (genotypes) that produce **traits** (phenotypes) more conducive to survival. Over time, the population changes to include more individuals with these **adaptations**, or helpful traits. Natural selection operates when an environment favors a trait, or increases the survival rates of those who have it. The population thus evolves to better adapt itself to local circumstances.

Darwin's theory included the following key points:

1. Populations have a powerful tendency to overpopulate. When they do, they outgrow the scarce resources of their environment. Darwin got this idea from reading Malthus on how population growth is affected by disease and famine.

2. At some point, populations tend to stabilize at a certain size due to competition for scarce resources. This is the "struggle for survival" that Darwin described.

3. In every population, there is a variation among individuals' ability to survive and reproduce. Mendel's work on genetics eventually provided an explanation for these variations.

4. Only the fittest individuals in a population survive and reproduce. These individuals out-compete others in the population.

5. Evolution occurs as traits that favor survival accumulate in the population. Parents pass these traits on to their children, the fittest of which reproduce and pass on their traits. Over generations, the population changes to include the most successful adaptations to the environment. It is important to remember that individual organisms do not change due to environmental pressures. What changes instead is the frequency of a particular allele in the population.

Five types of natural selection include the following:

- **Stabilizing selection** favors the more common traits of individuals as opposed to extreme or unusual variations. For example, human offspring tend to be about 6–8 pounds (2.7–3.6 kg) at birth. Individuals with much larger or much smaller birth weights have higher rates of infant mortality.

- **Directional selection** favors traits at one extreme of a range of possible traits. The result is that traits at the opposite extreme tend to disappear. The favored traits in turn become increasingly extreme, changing the population's overall **allele frequencies**. An example of directional selection is insects with resistance to pesticides. Resistant individuals tend to survive, while less resistant ones die. Over time, the entire population develops resistance.

- **Disruptive selection** favors more extreme traits over common ones. Over time, two sets of extreme traits can result in **balanced polymorphism**, with the population divided into two types. This division can finally result in the creation of two new species. In one example of disruptive selection, giraffes with the extreme trait of long necks outcompeted shorter-necked giraffes for scarce leaves in tall trees and survived in greater numbers. In the same way, shorter weeds tend to survive in suburban lawns because they are less likely to be mowed while taller weeds with better access to sunlight survive better in the wild.

- **Sexual selection** is the mating behavior in a population that produces more numerous and/or more fit offspring. **Female choice** means that females tend to strengthen the gene pool by choosing superior males with which to mate. Females respond to behaviors and traits (elaborate mating rituals, colorful plumage) that attract them to certain males. **Male competition**, on the other hand, means that males compete with other males for mating opportunities, or to produce quantities of offspring. They develop traits such as superior size or musculature, horns, and antlers that are assets in contests of strength to determine mating opportunities.

- **Artificial selection** is when humans breed plants and animals to produce individuals with desirable traits that can be used as breeding stock. (Since this does not occur naturally, it is not technically a part of natural selection.) For example, racehorses are bred for traits that increase speed. Cauliflower, broccoli, brussels sprouts, and kale were all bred from a single species of wild mustard by selecting for desired traits.

Other Mechanisms for Evolutionary Change

While Darwin proposed that natural selection was what caused a population to evolve, modern genetics has shown that other mechanisms also cause evolutionary change.

- **Genetic drift** is a random change in the gene pool. Alleles may increase or decrease purely by chance. In the **bottleneck effect**, a population is drastically reduced in size due to natural disaster or disease. The smaller population is then vulnerable to genetic drift as certain alleles have a greater effect on the population than usual. In the **founder effect**, a subgroup that migrates away from a larger population becomes subject to the effect of rare alleles.

- **Gene flow** is the migration of alleles into or out of a population. The usual result of gene flow is to increase the population's diversity.

- **Nonrandom mating** is the choice of a mate based on specific reasons, such as a preference for similar or different traits from oneself, preference for geographical nearness, or some other preference. **Inbreeding** (mating with relatives) and **sexual selection** (female choice of strong or aggressive males) are other forms of nonrandom mating.

- **Mutation** is the introduction into the gene pool of alleles that never existed before. Mutation is vital because it provides the basis for new variation. While some mutations may prove beneficial, most are harmful. Variation is also promoted by **genetic recombination**, in which the parental combination of alleles recombines to produce altered chromosomes in the offspring.

Inheritance Patterns and Mendel's Laws

In the mid-1800s, an Austrian monk named **Gregor Mendel** produced laws of heredity that established the field of **modern genetics**. Mendel bred thousands of pea plants in order to study inherited traits. By applying statistical analysis to his carefully recorded data, Mendel demonstrated how genetic variations occur in observable patterns.

To answer questions about heredity on the Florida Biology 1 End-of-Course Assessment, you must know the basics of **probability**. An event that is certain has a probability of 1; an event that cannot occur has a probability of 0. All other probabilities lie between 0 and 1. Probability cannot predict the outcome of a single event. Instead, it is used in large samples to predict an average outcome from certain circumstances. How likely is it that a blue-eyed mother and a brown-eyed father will have a blue-eyed child? Probability provides the answer.

The Rule of Multiplication

The probability of two independent events occurring is:

probability of first event × probability of second event

For example, the probability of getting heads on two coin flips involves two independent events. The chance of the first coin flip being heads is 1 : 2. The chance of the second coin flip also being heads is also 1 : 2. Therefore the probability that two coin flips will both be heads is $1/2 \times 1/2 = 1/4$.

The Rule of Addition

The probability of either of two mutually exclusive events occurring is:

probability of one event + probability of the other event

For example, the probability of rolling a die and getting either a 3 or a 4 is

$1/6 + 1/6 = 2/6$ or $1/3$.

Figure 5.3: Probability

Mendel carried out his experiments on pea plants, for which the allele for purple flowers is **dominant** *(P)* and the allele for white flowers is **recessive** *(p)*. If the offspring of crossed pea plants is **homozygous dominant**, it inherits two dominant alleles *(PP)* and the dominant trait (purple flowers) is exhibited. If it is **homozygous recessive**, it inherits two recessive alleles *(pp)* and the recessive trait (white flowers) is expressed. If it is **heterozygous**, it inherits one dominant allele and one recessive allele *(Pp)* and only the dominant trait is expressed. The **genotype** refers to an organism's entire set of alleles. The **phenotype** is how a gene is expressed in physical appearance, such as a purple flower or blue eyes. Think of the genotype as the blueprint and the phenotype as the final visible product.

In heredity experiments, the parents are called the *P* generation. The offspring from the crossing of the parent organisms is the F_1 generation. The offspring from crossings among the F_1 is called the F_2 generation.

Mendel's laws of heredity and other genetic principles include the following.

- The **law of dominance** says that when two organisms, each of which is homozygous for two different traits (such as purple flowers and white flowers), are crossed, the offspring produced will be **hybrid** (with two different alleles) but will express only the dominant allele. Thus, Mendel observed that hybrid plants did not result in a blending of traits (such as mottled purple-and-white flowers), but instead the plants inherited each trait intact. The recessive trait that is present but not expressed is said to be **latent**.

- The **law of segregation** states that the alternate alleles for a trait segregate (or separate) from each other during the formation of gametes and thus remain distinct. This law is best demonstrated by the **monohybrid cross**. This is a cross between two organisms that each are hybrid for one trait, a situation shown as *(Pp × Pp)*. Mendel found that the **phenotype ratio** for this type of cross is always 3 dominant to 1 recessive. He also found that the **genotype ratio** is always 1 to 2 to 1 — or in percentage terms, 25 percent homozygous dominant to 50 percent heterozygous to 25 percent homozygous recessive. The monohybrid cross can be illustrated by a Punnett square, as in Figure 5.4. A Punnett square shows all the possible outcomes of a genetic cross and helps in figuring the probability of a particular outcome.

	P	*p*
P	*PP*	*Pp*
p	*Pp*	*pp*

Figure 5.4: Punnett Square for a Monohybrid Cross

- The **testcross** is a method of finding the genotype of an organism showing the dominant trait. For example, a purple-flowered pea plant can be crossed with a white-flowered pea plant, a plant known to be homozygous recessive. If all the offspring have purple flowers, then the original plant must be homozygous dominant. If half of the offspring have purple flowers and half have white flowers, then the original plant must be heterozygous dominant.

- The **law of independent assortment** applies to a cross between two organisms that are hybrid for two or more traits. For example, pea plant seeds can be yellow (*Y*) or green (*y*) and their texture can be round (*R*) or wrinkled (*r*). This situation is called a **dihybrid cross**. The phenotype ratio for the 16 possible outcomes of the dihybrid cross is 9:3:3:1. In other words, for two pea-plant seed traits that behave independently, the possible outcomes are 9 round-yellow, 3 round-green, 3 wrinkled-yellow, and 1 wrinkled-green. The Punnett square for this dihybrid cross is shown in Figure 5.5.

	RY	*Ry*	*rY*	*ry*
RY	*RR YY*	*RR Yy*	*Rr YY*	*Rr Yy*
Ry	*RR Yy*	*RR yy*	*Rr Yy*	*Rr yy*
rY	*Rr YY*	*Rr Yy*	*rr YY*	*rr Yy*
ry	*Rr Yy*	*Rr yy*	*rr Yy*	*rr yy*

Figure 5.5: Punnett Square for a Dihybrid Cross

- **Codominance** is an inheritance pattern in which both inherited alleles are expressed. A good example of codominance are the MN blood groups found in humans.

- **Incomplete dominance** is when a gene's alleles are not dominant and recessive but instead produce a blending of the individual traits. Using snapdragons as an example, a red snapdragon *(R)* crossed with a white snapdragon *(r)* produces a pink snapdragon *(Rr),* which indicates that neither the red nor white color was dominant. Thus, the three kinds of inheritance form a continuum from complete dominance (dominant allele over recessive allele) at one end to codominance (both alleles expressed) at the other end, with incomplete dominance (blending of two alleles) lying between the two extremes.

- **Multiple alleles** is a situation in which there are more than two possible alleles for a gene. (Most genes in a population have two alleles, one dominant and one recessive.) For the ABO blood group in humans, there are three alleles, A, B, and O, which produce 6 possible genotypes to form 4 blood types. The A and B alleles are codominant. This situation means that only the O blood type is a "universal donor" that every person's immune system can tolerate. A person with blood type A, B, or AB must receive the same blood type in transfusion or else his or her immune system will respond by attacking the antigens of the foreign blood type. This results in **agglutination**, or clumping, which can be fatal.

- **Sex-linkage** refers to linked genes on the X chromosome. Humans have 46 chromosomes, 44 of which are **autosomes** and 2 of which are **sex chromosomes**. The sex chromosomes are X and Y, with most of the genes carried on the X chromosome, also called the sex chromosome. Females have two copies of the X chromosome (XX), while males have one X chromosome and one Y chromosome (XY). Sex-linked traits are carried on the X chromosome. A sex-linked genetic defect such as hemophilia *(h),* a disease in which blood does not clot properly, occurs only in a female who has two copies of the defective gene *($X^h X^h$).* A female with only one copy of the defective gene *($X^H X^h$,* with *H* a healthy gene) will not have hemophilia but is a carrier and can pass on the defective gene to offspring. Hemophilia occurs in males who inherit only one copy of the defective gene (X^hY). For this reason, sex-linked genetic defects appear much more frequently in males. Other such conditions due to gene mutation are cystic fibrosis, Huntington's disease, color-blindness, and sickle cell disease.

- **Polygenic inheritance** is the interaction of multiple genes to form a single phenotype. For example, height in humans is not limited to being either short or tall but is instead a **continuous variation**, or wide range, from very short to extremely tall. The opposite of polygenic inheritance is **pleiotropy**, in which one gene results in several phenotypes.

End-of-Chapter Quiz

1. Which of the following scientists theorized correctly about organisms changing over time, but was incorrect as to the method of this change?

    A. Alfred Russel Wallace

    B. Charles Darwin

    C. Jean-Baptiste de Lamarck

    D. Thomas Malthus

2. Rabbits are not native to Australia, having been brought there from England by sailors in the late eighteenth century. Yet rabbits have thrived in Australia to the point of becoming too numerous. In addition, rabbits and certain native Australian wallabies, although not closely related, resemble each other as to body structure and habits. Which idea about evolution is supported by these facts?

    A. Mass extinctions of species and the emergence of new species can be studied by examining the fossil record.

    B. Different species originally developed because of changes in some shared ancestral genetic code.

    C. Many species have body parts that look similar because they evolved from the same ancestral mammal.

    D. Species evolve in similar ways when they react to similar surroundings.

3. Which of the following is NOT a homologous structure?

    A. a moth wing

    B. a whale fin

    C. a human arm

    D. a bat wing

4. Which of the following was the most basic adaptation that distinguished hominids from gorillas and chimpanzees?

    A. the ability to speak

    B. the ability to use tools

    C. the ability to walk upright

    D. the ability to reason

5. **Which of the following is NOT a trend in the evolution of the hominid species?**

    A. smaller molars

    B. thicker skeletons

    C. smaller brow ridges

    D. larger brain size

6. **Most scientists now subscribe to the three-domain system of classifying organisms, which has replaced the five-kingdom system. Which is the main reason for this change?**

    A. research into DNA and evolutionary relationships

    B. close study of the fossil record

    C. discovery of microorganisms that differ in many ways from bacteria

    D. doubts about the role of evolution in changing organisms over time

7. **Which of the following is eukaryotic and heterotrophic, and has cell walls made of chitin?**

    A. animals

    B. plants

    C. fungi

    D. protozoa

8. **The evolutionary development of plants included a waxy outer covering called a cuticle. What is the main purpose of this covering?**

    A. protect the plant from ultraviolet radiation

    B. facilitate photosynthesis

    C. distribute water throughout the plant

    D. reduce the plant's tendency to dry out

9. In which kingdom are organisms grouped together more for shared features than true evolutionary relationships?

    A. Protista

    B. Fungi

    C. Plantae

    D. Animalia

10. Which of the following is *least* characteristic of a complex organism?

    A. cephalization

    B. symbiotic relationship

    C. bilateral symmetry

    D. specialized tissues and organs

11. In most animal embryos, the layer of tissue called the mesoderm develops into which of the following?

    A. nervous system

    B. skin

    C. digestive system

    D. blood and bones

12. What does the theory of endosymbiosis attempt to describe about the origins of life?

    A. how various sources of energy caused the formation of increasingly complex molecules

    B. how the absence of oxygen enabled the first organic molecules to remain stable

    C. how eukaryotes were formed from prokaryotes

    D. how some prokaryotes mutated into autotrophs able to manufacture their own food

13. Scientists agree that organic molecules were first created in a "primordial soup" filled with compounds that reacted with energy and remained stable due to the absence of oxygen. This theory resulted from the work of which of the following scientists?

    A.   A. I. Oparin

    B.   A. I. Oparin and J. B. S. Haldane

    C.   Stanley Miller and Harold Urey

    D.   Sidney Fox

14. Which of the following is NOT a part of Darwin's theory of natural selection?

    A.   Individual organisms change over time exclusively because of environmental pressures.

    B.   Evolution occurs due to the accumulation in a population of traits that favor survival.

    C.   In every population there exists a variation or disparity among individuals' ability to survive and reproduce.

    D.   Only the fittest individuals in a population survive and reproduce.

15. Darwin's theory of natural selection begins with the idea that populations have a powerful tendency to overpopulate and use up scarce resources. He developed this idea from reading which of the following?

    A.   Lamarck

    B.   Malthus

    C.   Mendel

    D.   Wallace

16. A hawk moth looks much like a crumpled and veined dead leaf, an appearance that helps to protect it from predators. This is an example of which of the following?

    A.   a balanced polymorphism

    B.   an allele

    C.   a mutation

    D.   an adaptation

17. **A population of mice features some with dark fur, some with white fur, and some with fur that appears gray. The population lives in an environment divided between patches of dark soil and areas of white rocks. As a result, the mice with dark fur are able to hide from winged predators in the dark soil, while the mice with white fur are able to hide among the white rocks. However, the gray mice stand out in that environment and are caught by predators in disproportionate numbers. This situation is an example of which form of natural selection?**

    A.   sexual selection

    B.   directional selection

    C.   disruptive selection

    D.   stabilizing selection

18. **Which of the following is a change in the genetic makeup of a population due to chance?**

    A.   genetic drift

    B.   gene flow

    C.   mutation

    D.   inbreeding

19. **What is the purpose of a testcross?**

    A.   to find the genotype of an organism displaying the dominant trait

    B.   to find the phenotype of a hybrid organism

    C.   to determine if an organism is homozygous recessive

    D.   to determine the phenotype ratio of a dihybrid cross

20. Look at the Punnett square. It shows the F_2 generation for a monohybrid cross of watermelons.

	W	w
W	WW	Ww
w	Ww	ww

The shape of the watermelons can either be long (*W*) or round (*w*). According to the results of this cross, how many of the watermelons would be long?

A. 1

B. 2

C. 3

D. 4

Answers to the Chapter Quiz

1. **C**

Lamarck was a French scientist who published his own theory of evolution in 1809, long before Darwin's work. He correctly believed that more complex organisms evolve from prior, less complex ones.

2. **D**

The similarity of rabbits and wallabies despite their not being closely related and their original distance from each other geographically, plus the ability of rabbits to thrive in a new environment that seems to be similar to their original one, supports the findings of biogeography about how widely divergent species can evolve in similar ways when reacting to similar environments.

3. **A**

Homologous structures are body parts in different species that have a similar appearance because they have evolved from a common ancestor. Insects, such as moths, are not closely related to the other animals listed, which are all mammals.

4. **C**

   Walking upright, or bipedalism, was the most basic adaptation that distinguished hominids from similar primates.

5. **B**

   The trend in hominid evolution is toward **less** robust skeletons with thinner bones.

6. **A**

   The change to the three-domain system reflected new information gained from a deeper understanding of DNA and phylogeny, or relationships based on evolution.

7. **C**

   Fungi are eukaryotes that are heterotrophic, or get energy from consuming organic material made by autotrophs. Their cell walls are made of a substance called chitin, not cellulose as in plants.

8. **D**

   The cuticle helps prevent desiccation, or drying out. Its main purpose is not to protect the plant from UV radiation. Leaves mainly aid in photosynthesis, and the vascular system distributes water throughout the plant.

9. **A**

   The organisms in Kingdom Protista share features that seem to be due to convergent evolution, in which similar traits arise independently. Thus these organisms are grouped together more for their shared features than close relationships through ordinary evolutionary processes.

10. **B**

    Symbiotic relationship is more characteristic of plants and fungi that depend on each other directly for life-giving nutrients. The other answer choices are characteristic of more complex animal life.

11. D

The mesoderm is the middle layer of germ-layer tissue. It develops into the blood and bones.

12. C

The theory of endosymbiosis describes the mutually beneficial symbiotic relationship between smaller prokaryotes, such as mitochondria, chloroplasts, and other organelles, and the larger prokaryotic cells inside which the organelles began to live. This relationship resulted in the formation of eukaryotes, which were more complex cells.

13. B

In the 1920s the Russian scientist Oparin and the British scientist Haldane each separately theorized about the conditions that led to the creation of the first organic molecules.

14. A

The theory of natural selection says that environmental pressures affect the frequency of particular alleles that tend to produce a traits more favorable to survival in the environment. The environment does not cause evolutionary change directly.

15. B

Thomas Malthus published a treatise on population growth and its related problems in 1798. Darwin developed his idea about overpopulation after reading this work.

16. D

The hawk moth's deceptive appearance is an example of an adaptation, or an advantageous trait that has evolved to help the organism survive.

17. C

This situation is an example of disruptive selection, in which more extreme traits (dark fur and white fur) are favored over common or intermediate ones (gray fur).

18. A

Genetic drift occurs when alleles in a population increase or decrease purely by chance, such as from migration or natural disasters.

19. A

In a testcross, a plant displaying the dominant trait is crossed with a plant known to be homozygous recessive. The results will determine if the original plant is homozygous dominant or heterozygous dominant.

20. C

The phenotypic frequencies of the monohybrid cross would be 3/4 long and 1/4 round because both *WW* and *Ww* genotypes produce long watermelons. Thus, three of the four watermelons would be long.

Chapter 6

Heredity and Reproduction

Your Goals for Chapter 6

1. You should be able to describe the process of DNA replication and/or its role in the transmission and conservation of genetic information.

2. You should be able to describe gene and chromosomal mutations in the DNA sequence.

3. You should be able to explain how gene and chromosomal mutations may or may not result in a phenotypic change.

4. You should be able to explain the basic processes of transcription and/or translation, and their roles in the expression of genes.

5. You should be able to explain that the basic components of DNA are universal in organisms.

6. You should be able to explain how similarities in the genetic codes of organisms are due to common ancestry and the process of inheritance.

7. You should be able to evaluate examples and/or explain the possible impact of biotechnology on the individual, society, and/or the environment.

8. You should be able to identify and/or describe the basic anatomy and physiology of the human reproductive system.

9. You should be able to describe the process of human development from the zygotic stage to the end of the third trimester and birth.

10. You should be able to differentiate the processes of mitosis and meiosis.

11. You should be able to describe the role of mitosis in asexual reproduction, and/or the role of meiosis in sexual reproduction, including how these processes may contribute to or limit genetic variation.

12. You should be able to describe specific events occurring in each of the stages of the cell cycle and/or phases of mitosis.

13. You should be able to explain how mitosis forms new cells and its role in maintaining chromosome number during asexual reproduction.

14. You should be able to explain how cancer (uncontrolled cell growth) may result from mutations that affect the proteins that regulate the cell cycle.

15. You should be able to describe the process of meiosis, including independent assortment and crossing over.

16. You should be able to explain how meiosis results in the formation of haploid gametes or spores.

Standards

The following standards are assessed on the Florida Biology 1 End-of-Course Assessment either directly or indirectly:

SC.912.L.16.3 Describe the basic process of DNA replication and how it relates to the transmission and conservation of the genetic information.

SC.912.L.16.4 Explain how mutations in the DNA sequence may or may not result in phenotypic change. Explain how mutations in gametes may result in phenotypic changes in offspring.

SC.912.L.16.5 Explain the basic processes of transcription and translation, and how they result in the expression of genes.

SC.912.L.16.8 Explain the relationship between mutation, cell cycle, and uncontrolled cell growth potentially resulting in cancer.

SC.912.L.16.9 Explain how and why the genetic code is universal and is common to almost all organisms.

SC.912.L.16.10 Evaluate the impact of biotechnology on the individual, society and the environment, including medical and ethical issues.

SC.912.L.16.13 Describe the basic anatomy and physiology of the human reproductive system. Describe the process of human development from fertilization to birth and major changes that occur in each trimester of pregnancy.

SC.912.L.16.14 Describe the cell cycle, including the process of mitosis. Explain the role of mitosis in the formulation of new cells and its importance in maintaining chromosome number during asexual reproduction.

SC.912.L.16.16 Describe the process of meiosis, including independent assortment and crossing over. Explain how reduction division results in the formation of haploid gametes or spores.

SC.912.L.16.17 Compare and contrast mitosis and meiosis and relate to the processes of sexual and asexual reproduction and their consequences for genetic variation.

The Process of DNA Replication

DNA replication is the making of an exact copy of the DNA molecule. This process takes place before cell division in all living organisms. It ensures that each new cell will contain the full amount of DNA material and thus allows for inheritance of traits. The important steps in DNA replication include the following.

- First, an overview: The DNA molecule consists of two strands in a spiral formation called a **double helix**. In DNA replication, the double helix separates, or "unzips," into a leading strand and a lagging strand. Each becomes a template (model) for a new, complementary strand. Thus two new molecules of DNA are formed. Each consists of one old template strand and one new complementary strand. This process is called **semiconservative replication**.

- Replication begins when the enzyme **helicase** unzips the DNA. This produces a Y-shaped **replication fork**. Proteins keep the separated strands from recombining.

- Another enzyme called **primase** starts the complementary strand with short segments of RNA called **RNA primers**.

- Yet another enzyme called **DNA polymerase** bonds to the RNA primers. The process of **elongation** begins. That is when DNA nucleotides are added to each complementary strand.

- The two complementary strands develop in different ways. The leading strand assembles in a continuous process as the DNA unwinds. The lagging strand assembles in short pieces called **Okazaki fragments**. These fragments are joined by **DNA ligase**. The result for each strand is a new and complete molecule of DNA.

Transcription and Translation

The function of DNA is to store genetic information. Genetic instructions in DNA cause cells to grow and develop in certain ways. This determines what kind of organism the cells will form, such as an oak, a mouse, or a human. As each cell develops, it may become part of a leaf stem, a mouse's whisker, or a human fingernail. All of this happens because of a chemical process called **protein synthesis**, in which enzymes and other proteins are formed from DNA. The two steps of this process are **transcription** and **translation**.

1. **Transcription** makes an RNA copy (a "transcription") of a DNA molecule. A single gene may be transcribed thousands of time. The main functions of RNA are to decode and express genetic information as protein. In transcription, three types of RNA are produced: messenger RNA (mRNA), transfer RNA (tRNA), and ribosomal RNA (rRNA). **Messenger RNA** sends the DNA "message" to the ribosome. **Transfer RNA** carries amino acids to the correct place on the mRNA template. **Ribosomal RNA** builds ribosomes from various proteins. In **RNA processing**, the mRNA is modified by a series of enzymes. The additions provide stability. The deletions remove **introns** by splicing, leaving only the **exons**, or expressed genetic sequences, to exit the nucleus.

2. In **translation**, RNA is translated into the language of amino acids, which are the building blocks of proteins. Ribosomes synthesize the proteins using the final mRNA transcript. The proteins bond together to form a growing polypeptide chain. Altogether, this process allows for **gene expression**, or the expression of different genetic traits in organisms.

DNA $\xrightarrow{\text{transcription}}$ mRNA $\xrightarrow{\text{translation}}$ protein

Figure 6.1. Transcription and Translation

The Genetic Code

The bonding that takes place in translation is accomplished with blocks of information that together make up the **genetic code**. The genetic code consists of 64 "triplets" of nucleotides, with each 3-letter code representing one amino acid. The 3-letter codes in the mRNA are called **codons.** For example, the codon AUG signals the *start* of translation. There are also three 3-letter codes in the tRNA that *stop* the bonding process and are called **anticodons**.

The genetic code is virtually universal for organisms. The vast majority of genes in microorganisms, plants, and animals have the same codons linked to the same amino acids and the same start and stop signals. A few exceptions have been found. Nevertheless, the fact that the basic components of DNA are nearly universal shows that organisms from bacteria to humans have a common ancestry and have evolved through the process of inheritance.

Figure 6.2. The Genetic Code

First Letter	Second Letter				Third Letter
	U	C	A	G	
U	Phenylalanine	Serine	Tyrosine	Cysteine	U
	Phenylalanine	Serine	Tyrosine	Cysteine	C
	Leucine	Serine	Stop	Stop	A
	Leucine	Serine	Stop	Tryptophan	G
C	Leucine	Proline	Histidine	Arginine	U
	Leucine	Proline	Histidine	Arginine	C
	Leucine	Proline	Glutamine	Arginine	A
	Leucine	Proline	Glutamine	Arginine	G
A	Isoleucine	Threonine	Asparagine	Serine	U
	Isoleucine	Threonine	Asparagine	Serine	C
	Isoleucine	Threonine	Lysine	Arginine	A
	Start: Methionine	Threonine	Lysine	Arginine	G
G	Valine	Alanine	Aspartic acid	Glycine	U
	Valine	Alanine	Aspartic acid	Glycine	C
	Valine	Alanine	Aspartic acid	Glycine	A
	Valine	Alanine	Aspartic acid	Glycine	G

Mutations

Sometimes errors occur in DNA replication. Such errors generally occur spontaneously and at random. An error that is not repaired becomes a **mutation**. When a sequence of genetic material in a DNA molecule does not exactly match the DNA molecule it was copied from, a mutation occurs.

- A mutation in a body cell, or **somatic mutation**, can result in a disease such as cancer. A somatic mutation may also be caused by radiation or chemicals, which are called **mutagens**. Somatic mutations do not occur in cells that give rise to gametes, so they are not passed on by sexual means and are not inherited by the next generation. For example, skin cells that develop cancer do not pass on the mutation. Desirable mutations, such as those for certain flowers and fruits, can be maintained by cloning procedures such as grafting mutant branches onto normal plants.

- A mutation in a cell that gives rise to gametes, or a germ cell, is called a **germinal mutation**. Some gametes will pass the mutation on to the next generation by sexual reproduction. A germinal mutation is not expressed in the carrier, only in the carrier's offspring. Thus a mutation in gametes may result in a phenotype change in the next generation. Since germinal mutations can affect the gene pool of an entire population, they are extremely important to the mechanism of natural selection.

Let's look more closely at what a mutation is. The most basic type is **point mutation**. It is an error in only one nucleotide. (Nucleotides are the organic molecules that make up the strands of DNA and RNA.) Forms of point mutation include the following.

- A **substitution** is when the DNA sequence has an incorrect nucleotide in place of a correct one.

- A **deletion** is when one nucleotide is left out of the DNA sequence.

- An **insertion** is when one nucleotide is added to the DNA sequence. Both a deletion and an insertion result in a **frameshift mutation**. All the nucleotides in the sequence are shifted by one place.

A point mutation or frameshift may alter a codon in a gene to a stop codon. This causes the translation to produce a **missense mutation** or a **nonsense mutation**. In a missense mutation, proteins may not be able to form into their proper shapes. Sickle cell disease, in which red blood cells bend into a sickle shape, is an example of a missense mutation.

Figure 6.3. Effects of Mutations

The following examples show how genetic mutations are the result of changes in the triplet code (groups of three letters, like the genetic code).

Correct Sequence

The big dog bit the fat cat.

Point Mutation by Substitution

The big dot bit the fat cat.

Point Mutation by Deletion (of "d")

The big ogb itt hef atc at.

Point Mutation by Insertion (of "m")

The bmi gdo gbi tth efa tca t.

Cells have developed systems that repair errors in DNA replication and correct mutations. These systems include the following.

- **Proofreading** is when an enzyme called DNA polymerase "proofreads" the newly copied strand of DNA to make sure each added nucleotide matches its counterpart on the model strand. Each incorrect nucleotide is replaced with the correct one.

- **Excision repair** is when enzymes remove and repair a nucleotide damaged by mutagens. The damaged nucleotide is replaced by one that is made using the complement strand as a template.

- **Mismatch repair** is the work of enzymes that remove a damaged segment of DNA and then repair the gap. It corrects errors that proofreading misses.

- **Recombination repair** mends double-stranded breaks in DNA.

Biotechnology

Biotechnology is the branch of science that manipulates genes in a laboratory. One of the basic tools of biotechnology is **recombinant DNA**, in which DNA from two different sources is combined into a single molecule. This process is possible because all organisms contain the same type of genetic material. Scientists now are able to use **genetic engineering** to remove, modify, or add genes to a DNA molecule. This changes the information the molecule contains and thus the kind or amount of proteins it can produce. Biotechnology's many potential uses can affect individuals, society, and the environment, as in the following.

- **Bioengineered crop plants** such as wheat, corn, potatoes, and cotton, can be fortified against diseases and pests with special genes, thus increasing crop yields. Certain fruits and vegetables can be engineered for better taste, texture, nutrients, and even color. Hybrid seeds can unite genotypes to make plants that are better adapted to certain growing conditions. Bioengineered crops may require less water, fertilizer, and chemical pesticides, thus helping the environment. These techniques have also been used to improve livestock breeding and develop vaccines for animals.

- **Biofertilizers** can employ microorganisms to add nitrogen to soils and increase their fertility. Genetically engineered bacteria can clean up toxic waste and oil spills by "eating" the unwanted products.

- In **gene cloning**, a specific sequence of DNA is isolated and reproduced. The technique is used to make helpful protein products such as insulin, which is a treatment for persons with diabetes, and certain vaccines. It can also be used to make numerous copies of a gene for medical research.

- In **human gene therapy**, a nonfunctioning gene in human cells is replaced with a functioning one. In theory, the replacement gene can develop antibodies to fight cancer and sexually transmitted diseases. So far scientists have had mixed results with gene therapy. Patients often become ill from the **vector** needed to introduce the new gene into their systems. Other times the gene produces the desired proteins for only a brief time. Much research into this technique remains to be done.

- In **DNA fingerprinting**, different fragments of DNA, or unique "markers," are used to identify criminals from blood or hair at the scene of a crime. Such DNA testing can also reveal the paternity of children.

While biotechnology has many benefits, it also raises practical and ethical concerns. Some of these include:

- **Reduced genetic diversity**. Bioengineered crops and animals may crowd out other possible genetic developments that could prove beneficial in unknown ways.

- **Safety of genetically modified foods**. There are persistent concerns about whether these foods are safe for humans, animals, or the environment. Scientists counter that gene transfers involve only single genes or small clusters of genes and therefore are narrowly targeted and safe.

- **Discrimination by DNA**. Biotechnology enables scientists to detect genetic defects and potential diseases in individuals. However, the possibility also exists that these individuals could suffer discrimination in the workplace or by insurance companies.

- **Bioterrorism**. Genetic engineering raises the possibility that a deadly bacteria or disease could be developed and used to attack a society through the water supply or some other means.

- **Interference with nature**. Some people believe that biotechnology is an immoral attempt to change the natural order of life on Earth. Thus, campaigns against genetically modified foods often refer to them as "Franken-foods," after Mary Shelley's Frankenstein, who created a dangerous monster.

Human Sexual Reproduction

Sexual reproduction includes the making of two kinds of **sex cells**, or **gametes**, and the processes that result in **fertilization**. Since the overall goal of reproduction is to pass on genes to the next generation, sexual reproduction has many drawbacks compared to asexual reproduction. We will review these a bit later. However, sexual reproduction does have the advantage of **variation**. With random mating and recombination of parents' chromosomes, new traits can emerge that strengthen the overall population.

The basic anatomy of the **human male reproductive system** includes the following.

- The **testis** is the male gonad, where the male gametes, called **sperm**, are produced. Each male has two **testes**. The testes are contained in the **scrotum**, a sac located outside the abdominal cavity, where cooler temperatures enable sperm to survive.

- The **seminiferous tubules** are where sperm is produced in the testes. **Interstitial cells** in the testes produce male sex hormones including testosterone.

- The **epididymis** is the coiled tube in each testis where sperm mature and are stored.

- The **vas deferens** is one of two muscular ducts that carry sperm from one epididymis to the **urethra**, a tube running through the penis. During ejaculation, the penis emits sperm through the urethra.

- Also during ejaculation, the **seminal vesicles** secrete mucus (a liquid medium for sperm), fructose sugar (energy source for the sperm), and prostaglandin (a hormone that stimulates uterine contractions) into the vas deferens.

- The **prostate gland** is a large gland that secretes semen directly into the urethra. The milky fluid helps neutralize the acidity of any urine left in the urethra.

The basic anatomy of the **human female reproductive system** includes the following.

- The **ovary** is the organ where the female gamete, or **egg**, is produced. Eggs are also called **ova** (singular: ovum). Each female has two ovaries.

- The **oviduct** is where fertilization occurs. The egg moves through the oviduct to the uterus after ovulation. The oviduct is also called the **fallopian tube**. Each female has two oviducts, one for each ovary.

- Inside the **uterus,** the fertilized egg, or **blastocyst**, is implanted on the inside wall. There the embryo develops for a nine-month **gestation** period until birth.

- The **endometrium** is the lining, or inside wall, of the uterus. It thickens monthly in preparation for a fertilized egg being implanted.

- The **vagina** is the birth canal. During labor and delivery, the baby passes through the **cervix**, or opening in the uterus, and into the vagina.

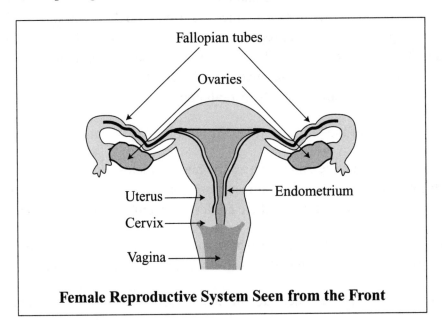

Female Reproductive System Seen from the Front

Figure 6.4. The Human Female Reproductive System

In human females, two hormonal cycles are involved in reproduction. The **ovarian cycle** carries out the production of the egg and its release in the middle of the cycle, an activity called **ovulation**. The **menstrual cycle** prepares the uterus for implantation of the fertilized egg by thickening the endometrium, or uterine wall. If implantation does not occur, this thickened inside wall is shed. These cyclical processes are started and stopped by the release of certain hormones. In the **follicular phase**, or stage of positive feedback, the hormone **estro-**

gen causes the release of **luteinizing hormone (LH),** which in turn causes more estrogen to be released. Hormone levels continue to rise until ovulation occurs. In the **luteal phase**, or stage of negative feedback, LH causes estrogen and progesterone to be secreted. Once these hormones reach a certain high level, the pituitary and hypothalamus shut down, and hormone production ceases.

The Process of Human Development

Human development from fertilization to birth is usually divided into three periods called **trimesters.**

First Trimester

- **Fertilization** is the fusion of sperm and egg nuclei, creating a **zygote**. This is the first cell of the new offspring.

- **Cleavage** begins to occur about 30 hours after fertilization. The zygote undergoes rapid cell division, from one to two, two to four, etc. By day 6, the grouping cells have formed a fluid-filled **blastocyst**, which attaches to the uterine wall. This is called **implantation**.

- **Gastrulation** occurs in the second week after fertilization. It reorganizes the cells of the early embryo into three layers of tissue: endoderm, mesoderm, and ectoderm. The first **somites** appear, which are bands of body cells that will become muscles, vertebrae, and connective tissue.

- Also in the second week, the **placenta** forms. The placenta provides nourishment for the embryo, protects it from certain toxic molecules, and releases hormones to prevent ovulation. The **umbilical cord** connects the placenta to the developing embryo. The umbilical cord consists of three blood vessels: two small arteries that send blood to the placenta and a large vein that returns blood to the embryo. While the mother's blood and the embryo's blood do not mix, certain substances, such as drugs and alcohol, can pass from the mother's bloodstream to the embryo's. The placenta includes two layers of membrane. The outer layer surrounds the embryo. The inner layer develops into the **amniotic sac**, usually by about day 10–12. The amniotic sac fills with a clear liquid called the **amniotic fluid** and expands to enclose the developing embryo, which floats inside. The fetus will "breathe" the fluid in order to develop its lungs. Amniotic fluid also promotes easier fetal movement, cushions the fetus against jars to the mother's abdomen, and aids the development of the fetus's skeleton and muscles.

- In the third week, cells continue to differentiate into various tissues, such as blood vessels and intestines.

- In the fourth week, **organogenesis** begins. All the organ systems begin to develop. The eyes form and the heart beats for the first time.

- During the second month, the major organs develop in the abdominal cavity and the limbs begin to assume their final shape.

- By the third month, the embryo has become a distinctly human-looking **fetus**. As its nervous system develops, the fetus begins to move its limbs and make facial expressions.

Second Trimester

- By the fourth month, the fetus's fingers and toes are defined. Bones and teeth become denser. With the genitalia fully formed, the sex of the fetus can be determined.

- By the fifth month, the fetus begins to develop body fat and moves its developing muscles. The first movement the mother feels is called "quickening."

- By the end of the sixth month, the fetus is about 300 mm (12 in) long and weighs about 600 g (1.3 lb), with most of its pre-birth growth yet to come. Born prematurely at this stage, the fetus could only survive with special medical care.

Third Trimester

- By the end of the seventh month, the fetus has added more body fat and weighs about 900–1800 g (two to four pounds). The fetus has fully developed hearing and may be startled by loud noises. The fetus could probably survive a premature birth at this stage.

- By the end of the eighth month, most of the fetus's internal organs are well developed. Brain and nerve cell development is rapid.

- By the end of the ninth month, the fetus's lungs are almost fully formed. Fetal reflexes include blinking, closing the eyes, and reacting to light and sounds. The fetus changes position to prepare for birth, dropping down in the pelvis with the head facing toward the birth canal. The fetus is about 46–51 cm (18 to 20 inches) and weighs about 3.2 kg (seven pounds).

- **Labor** begins when the uterus starts contracting. This occurs due to hormones that are released in a cycle of positive feedback. The contractions force the fetus downward toward the **cervix**, which is the lower portion of the uterus. The rate of contractions increases from a few every hour to one every 2–3 minutes. The final strong contractions, with the help of the mother's pushing, expel the baby through the dilated cervix and into the birth canal.

Mitosis and Asexual Reproduction

Asexual reproduction is when offspring are produced from a single parent. In **cell division**, a single cell divides to become two cells. Each offspring cell is identical to the parent. Simple organisms such as protozoa reproduce by cell division. More complex, multicellular organisms use cell division to grow or to replace tissues.

The process of cell division in more complex eukaryotic cells is called the **cell cycle**. To help you understand, it is divided here into five main phases, or steps. In reality, however, the process is continuous, without separate steps. The first three phases of the cell cycle are part of **interphase.** This is the activity in between actual cell divisions. Cells spend most of their time in interphase.

- **G_1 phase:** The new cell grows to mature size and may begin to carry out its specific function.

- **S phase:** If the cell is going to divide again, it copies its chromosomes during the S phase by the process of DNA replication (as we saw earlier).

- **G_2 phase:** Once the DNA is replicated, the cell enters G_2, during which it prepares for cell division.

The last two phases of the cell cycle are part of **cell division**. This will result in the production of two nearly identical cells. The cell that divides is a **diploid cell**, which contains two complete sets (2n) of chromosomes.

- **Mitosis:** This is the division of the nucleus, which leads to the separation of the chromosomes that were previously duplicated in the S phase. The resulting **chromatids**, or daughter cells, each have one copy of each chromosome. In other words, one cell with 2n chromosomes divides into two separate cells, each with 2n chromosomes. Thus mitosis is important in maintaining the chromosome number during asexual reproduction. Mitosis consists of four main stages.

  — In **prophase**, coiled bundles of DNA and proteins called **chromatin** condense into chromosomes. Each chromosome has two **chromatids**, which are joined at a centromere. The nuclear membrane breaks down and disappears. A cytoskeletal structure forms, called the **mitotic spindle**, which will be used to separate the chromatids. Next, two **centrosomes** are synthesized. In animal cells these contain small cylindrical bodies called **centrioles**. The centrisomes move to opposite sides of the cell. Spindle fibers, made of **microtubules**, radiate outward from the centrosomes. They form a bridge called the **spindle apparatus**.

— During **metaphase**, the chromatids line up across the center of the cell, along the metaphase plate. This is not an actual plate, but rather the future axis for cell division.

— In **anaphase**, the chromatids separate from one another. At this point each chromatid is considered to be an individual chromosome. The kinetochore fibers pull one copy of each chromosome to one pole and the rest to the other side of the cell.

— In **telophase**, the last stage of mitosis, the mitotic spindle disassembles and the chromosomes unwind from their highly compacted state. A new nuclear membrane forms and surrounds each new complete set of chromosomes. Thus telophase is a reversal of prophase and returns the cell to the interphase state.

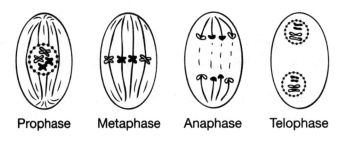

Prophase   Metaphase   Anaphase   Telophase

Figure 6.5. The Stages of Mitosis

• **Cytokinesis:** This is the division of the cytoplasm following mitosis. In cytokinesis, the two newly formed nuclei become incorporated into separate cells. In animal cells, the microfilaments of the cytoskeleton form a **cleavage furrow** in the center of the cell. This is like a constricting strap, which creates an indentation and then eventually pinches the cell into two separate cells.

Cancer is a disease caused by uncontrolled division of human cells. It basically is a failure to control the cell cycle. Mutations in genes that encode the steps of cell division can cause damaged cells to divide. If special proteins fail to repair the damaged cells or eliminate them, the cells can accumulate into cancerous tumors.

Meiosis and Sexual Reproduction

As we have seen, sexual reproduction is the union of sex cells called gametes to produce a zygote. Both sex cells — the egg and the sperm — are **haploid cells** that contain half the number of chromosomes as diploid cells. When the haploid sex cells unite, they form a zygote that is diploid ($n + n = 2n$). The zygote then divides by mitosis many times to produce a multi-cellular organism composed of diploid cells. This is how nature maintains the proper number of chromosomes in organisms.

Meiosis produces haploid cells from a diploid cell by two rounds of cell division: **meiosis I** and **meiosis II**. Each round includes stages of prophase, metaphase, anaphase, and telophase. The basic process of meiosis is described in the following steps.

- Like mitosis, meiosis is preceded by an S phase in which all the chromosomes are copied. The two copies, called chromatids, are held together at their centromeres.

- **Meiosis I** is the cell division in which homologous pairs of chromosomes are separated from one another into two cells that are haploid. It can be divided into four stages.

Prophase I is like the prophase of mitosis in certain ways (see Figure 6.5.). The chromosomes are condensed, the nuclear envelope disassembles, and a spindle forms. However, prophase I features a process called **crossing over**, in which homologous (maternal and paternal) chromosomes pair and exchange DNA. This pairing of homologues is called **synapsis**. The result is that each pair of homologues has four units, called a **tetrad**. In the chromosomes that are produced, maternal and paternal DNA are mixed.

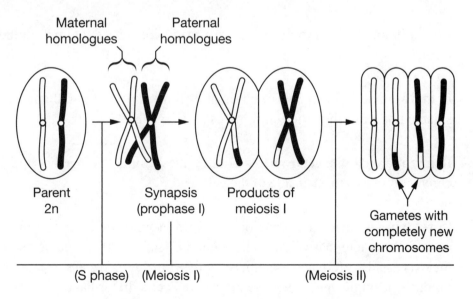

Figure 6.6. Crossing Over in Meiosis I

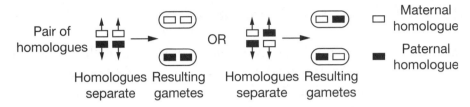

Depending on how homologues align during meiosis I, gametes with different combinations result.

Figure 6.7. Independent Assortment of Homologous Chromosomes in Meiosis I

— During **metaphase I** and **anaphase I**, there is **independent assortment** of homologous chromosomes. This creates a variety of outcomes (that is, gametes) that contain *different combinations* of the organism's maternal and paternal chromosomes. (Mendel discovered the law of independent assortment with his experiments on dihybrid crosses.)

— During **telophase I**, the movement of chromosomes is completed. In some species, cytokinesis follows telophase I.

• **Meiosis II** is a second round of cell division that follows meiosis I. Meiosis II is like a normal mitosis division. There is no DNA replication between meiosis I and meiosis II. Meiosis II occurs in each of the two new cells. It also includes four stages.

— In **prophase II**, the chromosomes are already condensed and new spindle fibers form.

— In **metaphase II**, each pair of chromatids lines up in the middle of the cell, and spindle fibers attach to the centromeres of each pair.

— In **anaphase II**, the centromeres holding the chromatids together split, and one chromatid moves to each side of the cell.

— In **telophase II**, nuclear envelopes reform around the chromosomes. Cytokinesis follows telophase II, which results in gametes. If the gametes are sperm, meiosis usually produces four sperm cells. If the gametes are ova, meiosis often produces a single egg, while the other three cells die or have other functions in reproduction.

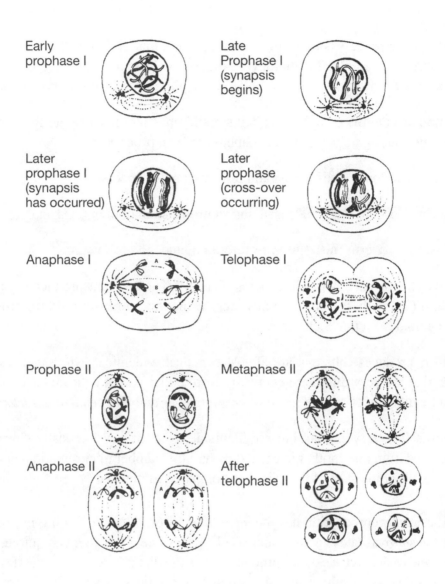

Early prophase I

Late Prophase I (synapsis begins)

Later prophase I (synapsis has occurred)

Later prophase (cross-over occurring)

Anaphase I

Telophase I

Prophase II

Metaphase II

Anaphase II

After telophase II

Figure 6.8. Meiosis I and Meiosis II

Comparison of Mitosis and Meiosis

Similarities between mitosis and meiosis include the following.

- All chromosomes are replicated during the S phase of the interphase that precedes both mitosis and meiosis. Copies of the chromosomes are called chromatids in both processes. The chromatids are attached to each other at their centromeres in both processes.

- The replication of chromosomes results in a doubling of the total amount of DNA within the cell that begins mitosis or meiosis. The amount of DNA present at the start of each process is twice the amount present in a diploid cell of the organism. In humans, for example, $2n$ (diploid) $= 46$, so 46 chromosomes are present in diploid cells, and 92 chromatids are present at the beginning of both mitosis and meiosis.

- Components in the cytoplasm called spindle fibers are responsible for moving chromosomes during metaphase and anaphase in both processes.

- Nuclear envelopes disassemble and reform in both processes.

- The chromosomes are condensed during prophase in both mitosis and meiosis.

Differences between mitosis and meiosis include the following.

- Mitosis has one division, while meiosis has two. The two cells produced by mitosis are diploid ($2n$) with 46 chromosomes each, while the four cells resulting from meiosis are haploid (n) with 23 chromosomes each.

- Mitosis produces cells that are almost genetically identical, while meiosis produces cells that are very different genetically from either parent or from each other. These genetic differences are the result of *crossing over* and *independent assortment*.

- Meiosis II is very similar, but not identical, to mitosis. While sister chromatids are separated from one another in each, only half the number of chromatid pairs is present in the cells at the start of meiosis II as compared to mitosis.

Overall, asexual reproduction has the *advantage* of producing offspring in greater numbers so that the survival rate is greatly increased. Also, since no partner is required, reproduction is faster and easier. Yet asexual reproduction has the distinct *disadvantage* of not producing variation or diversity. Only in sexual reproduction can the genes of offspring be improved through the mixing of the parents' genetic information.

Organism	Multicellular Form(s)	Meiosis Produces Haploid Cells	Gametes Produced by Meiosis	Gametes Produced by Mitosis
Animals	Diploid only	Always	Yes	No
Fungi and some algae	Haploid only	Always	No	Yes
Plants and some algae	Diploid and haploid forms	Always	No	Yes

Figure 6.9. Comparison of Sexual Life Cycles

End-of-Chapter Quiz

1. **How does DNA replication help to conserve genetic information?**

    A. by encoding information that causes cells to grow and develop in certain ways

    B. by making an exact copy of a DNA molecule for the next generation

    C. by making an RNA copy of a DNA molecule

    D. by combining fragments of DNA into new combinations

2. **RNA processing is a part of transcription in which messenger RNA is modified by a series of enzymes. What is the purpose of the deletions from the mRNA?**

    A. to build ribosomes from a variety of proteins

    B. to provide added stability for the mRNA

    C. to allow only the expressed genetic sequences to leave the nucleus

    D. to carry amino acids to the correct location on the mRNA template

3. **Insulin is a natural human product that is deficient in people with diabetes. The human gene for insulin has been inserted into E. coli DNA to produce synthetic insulin for diabetes treatment. Why can the E. coli bacteria accept a human gene and then produce a human protein?**

    A. Bacteria cells are identical in structure to human cells.

    B. The basic components of DNA are the same in bacteria and humans.

    C. DNA replication occurs in the exact same way in both bacteria cells and human cells.

    D. Chromosomes are identical in bacteria cells and human cells.

4. **Which of the following indicates that all organisms can be traced back to a common ancestry?**

    A. The genetic code consists of nucleotides in triplet code.

    B. Almost all genes in microorganisms, plants, and animals have the same codons.

    C. Microorganisms contain codons and anticodons.

    D. There are a few organisms that respond differently to the start and stop signals in the genetic code.

5. **What causes a mutation?**

    A. the translation of RNA into the language of amino acids

    B. the production of a complementary strand of DNA

    C. frequent replication of DNA

    D. an error in DNA replication

6. **Which of the following may result in a phenotype change in the next generation?**

    A. a somatic mutation

    B. a germinal mutation

    C. either a somatic mutation or a germinal mutation

    D. any mutation due to exposure to radiation or chemicals

7. **A point mutation is the result of which of the following?**

    A. an error in a single nucleotide

    B. errors in a string of nucleotides

    C. an incorrect nucleotide replaced by a correct one

    D. mismatch repair by enzymes that remove a segment of DNA

8. **Bioengineered crop plants such as wheat and corn can be fortified against damaging insects to increase crop yields. Yet some experts have expressed concerns about these modified plants. Which of the following might result from increased use of bioengineered crop plants?**

    A. an increased chance of contaminating ground water supplies

    B. an increase in the need for strong pesticides

    C. a decreasing amount of diversity in the genes of crop plants

    D. an increasing amount of diversity in the genes of crop plants

9. **Look at the diagram below of the human female reproductive system.**

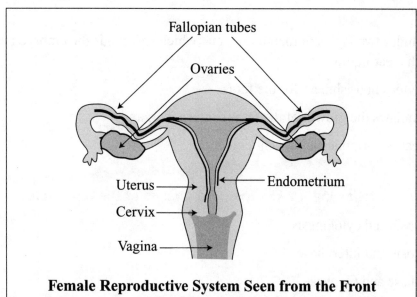

Fallopian tubes

Ovaries

Uterus

Endometrium

Cervix

Vagina

Female Reproductive System Seen from the Front

In which of the following does fertilization of the ovum occur?

A. fallopian tube

B. ovary

C. uterus

D. placenta

10. **Which of the following is the name for human male gametes?**

A. sperm

B. gonads

C. testes

D. seminal vesicles

11. **In the process of human development, what happens when cleavage begins?**

A. The placenta forms.

B. The embryo's cells reorganize into three different layers of tissue.

C. The blastocyst attaches to the wall of the uterus.

D. The zygote undergoes rapid cell division.

12. **Which of the following is NOT true about the role of the placenta in human development?**

    A. includes two layers of membrane, one which surrounds the embryo and one filled with clear liquid

    B. provides nourishment for the fetus

    C. stimulates the growth of the fetus's internal organs

    D. releases hormones to prevent ovulation

13. **Which of the following are the last two phases of the cell cycle?**

    A. mitosis and cytokinesis

    B. mitosis and interphase

    C. S phase and G_2 phase

    D. anaphase and telophase

14. **The role of mitosis in asexual reproduction has what effect on genetic variation?**

    A. It greatly increases genetic variation.

    B. It limits genetic variation.

    C. It prevents genetic variation from occurring.

    D. It has no effect on genetic variation.

15. **The chromatids separate during which phase of mitosis?**

    A. prophase

    B. metaphase

    C. anaphase

    D. telophase

16. **Which of the following is responsible for the onset of cancer?**

    A. breakdown and disappearance of the nuclear membrane in cells

    B. failure of human cells to divide

    C. uncontrolled division of damaged human cells

    D. union of an unhealthy gamete with a healthy gamete

17. During cytokinesis, two separate cells are formed when microfilaments in the cytoplasm form a sort of constricting belt in the center of the cell that pinches the cell in two. This describes which of the following?

    A. cell cycle

    B. mitotic spindle

    C. synapsis

    D. cleavage furrow

18. Which of the following is most similar to the process of mitosis?

    A. meiosis

    B. meiosis I

    C. meiosis II

    D. prophase I

19. In the meiotic process called crossing over, homologous chromosomes pair together and exchange DNA. Biologically, what is the main advantage of this process?

    A. increased variety of genetic combinations

    B. exact duplication of homologous chromosomes

    C. introduction of beneficial mutations

    D. decreased number of genetic combinations

20. Mitosis and meiosis are processes of cell reproduction that differ in certain important ways. Which of the following results from meiosis but NOT mitosis?

    A. two diploid daughter cells

    B. four haploid daughter cells

    C. a single stage of cell division

    D. daughter cells that are identical to the parent cell

Answers to the Chapter Quiz

1. **B**

   The purpose of DNA replication is to conserve the entire genome for the next generation by making an exact copy of the DNA molecule. Answer choice A describes what DNA is. Answer choice C describes transcription. Answer choice D is not a correct description of DNA replication.

2. **C**

   Deletions during RNA processing remove introns by splicing, which allows only the exons, or expressed genetic sequences, to emerge from the nucleus.

3. **B**

   The genetic code is almost universal for all organisms. This means that the basic components of DNA are much the same for bacteria such as *E. coli* as for humans.

4. **B**

   The fact that microorganisms, plants, and animals all have DNA with codons and anti-codons linked to the same amino acids and the same start and stop signals supports the idea that all these organisms share a common ancestry.

5. **D**

   When an error in DNA replication occurs and is not repaired, the result is a mutation.

6. **B**

   A germinal mutation is not expressed in the carrier, but only in the carrier's offspring. Thus it may result in a phenotype change in the offspring. A somatic mutation does not occur in cells that give rise to gametes, so it is not passed on to the next generation. Mutation due to exposure to radiation or chemicals is a kind of somatic mutation that is not passed on.

7. **A**

   A point mutation is the most basic type of mutation and results from an error in only one nucleotide. The error may be substitution, deletion, or insertion of a nucleotide.

8. **C**

   By focusing too much on developing one aspect of the crop plants — i.e., their resistance to insects—such use of bioengineered crop plants could decrease genetic diversity.

9. **A**

   Fertilization, or the fusion of sperm and egg nuclei, occurs in the fallopian tube, or oviduct.

10. **A**

    The male sex cells or gametes are called sperm. Gonads or testes are where sperm is produced in the male reproductive system. Seminal vesicles secrete a liquid medium for sperm.

11. **D**

    Cleavage is the beginning of mitotic cell division in the zygote, which proceeds rapidly.

12. **C**

    The placenta plays no particular role in the growth and development of the fetus's internal organs other than generally providing nourishment.

13. **A**

    Mitosis and cytokinesis, which together are part of cell division, form the last two phases of the cell cycle. The result of these two phases is the production of two nearly identical new cells.

14. **B**

    Since mitosis is the production of two identical cells from a single parent cell, it leads to very little genetic variation. In mitosis, genetic variation only occurs rarely and by chance.

15. **C**

    During anaphase, the chromatids separate from one another, and spindle fibers pull one copy of each chromosome to each of two poles on opposite sides of the cell.

16. **C**

Cancer occurs when human cells that are damaged by mutation divide uncontrollably and do not respond to enzymes that attempt to repair them or eliminate them. The cells can combine into cancerous tumors.

17. **D**

The cleavage furrow is the surface indentation of the cell that begins the process of cleavage, in which a single cell divides into two cells. Proteins in the cytoplasm, such as actin and myosin, apparently cause the constriction of the microfilaments that begins the process.

18. **C**

Meiosis II, in which sister chromatids line up in the middle of the cell and then separate and migrate to opposite poles of the cell, is much like normal mitosis. Unlike mitosis, the entire process of meiosis (including meiosis I and II) includes two processes of cell division.

19. **A**

In meiosis, the process of crossing over, or genetic recombination, allows for the shuffling of genes and an almost endless variety of possible genetic combinations. This is an important advantage with regard to natural selection.

20. **B**

The process of meiosis ends with four haploid daughter cells, each with half the normal number of chromosomes, as opposed to the process of mitosis that ends with two diploid daughter cells, each with a complete set of chromosomes. Also, meiosis takes place in two stages of cell division, while mitosis has only one stage.

Chapter 7

Ecology

Your Goals for Chapter 7

1. You should be able to use data and information about population dynamics, abiotic factors, and/or biotic factors to explain and/or analyze a change in carrying capacity and its effect on population size in an ecosystem.

2. You should be able to explain that different types of organisms exist within aquatic systems due to chemistry, geography, light, depth, salinity, and/or temperature.

3. You should be able to describe the potential changes to an ecosystem resulting from seasonal variations, climate changes, and/or succession.

4. You should be able to identify positive and/or negative consequences that result from a reduction in biodiversity.

5. You should be able to assess the reliability of sources of information according to scientific standards.

6. You should be able to describe the energy pathways through the different trophic levels of a food web or energy pyramid.

7. You should be able to analyze the movement of matter through different biogeochemical cycles.

8. You should be able to predict how the actions of humans may impact environmental systems and/or affect sustainability.

9. You should be able to evaluate possible environmental impacts resulting from the use of renewable and/or nonrenewable resources.

10. You should be able to identify ways in which a scientific claim is evaluated (e.g., through scientific argumentation, critical and logical thinking, and/or consideration of alternative explanations).

Standards

The following standards are assessed on the Florida Biology 1 End-of-Course Assessment either directly or indirectly:

SC.912.L.17.2 Explain the general distribution of life in aquatic systems as a function of chemistry, geography, light, depth, salinity, and temperature.

SC.912.L.17.4 Describe changes in ecosystems resulting from seasonal variations, climate change, and succession.

SC.912.L.17.5 Analyze how population size is determined by births, deaths, immigration, emigration, and limiting factors (biotic and abiotic) that determine carrying capacity.

SC.912.L.17.8 Recognize the consequences of the losses of biodiversity due to catastrophic events, climate changes, human activity, and the introduction of invasive, non-native species.

SC.912.L.17.9 Use a food web to identify and distinguish producers, consumers, and decomposers. Explain the pathway of energy transfer through trophic levels and the reduction of available energy at successive trophic levels.

SC.912.L.17.11 Evaluate the costs and benefits of renewable and nonrenewable resources, such as water, energy, fossil fuels, wildlife, and forests.

SC.912.L.17.13 Discuss the need for adequate monitoring of environmental parameters when making policy decisions.

SC.912.L.17.20 Predict the impact of individuals on environmental systems and examine how human lifestyles affect sustainability.

SC.912.E.7.1 Analyze the movement of matter and energy through the different biogeochemical cycles, including water and carbon.

SC.912.N.1.3 Recognize that the strength or usefulness of a scientific claim is evaluated through scientific argumentation, which depends on critical and logical thinking, and the active consideration of alternative scientific explanations to explain the data presented.

SC.912.N.1.4   Identify sources of information and assess their reliability according to the strict standards of scientific investigation.

HE.912.C.1.3   Evaluate how environment and personal health are interrelated.

Population and Carrying Capacity

Ecology is the study of how organisms interact with their physical environment and with each other. Important terms for the study of ecology include the following.

- A **population** is a group of individuals all belonging to the same species and living in the same area. There are populations of bacteria, of blue spruce, of raccoons, and of humans. **Size** refers to the total number *(N)* of individuals in a population. **Density** refers to the number of individuals per square unit. Sampling techniques are scientists' tools for estimating density in an area.

- Scientists also examine **dispersion**, which is how evenly individuals are distributed in an area. **Dispersion patterns** (Fig. 7.1) can be uniform (as with species that are territorial), random (as with plant seeds blown by the wind), or clumped (as with species that flock, swarm, or school).

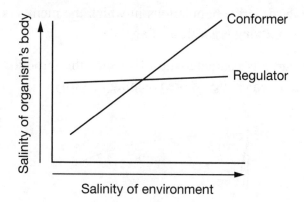

Figure 7.1. Population Dispersion Patterns

- **Age structure** (Fig. 7.2) is how individuals are weighted by age in a given population. It is determined by birth rates, death rates, and life expectancy. A population with a greater number of younger, reproductively active members will generally increase in size more rapidly than an aging population. As life expectancy increases, the number of older members in a population is expected to increase.

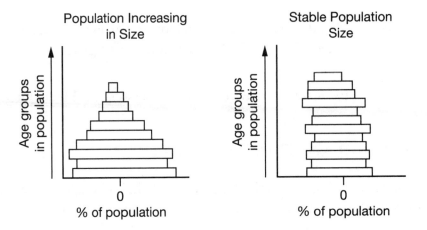

Figure 7.2. Age Structure in Two Different Populations

• A graph called a **survivorship curve** (Fig. 7.3) shows the expected mortality (death) rates of members of a population over their potential life span.

— In a population with a *Type 1* curve—characteristic of species that have few young and invest a lot of energy caring for them—survivorship is high for early and midlife individuals, and mortality is high for old age, indicating that most members of the population live out their potential, maximum life span.

— *Type II* curves describe populations in which the members have more or less the same chance of dying regardless of age.

— A *Type III* curve is characteristic of species that produce large numbers of offspring, most of which die before reaching maturity.

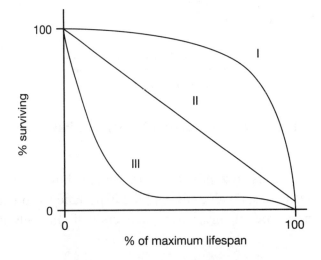

Figure 7.3. Survivorship Curves

- A **community** is made up of all the populations living in one area.

- An **ecosystem** includes all the organisms in a certain area, their relationships as a community, and the abiotic factors that make up their physical environment.

- **Abiotic factors** are nonliving environmental features, including water, sunlight, wind, temperature, and humidity. These can also include chemical factors such as soil minerals and water salinity. The kind of area where an organism usually lives is its **habitat**. The habitat includes biotic (living) and abiotic factors that enable the organism to survive.

- The **biosphere** consists of the global ecosystem, or all the areas of the Earth containing living things. It includes land, water, and air.

The study of **population growth** consists of the following terms and ideas.

- **Biotic potential** describes the maximum possible growth rate of a population under ideal conditions of unlimited resources and no growth restrictions. It includes such factors as age required for reproduction, number of offspring per reproductive event, frequency of reproduction, survival of offspring to reproductive maturity, and average length of reproductive career. It is also called the **intrinsic rate** of growth.

- **Carrying capacity** refers to the maximum number of individuals that a certain habitat can support.

- **Limiting factors** are factors that prevent a population from growing to its biotic potential. They can be density-dependent, becoming worse as population increases, or density-independent, occurring without regard to population. **Density-dependent factors** include disease and parasites, predators and competition for scarce resources, and toxic effects of chemicals or waste. All of these effects become more severe as populations grow. **Density-independent factors** include natural disasters and extreme weather events such as tornadoes and hurricanes. Limiting factors are often categorized as biotic (predators, food sources, competing organisms) or abiotic (soil nutrients, air temperature, sunlight intensity).

- The **growth rate** *(r)* of a population is shown by the following equation, in which *N* is the present population size, *t* is a given interval of time, and *r* is the rate of increase or decrease (births – deaths). The variable *d* means "change in," as in "change in population size." When deaths exceed births, the rate is negative and the population will decrease.

$$\frac{dN}{dt} = rN$$

- **Immigration** is when organisms move into an area. **Emigration** is when organisms move out of an area. (Notice that both words have the root *migrate*.) Rates of immigration and emigration are used to calculate the size of a population.

- Two basic patterns of population growth are **exponential growth** and **logistic growth** (Fig. 7.4). Exponential growth results when a population has no limiting factors such as competitors, predators, or parasites. The reproductive rate is greater than zero. Plotted on a graph against time, the line for exponential growth is a J-shaped curve that rises quickly. Logistic growth is when limiting factors restrict the population size to the habitat's carrying capacity. The line for logistic growth is an S-shaped curve showing that as the size of the population increases and the carrying capacity is reached, the reproductive rate decreases and growth levels out.

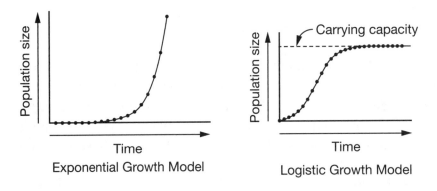

Figure 7.4. Exponential and Logistic Growth Models

- Small populations are more likely to become extinct than larger ones. Inbreeding reduces the number, health, and genetic variability of offspring. Also, a local natural disaster could eliminate the entire population.

- The human population began exponential growth about a thousand years ago. This was due mainly to increases in the food supply, reduction of diseases and human wastes, and increases in possible habitat due to better methods of building, weaving, heating, cooling, and even cooking. Since the 1960s, the population growth rate has slowed in many developing countries. In general, countries that are more developed have lower rates of population growth.

Changes in Ecosystems

Ecosystems can undergo major changes due to factors such as the following.

- **Climate change** can cause species to migrate or even become extinct. Most plants and animals require very specific climate conditions to thrive and reproduce. Climate change that thins or eliminates certain plants may affect the food source of animals and thus the entire food chain. The loss of a single species may be devastating to a whole area. Warmer and more acidic seawater can damage coral reefs in shallow tropical waters, which in turn affects the habitat of many other sea creatures. Climate change can also affect **seasonal variations** in temperature, air circulation, and rainfall that might disrupt the normal cycles of certain plants and animals. Most scientists believe that climate change is the result of **global warming** caused by the burning of carbon fuels. This has caused an increase in levels of atmospheric carbon dioxide, which in turn has raised air temperatures due to the **greenhouse effect**.

- **Succession** is the gradual progression of different communities onto virgin land or onto habitat that is recovering from natural or manmade disturbances. Succession involves species changing the environment over time. **Primary succession** is mostly soil building on newly formed or newly exposed rock. As the rock breaks down from repeated freeze and thaw, it mixes with organic matter from **pioneer organisms** such as bacteria, algae and lichens. Eventually small amounts of soil are produced, which in turn support small plants and insects. These are followed by larger plants and animals, until the area becomes a stable **climax community**. Should a natural disaster hit, the ecosystem may be destroyed and the process will begin again. **Secondary succession** is when a natural disaster occurs and leaves the fertile soil intact. For example, a fire might destroy a large tract of forest, yet the burned area can be covered with new vegetation within a year or two.

- **Introduction of invasive non-native species** can disrupt an ecosystem over time. The invasive species might be a plant, an animal, an insect, or a disease. It might be introduced to the new ecosystem on purpose or by accident. Most species fail to survive when transplanted to a new area, but some thrive to become dangerous pests. In an earlier chapter, we saw how English sailors introduced a non-native species of rabbit to Australia in the late 1700s, resulting in an overpopulation of rabbits that continues to be troublesome today.

- **Catastrophic events** such as floods, earthquakes, tornadoes, hurricanes, volcanic eruptions, fires, and ice storms can severely damage or even destroy an ecosystem.

- **Human activity** can harm ecosystems in various ways. For example, in a process called **eutrophication**, freshwater lakes are disrupted by the runoff of sewage and fertilizers. These increase the nutrients in lake waters, which results in runaway growth of algae and other plants. Soon shallow areas are filled with weeds, and organic sediment raises the level of the entire lake. The decomposing of dead organic material uses up oxygen, which in turn causes fish to die. The cycle can eventually wipe out the entire lake, converting it to dry land.

There are other ways that human activity can contribute to **species extinctions**. The expansion of cities and suburbs can disrupt or destroy habitats, and overharvesting of fish and other wildlife can affect the food chain. Many scientists believe that, as the number of extinctions grows, the effects of species loss—and **loss of biodiversity**—will rival the effects of such human-caused problems as air pollution and acid rain.

Aquatic Ecosystems

Aquatic ecosystems cover more of the Earth's surface than terrestial ecosystems. **Saltwater life zones** include the oceans, which cover more than 70% of the Earth's surface and contain about 3% salt concentration. They are divided into the following zones.

- The **coastal zone** is at the shorelines of oceans. Coastal zones contain 90% of all marine species and are the most nutrient-rich areas of the oceans. These zones include:

  — estuaries, where oceans meet rivers

  — intertidal zones, where oceans meet land

  — continental shelves, which are the shallow ocean areas surrounding continents

  — coral reefs, which are masses of coral at or just below the ocean surface

  Only the upper layer of the coastal zone (about 30 meters or 100 feet below the water's surface) will support photosynthesis. This is because sunlight can only filter down to this depth. Sea life that relies on photosynthesis, such as algae and plankton, can survive only at this upper level. Oxygen released by photosynthesis supports a wide variety of fish and other aquatic organisms in the upper layer. Nutrients, such as nitrates, phosphates, and iron, are plentiful in shallow waters but are in short supply at lower depths. Species living in the coastal zone include plankton, clams, oysters, mussels, crabs, sea anemones, whelks, and sea stars. Farther out, at the end of the continental shelf, there is even richer biodiversity. In warmer waters coral reefs thrive. Other species in this outer zone include sponges, mollusks, sea turtles, squid, and many species of fish.

- The **open ocean zone** is divided into three layers based on the penetration of sunlight. The upper layer has low levels of nutrients but high levels of oxygen from producer species. The upper level includes whales, dolphins, sea turtles, and many invertebrates such as shrimp and oysters. Water temperature is coldest in the lower ocean layer, between 1,500 and 10,000 meters. It is very dark at these depths, with no producer species due to lack of sunlight. At the bottom of the sea, decomposer species break down organic material into nutrients. Only about 10% of all ocean species are found in the open ocean zone.

Freshwater life zones are large bodies of standing water such as lakes and ponds. Like saltwater zones, they have different life forms at different depths. The most productive area is near the shore, where rooted and floating plants thrive due to the abundant sunlight and nutrients such as nitrogen and phosphorus that accumulate from rain and snow run-off. There are also algae and plankton, decomposing organisms, and species such as fish, frogs, and insects. Away from the shore, most fish still live at the depth to which sunlight penetrates. Fewer fish can survive at the lower level, which is much darker and cooler. At the bottom of freshwater lakes and ponds, decomposers cycle nutrients from organic material.

Energy Flow in an Ecosystem

Now let's examine how energy is produced and utilized in an ecosystem. Plants and animals are organized into groups called **trophic levels**. A trophic level is an organism's nutritional position in a food chain. In other words, each trophic level has its own main energy source. Energy flows through an ecosystem from lower trophic levels to higher trophic levels. Trophic levels include the following.

- **Producers** are autotrophs that convert energy from sunlight into chemical energy. Plants are the major producers in ecosystems on land. Photosynthetic bacteria and protists are the major producers in aquatic ecosystems.

- **Primary consumers** are herbivores that eat the producers.

- **Secondary consumers**, or primary carnivores, eat the primary consumers.

- **Tertiary consumers**, or secondary carnivores, eat the secondary consumers. If they are scavengers, such as vultures or hyenas, they may eat the meat left by the primary carnivore.

At the upper trophic levels, there are **omnivores** that eat both consumers and producers. There are also **detrivores** such as earthworms, insects, jackals, and vultures that eat dead plants and animals. **Decomposers** are tiny detrivores such as bacteria and fungi.

Only about 10% of the energy available at one trophic level is converted into biomass in the next trophic level. This is due to energy lost in the following ways.

- Heat is lost each time a chemical reaction occurs within an organism.

- Cellular respiration and other processes do not produce biomass directly.

- Energy is lost as waste, such as urine and feces.

- Not all organisms at a lower level are consumed by organisms at the next higher level.

- Some parts of an organism's biomass cannot be eaten or digested, such as bones, teeth, or cellulose (for some consumers).

An energy level diagram (Fig. 7.5) or energy pyramid shows the feeding patterns of related populations. Each horizontal section represents a trophic level. Because of energy lost at each trophic level, there are usually no more than five trophic levels in a food chain.

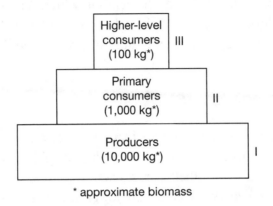

* approximate biomass

Figure 7.5. Three Trophic Levels

Two kinds of charts called food chains and food webs show the flow of energy between specific organisms in a community.

- A **food chain** is a linear flow chart showing which organisms eat other organisms. It pictures a single energy path from a producer to a primary consumer to a secondary consumer, and so forth.

- A **food web** is an expanded version of a food chain. For example, it shows all the major plants in an ecosystem, the animals that eat the plants, and the animals that eat those animals. Detrivores and decomposers may also be shown. Arrows connect the eaten organisms to the ones that eat them, thus showing the direction of energy flow.

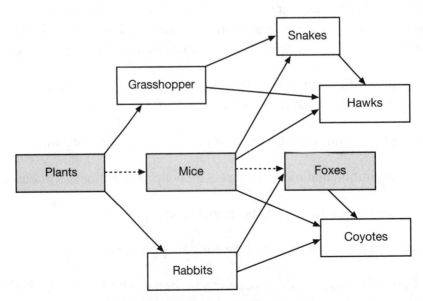

Figure 7.6 A Food Chain (---→) Within a Food Web (——→)

Chemical Cycles

Biogeochemical cycles recycle elements such as water, carbon, nitrogen, and phosphorus. The elements move from the environment to living things and back to the environment.

- In the **water cycle** (Fig. 7.7), water is stored in oceans, groundwater, glaciers, and the air (as water vapor). Plants take in water from the soil, and animals drink water or eat organisms that are mostly made of water. In **transpiration**, plants release water vapor into the air. Water also evaporates from soil and from organisms when they sweat, exhale, or produce waste. The water vapor condenses to form precipitation. Rain falling on land percolates through the soil to become groundwater or runs off, returning to larger bodies of water.

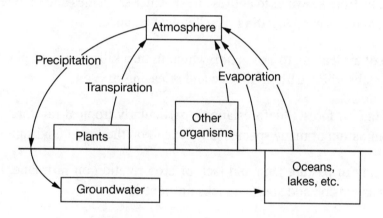

Figure 7.7. The Water Cycle

- In the **carbon cycle** (Fig. 7.8), carbon is used to build organic compounds. This occurs through the processes of photosynthesis, cellular respiration, and combustion. Carbon is stored in the atmosphere as CO_2, in fossil fuels such as oil and coal, and in peat and other organic material. Plants use CO_2 in photosynthesis, while animals consume plants or other organisms. Plants and animals return CO_2 to the atmosphere by cellular respiration and decomposition. CO_2 is also released when wood or fossil fuels are burned.

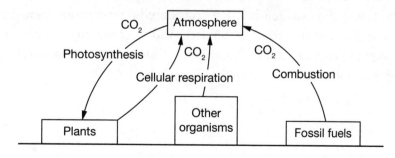

Figure 7.8. The Carbon Cycle

Renewable and Nonrenewable Resources

Renewable resources are those that can reproduce or be replenished. For example, fresh water is renewed through the water cycle, and oxygen is renewed by photosynthesis and cellular respiration of plants and trees. Livestock and fish are organisms that reproduce, as are trees and crop plants. Yet even renewable resources can be damaged or ruined if not managed properly, as in these examples.

- Pollution of fresh water with chemical dumps, spills, or from problems associated with drilling for oil or natural gas

- Pollution of seawater and damage to marine life due to desalination processes that remove salts from seawater to address fresh water shortages and then return the recovered salts to the ocean, upsetting the chemical balance

- Pollution of air leading to **acid rain**, which in turn kills trees and plants and prevents them from absorbing carbon dioxide and releasing oxygen

- Clear-cutting of forests (deforestation), particularly tropical rainforest, which results in the elimination of many species that depend on the forest environment

- Over-grazing of pasture land and lack of crop rotation on farmland, leading to such problems as erosion and soil that lacks nutrients

- Over-fishing and over-harvesting of wildlife, which can deplete species or drive them into extinction

Nonrenewable resources are limited in quantity or cannot be replaced as quickly as they are used up. These include oil, coal, and natural gas. Drilling for oil, or petroleum, can threaten wildlife habitats (with infrastructure for well sites) and waterways (with oil spills). Burning petroleum for fuel creates air pollution and increased greenhouse gas emissions. Extracting coal from surface and below-surface mines can cause ground levels to lower and erosion to occur. Burning coal for fuel also contributes to pollution and greenhouse gases. Natural gas burns cleaner than oil or coal, but drilling for it can also affect wildlife and groundwater. Nuclear energy, which is often considered a renewable resource, requires uranium, a radioactive element that must be mined. And while nuclear energy is less harmful to the air and upper atmosphere than oil and coal, it also produces radioactive waste that is deadly to ecosystems and must be disposed of somehow.

End-of-Chapter Quiz

1. **Which of the following categories includes all the others?**

   A. species

   B. community

   C. ecosystem

   D. population

2. **Currently the age structure in Japan is weighted towards older people. This will probably lead to which of the following?**

   A. very slow growth or even decrease in population

   B. very rapid growth in population

   C. a decrease in life expectancy over the long term

   D. higher birth rates than death rates for the foreseeable future

3. **Look at the survivorship curves below.**

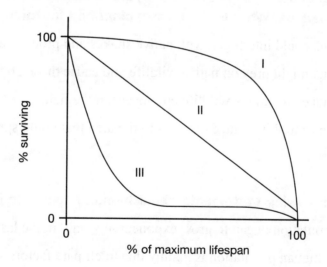

   Curve III on the graph *best* describes which of the following situations?

   A. a species with low death rates in young and middle age members

   B. a species whose members have much the same chance of dying at any age

   C. a species that produces large numbers of offspring, most of which die before reaching maturity

   D. a species that produces few offspring and invests a lot of energy caring for them

4. **Which of the following is NOT an abiotic factor in an environment?**

   A. temperature

   B. food plants

   C. water salinity

   D. sunlight

5. **The following are all factors that limit the growth of a population. Which of the factors is density-independent?**

   A. predators

   B. disease

   C. competition for scarce resources

   D. random forest fires

6. **Burmese pythons are native to Southeast Asia, yet they are now found in the Florida Everglades. It is thought that the pythons were brought to the United States as pets and then released into the wild. Florida biologists have authorized a hunting contest to thin out the python population, which now numbers in the ten thousands. What is the best explanation for taking this approach?**

   A. The pythons could interbreed with native snakes and produce a dangerous hybrid.

   B. The pythons might prey on native wildlife and cause those populations to decline.

   C. The pythons could attack wildlife employees in the field.

   D. The pythons could introduce diseases to the area that could spread to the human population.

7. **Which of the following statements about human population is correct?**

   A. Human population began to grow exponentially only in the last century.

   B. Growth in human population is mainly due to climate factors.

   C. Developed countries are more likely to experience high rates of population growth.

   D. Inventions that helped people live in extreme conditions have contributed to growth in the human population.

8. **Look at the population graph below.**

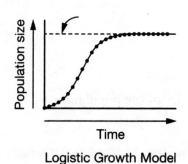

Logistic Growth Model

What population factor does the dotted line represent?

A. carrying capacity

B. limiting factors

C. migration

D. lack of competitors

9. **Which of the following is the *most important* aspect of primary succession in an ecosystem?**

A. natural disaster

B. climate change

C. soil building

D. water recycling

10. **What is the usual cause of a harmful increase in the nutrients in a freshwater lake?**

A. global warming

B. runoff of fertilizers and sewage

C. loss of biodiversity

D. seasonal variations in rainfall

11. Wolves that travel and hunt in packs exhibit which dispersion pattern?

    A.   uniform

    B.   random

    C.   clumped

    D.   It depends on the density of the population.

12. Which of the following is the kind of area where an organism typically lives, including the biotic and abiotic factors that enable it to survive?

    A.   climax community

    B.   ecosystem

    C.   biome

    D.   habitat

13. Which of the following eat producer organisms in a food chain?

    A.   detrivores

    B.   herbivores

    C.   primary carnivores

    D.   secondary carnivores

14. About what percentage of the energy available at one trophic level is converted into biomass at the next trophic level?

    A.   1%

    B.   10%

    C.   50%

    D.   98%

15. In the following energy-level diagram, the horizontal bar for each trophic level represents the relative number of organisms at that level.

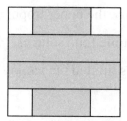

Which of the following descriptions *best* fits this diagram?

A. fewer organisms at the producer and tertiary consumer levels

B. fewer organisms at the primary consumer and secondary consumer levels

C. a concentration of organisms at the lowest and highest trophic levels

D. an even distribution of organisms at all trophic levels

16. **Look at the following food chain for the African savanna.**

grass ——> antelope ——> lion ——> ?

Which of the following would *most likely* be the next link in this food chain?

A. grass

B. zebra

C. vulture

D. elephant

17. **Which of the following are found in the lowest layer of the ocean?**

A. producer species dependent on sunlight for photosynthesis

B. decomposers that break down organic material

C. whales, dolphins, and sea turtles

D. invertebrate organisms such as oysters and shrimp

18. **Why does a food chain generally have no more than five trophic levels?**

    A. There is a loss of energy at each trophic level.

    B. There is no way to determine the upper trophic levels.

    C. Many organisms have multiple food sources.

    D. The loss of biodiversity has limited the variety of organisms.

19. **Which of the following is NOT one of the ways that the carbon cycle adds CO_2 to the air?**

    A. cell respiration

    B. burning of fossil fuels

    C. photosynthesis

    D. decomposition of dead organisms

20. **Tropical rainforests are renewable resources in theory, since plants and trees can reproduce. What human activity is the main threat to the viability of tropical rainforests and the species that depend on them?**

    A. global warming due to burning of fossil fuels

    B. over-harvesting of wildlife in tropical forests

    C. industrial pollution resulting in acid rain

    D. clear-cutting of forests

Answers to the Chapter Quiz

1. **C**

   From most general category to most specific, organisms can be grouped as ecosystem, community, species, population, and individual. Ecosystem is the most general category because it includes not only community relationships but also abiotic or nonliving factors in the environment.

2. **A**

   An aging population increases in size much less rapidly than a younger, reproductively active population. In fact, it may actually decrease in size, as is occurring today in Japan.

3. **C**

Curve III shows high mortality among young members. This is characteristic of many species of fish, which release thousands of eggs, rely on external fertilization, and are not involved in parenting.

4. **B**

"Abiotic" means nonliving. The only environmental factor listed that is not nonliving is food plants.

5. **D**

Density-independent factors include natural disasters, such as earthquakes and naturally occurring fires, and extreme weather events.

6. **B**

The introduction of an invasive, non-native species such as Burmese pythons into the Florida Everglades threatens the native wildlife, such as raccoons and possums, with a predator that is not a natural part of the ecosystem. Some species have declined more than 95% due to the pythons.

7. **D**

Such innovative methods as building climate-adapted structures, weaving warmer clothes, and heating and cooling structures more efficiently have contributed to human population growth by allowing people to settle in very warm and very cold environments.

8. **A**

The dotted line represents the point at which the habitat's carrying capacity is reached and population growth levels out. Limiting factors contribute to the carrying capacity in logistic growth, which is shown in this graph.

9. **C**

In primary succession, soil building occurs on newly formed or newly exposed rock. This is the result of the rock breaking down because of freeze and thaw and mixing with organic matter from pioneer organisms such as bacteria, lichens, and algae.

10. **B**

   The runoff of human-produced fertilizers and sewage can lead to a rapid increase in the level of nutrients for a freshwater lake. When the amount of nutrients is too great, algae and other plants grow too rapidly, choking shallow areas with vegetation and initiating a cycle of decline for the lake.

11. **C**

   A clumped dispersion pattern indicates that wolves form packs for hunting and breeding. Wolves that hunt alone would be likely to stake out their own individual territories and thus would be more evenly distributed in a uniform dispersion. Knowing the density of the population alone (individuals per square kilometer, for example) doesn't explain how the population is dispersed in the area.

12. **D**

   The kind of place where an organism usually lives is its habitat. The habitat includes other organisms that live in the area, including food plants or prey, as well as the physical and chemical factors that make up the environment.

13. **B**

   Herbivores, or animals that eat plants, are the primary consumers of producers, or plants that convert sunlight into chemical energy. They are at the second trophic level of an energy level pyramid.

14. **B**

   Only about 10% of the energy available at one trophic level is converted into biomass in the next level. This is because of energy that is lost in a variety of ways, including heat loss, energy lost as waste, and indigestible parts of an organism's biomass such as bones and teeth.

15. A

The lower bar represents the producer level and the upper bar represents the tertiary consumer level. Notice that each of those bars is shorter than the middle two bars, indicating fewer organisms at those levels of energy.

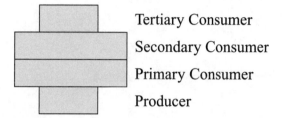

Tertiary Consumer

Secondary Consumer

Primary Consumer

Producer

16. C

The next link in the food chain after a lion eats an antelope would be a scavenger such as a vulture that consumes the meat left by the primary carnivore (lion).

17. B

In the extremely cold and dark layer at the bottom of the ocean, where lack of sunlight prevents producer species from living, decomposer species exist on organic material that drifts down from the ocean layers above.

18. A

A food chain is usually limited to no more than five trophic levels because of a nearly 90% loss of energy at each trophic level. Loss of energy is caused by such factors as heat loss from chemical reactions, energy lost as waste, and the fact that not all lower level organisms are consumed by organisms at the next higher level.

19. C

Photosynthesis is part of the carbon cycle, but it *removes* carbon from the air and adds oxygen.

20. D

Clear-cutting of tropical rainforests to provide new land for farming and grazing is the main threat to tropical rainforests and their dependent species. It is estimated that in the 1980s 21,000 square miles of tropical rainforest in South America (mainly Brazil) were deforested (cut down or burned) each year—an area about the size of North Carolina.

Chapter 8

Matter and Energy Transformations

Your Goals for Chapter 8

1. You should be able to identify and/or describe the basic molecular structure of carbohydrates, lipids, proteins, and/or nucleic acids.

2. You should be able to describe the primary functions of carbohydrates, lipids, proteins, and/or nucleic acids in organisms.

3. You should be able to explain how enzymes speed up the rate of a biochemical reaction by lowering the reaction's activation energy.

4. You should be able to identify and/or describe the effect of environmental factors on enzyme activity.

5. You should be able to explain how the products of photosynthesis are used as reactants for cellular respiration and vice versa.

6. You should be able to explain how photosynthesis stores energy and cellular respiration releases energy.

7. You should be able to identify the reactants, products and/or the basic function of photosynthesis.

8. You should be able to identify the reactants, products and/or the basic functions of aerobic and anaerobic cellular respiration.

9. You should be able to connect the role of adenosine triphosphate (ATP) to energy transfers within the cell.

10. You should be able to explain the properties of water at a conceptual level.

11. You should be able to explain how the properties make water essential for life on Earth.

Standards

The following standards are assessed on the Florida Biology 1 End-of-Course Assessment either directly or indirectly:

SC.912.L.18.1	Describe the basic molecular structures and primary functions of the four major categories of biological macromolecules.
SC.912.L.18.7	Identify the reactants, products, and basic functions of photosynthesis.
SC.912.L.18.8	Identify the reactants, products, and basic functions of aerobic and anaerobic cellular respiration.
SC.912.L.18.9	Explain the interrelated nature of photosynthesis and cellular respiration.
SC.912.L.18.10	Connect the role of adenosine triphosphate (ATP) to energy transfers within a cell.
SC.912.L.18.11	Explain the role of enzymes as catalysts that lower the activation energy of biochemical reactions. Identify factors, such as pH and temperature, and their effect on enzyme activity.
SC.912.L.18.12	Discuss the special properties of water that contribute to Earth's suitability as an environment for life: cohesive behavior, ability to moderate temperature, expansion upon freezing, and versatility as a solvent.

Basics of Biochemistry

The **atom** is the building block of all matter. An atom consists of the subatomic particles **protons, neutrons**, and **electrons**. The nucleus of an atom contains protons, which have a positive charge, and neutrons, which have a neutral charge. Negatively charged electrons are outside the nucleus. An atom in its natural state has a neutral state because its number of protons (+) equals its number of electrons (–). **Molecules** are formed from two or more atoms held together by the interaction of their electrons, called a chemical bond.

- An **ionic bond** forms between two atoms by the transfer of one or more electrons from one atom to the other.

- A **covalent bond** forms between two atoms when they share electrons. In **nonpolar covalent bonds**, electrons are shared equally. In **polar covalent bonds**, electrons are shared unequally, resulting in a negative pole and a positive pole.

- A **hydrogen bond** is a weak bond between molecules. It results when a positively charged hydrogen atom in a covalent molecule is attracted to the negative charge of a separate covalent molecule.

Biological Macromolecules

Since all living organisms are composed of matter, the basic rules of chemistry apply to them. This area of study is called **biological chemistry**. All organisms require an input of energy from the environment, as well as the means to control and use that energy. Organisms generally convert the energy they obtain to ATP, which is the cell's power source for all life processes. These processes include **biosynthesis**, or the chemical reactions that produce the organic molecules that compose an organism's cells.

Organic molecules are those that include carbon atoms. Large organic molecules are called **macromolecules** and may consist of hundreds or thousands of atoms. Macromolecules are usually **polymers**, which are chains of repeated similar units called **monomers**. Of carbon's six electrons, four are available to bond with other atoms. In diagrams, these bonds are represented by four lines, with each line standing for a pair of shared electrons (one from the carbon atom and one from the other atom). The similar clusters of atoms in organic molecules are called **functional groups**. Molecules in each functional group have similar properties.

The four major categories of biological macromolecules are the following.

- **Carbohydrates** are classified as monosaccharides, disaccharides, and polysaccharides depending on the number of sugar molecules. They contain carbon, hydrogen, and oxygen in the ratio 1:2:1. Carbohydrates contain many carbon-hydrogen bonds, which release energy upon oxidation. This makes carbohydrates excellent for storing energy.

  — **Monosaccharides** are the monomers of carbohydrates. They are simple **sugars** having the basic formula $(CH_2O)_n$ with n any number of carbon atoms from 3 to 8. Glucose (Fig. 8.1) and fructose are **isomers** that each have the formula $C_6H_{12}O_6$ (or $n = 6$), but with different arrangements of carbon atoms. Sugars are often the building blocks for larger molecules.

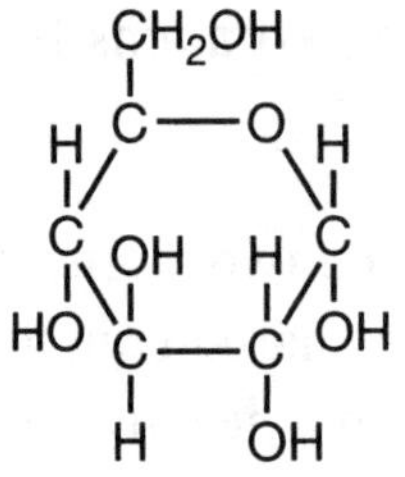

Figure 8.1. Glucose — Example of a Monosaccharide

— **Disaccharides** are usually made by linking two monosaccharides together. For example, sucrose (common table sugar) is made from the monosaccharides glucose and fructose (Fig. 8.2). Lactose (milk sugar) is made from glucose and galactose. Disaccharides are the **transport forms** that organisms use to move glucose from place to place. In plants, the transport form is sucrose. For many mammals, the transport form is lactose, which provides offspring with a source of energy. (In humans, glucose circulates as a simple monosaccharide.)

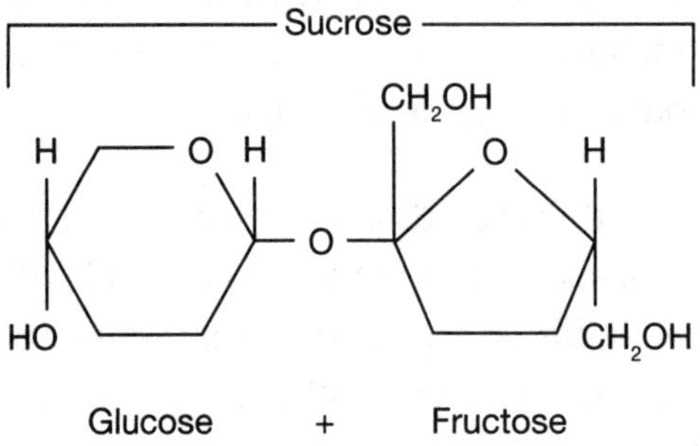

Figure 8.2. Sucrose — A Disaccharide Formed from Glucose and Fructose

— **Polysaccharides** are made of a series of connected monosaccharides in long branches or straight chains. Polysaccharides are polymers formed from chains of repeating monomers. **Starch** and **glycogen** are polymers of glucose used for energy storage in plants and animals respectively. **Cellulose** is a polymer of glucose found in the cell walls of plants.

• **Lipids** are molecules that are insoluble in water and are composed of glycerol and fatty acids. Animal fat is one kind of lipid. Oils such as coconut oil, olive oil, and corn oil are another. Waxes such as beeswax are yet another kind of lipid. The three main categories of lipids are the following.

— Fats, or **triglycerides**, are excellent energy-storage molecules consisting of one glycerol molecule with three fatty acid molecules attached. **Saturated fatty** acids have a single covalent bond between each pair of carbon atoms. They are more likely to remain solid at room temperature. **Unsaturated fatty acids** have one or more double bonds and are more likely to be fluid at room temperature. **Polyunsaturated fatty acids** have two or more double covalent bonds.

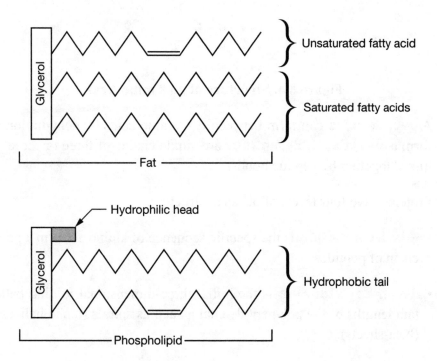

Figure 8.3. Structure of a Fat and a Phospholipid

— **Phospholipids** are molecules that make up the bilayer formation of cell membranes. Phospholipids consist of one glycerol molecule with two fatty acid molecules and a phosphate group attached. A phospholipid molecule has a polar "head" that is the phosphate group and two long nonpolar "tails." This structure, with both water-soluble and water-insoluble elements, is essential to phospholipids' function in the cell membrane. Wax and steroids, including cholesterol, are examples of lipids with more complex structures and a variety of functions.

• **Proteins** are polymers made of different combinations of 20 commonly occurring amino acid monomers. They are the most diverse group of macromolecules, both in chemical structure and function. Proteins' amino acid building blocks were probably among the first molecules to form on Earth.

— **Amino acids** share the same basic structure. Each amino acid has a central carbon atom covalently bonded to four atoms or groups of atoms called functional groups. One of the four is always a hydrogen atom. A carboxyl (acidic) functional group

(– COOH) and an amine (basic) functional group (– NH_2) are always present. The fourth component bound to the central carbon atom is a variable R group, which is different for each amino acid.

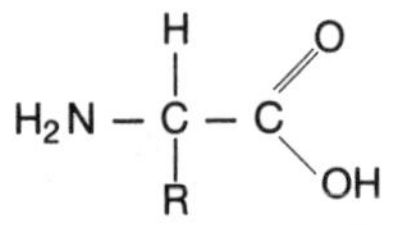

$$H_2N - \overset{\overset{\displaystyle H}{|}}{\underset{\underset{\displaystyle R}{|}}{C}} - C\overset{\displaystyle O}{\underset{\displaystyle OH}{\diagdown}}$$

Figure 8.4. Structure of an Amino Acid

— A **peptide bond** can form between two amino acids by dehydration synthesis to form a **dipeptide. Polypeptides** are single chains of three or more amino acids linked together by peptide bonds.

— Proteins have four levels of physical structure.

• **Primary structure** is the specific sequence of amino acids in a polypeptide, or chain of peptides.

• **Secondary structure** is the initial three-dimensional folding patterns of certain lengths of the polypeptide chain, such as spirals (alpha helices) and pleats (beta-sheets).

• **Tertiary structure** refers to the overall three-dimensional shape into which a polypeptide eventually folds.

• **Quaternary structure** refers to a protein formed from two or more folded peptide chains.

— **Protein functions** are too numerous to list here. Some of the most important functions include the following.

• **Catalyzing enzymes** are proteins with a three-dimensional globular shape that fits closely around other molecules. Enzymes activate metabolic reactions and speed up their rate. In order for a chemical reaction to occur, molecules must first collide and then maintain enough energy, called **activation energy**, to set off the formation of new chemical bonds. Enzymes are vital catalysts that accelerate the rate of a chemical reaction by lowering its required activation energy. Catalyst enzymes themselves are not changed by the chemical reaction, and thus can repeat the process over and over. Enzymes require certain environmental factors to work efficiently. These factors include temperature, pH levels, and concentration. For example, human enzymes work best at normal body temperature (98.6°). At temperatures above 104° enzymes lose their three-dimensional shape as hydrogen and peptide bonds start to break down. Certain digestive enzymes become active only at low levels of pH (extremely acidic). Also, as the enzyme concentration increases, the rate of enzyme activity increases until it reaches a constant level. With more enzymes available, more substrates are broken down in less time. (Substrates are molecules on which enzymes act.) The level becomes constant when substrates to be broken down are outnumbered by enzymes.

- **Defensive proteins** are the basis of the body's endocrine and immune systems. They recognize invading microbes and cancer cells.

- **Storage proteins** bind with iron and calcium to store these materials.

- **Transport proteins** move materials into and out of cells. Hemoglobin transports oxygen in the blood, and myoglobin moves oxygen in muscles.

- **Support proteins** provide structural support. These include collagen for cartilage, keratin for hair and nails, and fibrin for blood clots.

- **Motion proteins** such as myosin and actin cause muscles to contract. Similar proteins play important roles in moving materials within cells.

- **Messenger proteins** provide means for cells in one part of the body to communicate with cells in another part. Many of these very small proteins are hormones that regulate certain activities in the body. For example, insulin regulates glucose metabolism, and vasopressin stimulates kidneys to reabsorb water.

- The **nucleic acids** — DNA and RNA — are made from monomers called **nucleotides**. **DNA** (deoxyribonucleic acid) is the molecule that stores a cell's genetic information. DNA passes on genetic instructions to **RNA** (ribonucleic acid). RNA decodes and expresses genetic information as protein. A nucleotide has three parts: a nitrogen base, a five-carbon sugar (either deoxyribose in DNA or ribose in RNA), and a phosphate group.

  — One of four nitrogen bases is present in each nucleotide. Adenine, thymine, cytosine, and guanine are found in DNA. Adenine, uracil, cytosine, and guanine are found in RNA.

  — **ATP** (adenosine triphosphate) is a nucleotide that donates its energy to a wide variety of biochemical reactions and other processes within cells. ATP carries its energy in high-energy phosphate bonds.

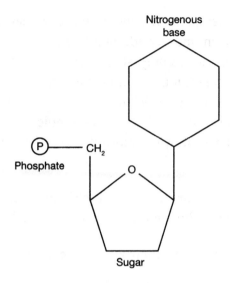

Figure 8.5. Structure of a Nucleotide

Photosynthesis

Photosynthesis is the process by which energy in sunlight is converted into energy in the form of chemical bonds, particularly glucose. In eukaryotes, photosynthesis takes place in chloroplasts. In prokaryotes, it occurs in the plasma membrane and the cytoplasm. The overall equation for photosynthesis is

$$6CO_2 + 6H_2O + \text{light energy} \longrightarrow C_6H_{12}O_6 + 6O_2$$

In a chemical reaction like photosynthesis, the **reactants** are chemical compounds that are consumed or acted upon to make the products. As you can see in the equation above, the reactants of photosynthesis are carbon dioxide and water, while the end products are glucose and oxygen. Photosynthesis has two main steps. The absorption and conversion of light energy to ATP and NADPH are called the **light reactions**. The use of ATP and NADPH to convert CO_2 to sugars is called the **light-independent reactions**.

- The light reactions take place in the thylakoid membrane, where photosynthetic pigments absorb light energy. Chlorophyll *a* is the main photosynthetic pigment, while Chlorophyll *b* and carotenoids are accessory pigments. The latter two allow leaves to capture a wider spectrum of visible light than chlorophyll alone.

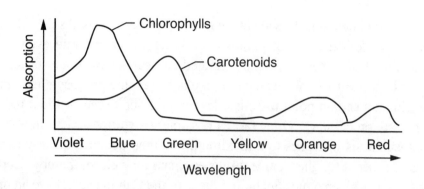

Figure 8.6. Absorption Spectra of Photosynthetic Pigments

- The energy gathered from the light reactions is stored by forming ATP, the compound that cells use to store energy.

- The light-independent reactions occur in the stroma within the chloroplast. This reaction converts CO_2 to glucose. It doesn't rely on light in order to take place, but it does require the products of the light reactions, which are ATP and NADPH.

- The main activity of the light-independent reactions is the **Calvin cycle** (Fig. 8.7). This is the cyclical process in which the 3-carbon sugar phosphoglyceraldehyde (PGAL) is produced. The process is called **carbon fixation**, because the Calvin cycle uses CO_2 and energy from ATP to "fix" the CO_2 (that is, incorporate it) into the 3-carbon sugar PGAL.

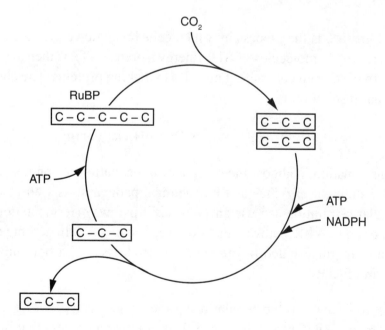

Figure 8.7. The Calvin Cycle

- Certain environmental factors affect the rate of photosynthesis. As the **intensity of light** increases, so does the rate of photosynthesis. However, the rate eventually levels off because the photosystems become saturated and cannot work any faster. Similarly, as the **concentration of CO_2** available to a plant rises, the photosynthetic rate increases. But again, at a certain point there is a leveling off due to the fact that the Calvin cycle enzymes are processing CO_2 as fast as possible. As **temperature increases**, the rate of photosynthesis increases to a maximum and then declines quickly as temperatures increase further. At higher temperatures, stomata may close, thereby decreasing available CO_2. Also, all enzymes, including those of the Calvin cycle, have an optimum temperature at which they process substrates at the highest possible rate.

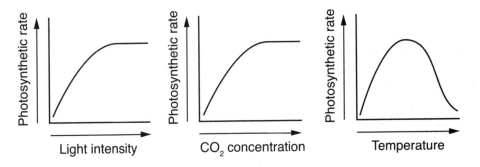

Figure 8.8. Environmental Effects on Photosynthesis

Cellular Respiration

Cellular respiration is the process by which cells break down glucose to extract energy and transfer that energy to molecules of ATP. Energy stored in ATP is then available for a variety of cellular activities, from contracting muscles to making proteins. The chemical equation for aerobic cellular respiration is

$$C_6H_{12}O_6 + 6O_2 \longrightarrow 6CO_2 + 6H_2O + energy$$

Although this equation is almost the reverse of the equation for photosynthesis, the two processes involve different enzymes and biochemical pathways, as well as different organs of the cell. Cellular respiration can use an **anaerobic** pathway (fermentation) that does not require oxygen, or an **aerobic** pathway that does require oxygen. In aerobic cellular respiration, the reactants are glucose and oxygen and the products are carbon dioxide, water, and energy in the form of ATP.

- Both anaerobic and aerobic cellular respiration begin with **glycolysis**. This step does not require oxygen. Glycolysis (Fig. 8.9) is a ten-step process that breaks down glucose to make **pyruvate** or **pyruvic acid** and releases ATP. This process occurs in the cell's cytoplasm.

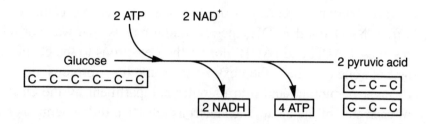

Figure 8.9. Glycolysis

- In **aerobic respiration**, the anaerobic phase of glycolysis is followed by a two-step phase that requires oxygen. The two steps in this aerobic phase are the Krebs cycle and the electron transport chain, which occur within the mitochondria.

- In the **Krebs cycle** (Fig. 8.10), pyruvic acid molecules produced by glycolysis are processed to release the energy stored in their molecular bonds. Before entering the Krebs cycle, the pyruvic acid molecules convert to Acetyl-CoA, which combines with oxaloacetic acid to produce citric acid. (That is why the Krebs cycle is sometimes called the citric acid cycle.) During each turn of the Krebs cycle, two CO_2, one ATP, three NADH, and one $FADH_2$ are produced. This releases a great deal of energy, as NADH is a particularly energy-rich molecule. At the end of the cycle, oxaloacetic acid, which was one of the first reactants, is regenerated to begin the cycle again. The CO_2 produced in the Krebs cycle is a waste product and is exhaled.

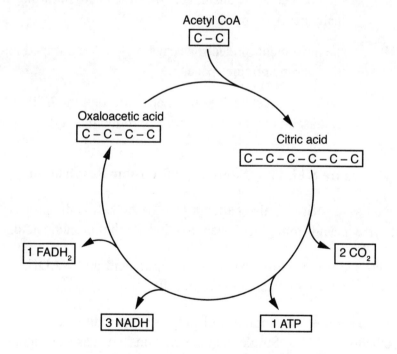

Figure 8.10. The Krebs Cycle

- The **electron transport chain** is the last stage of aerobic cellular respiration. It extracts from NADH and $FADH_2$ the remaining energy that was not released in the first two stages. NADH and $FADH_2$ donate their electrons to the chain, which carries electrons from one protein to the next. At the same time, protons are pumped across the cell's inner membrane and into its outer compartment by the electron transport chain. At each step of the chain, the electrons release a little energy as ATP. A proton gradient and electric-charge gradient create reserves of potential energy, like the water behind a dam is stored energy. Eventually the electrons with some protons are added to oxygen. This produces water, another waste product of cell respiration.

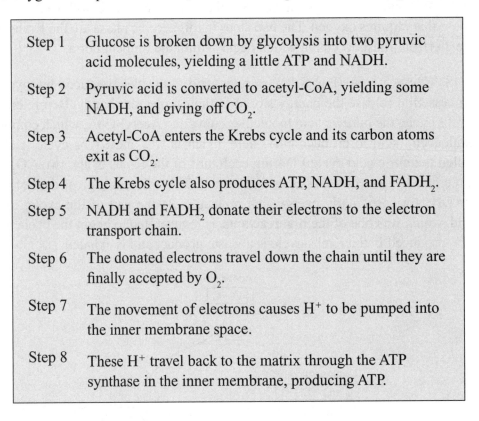

Step 1	Glucose is broken down by glycolysis into two pyruvic acid molecules, yielding a little ATP and NADH.
Step 2	Pyruvic acid is converted to acetyl-CoA, yielding some NADH, and giving off CO_2.
Step 3	Acetyl-CoA enters the Krebs cycle and its carbon atoms exit as CO_2.
Step 4	The Krebs cycle also produces ATP, NADH, and $FADH_2$.
Step 5	NADH and $FADH_2$ donate their electrons to the electron transport chain.
Step 6	The donated electrons travel down the chain until they are finally accepted by O_2.
Step 7	The movement of electrons causes H^+ to be pumped into the inner membrane space.
Step 8	These H^+ travel back to the matrix through the ATP synthase in the inner membrane, producing ATP.

Figure 8.11. Flow Summary of Aerobic Respiration

- **Anaerobic respiration** is also called **fermentation**. It is the process by which cells convert pyruvic acid from glycolysis into ethyl alcohol or lactic acid.

- Two of the end products of glycolysis, pyruvic acid and NADH, can be processed anaerobically in the cytoplasm of certain cells.

- **Alcoholic fermentation** includes glycolysis plus additional reactions that produce NAD^+, ethanol, and CO_2. Single-celled organisms, such as yeast and some plant cells, have special enzymes to carry out alcoholic fermentation. Yeast is used in bread making because CO_2 gas causes the bread to rise. The ethanol is removed by subsequent baking. Yeast is also used in making beer because it produces ethanol. CO_2 in an enclosed container produces carbonation.

- **Lactic acid fermentation** includes glycolysis plus an additional reaction that generates NAD+ and lactic acid. Certain fungi, bacteria, and muscle cells have special enzymes that carry out lactic acid fermentation. In the manufacture of dairy products, such as cheese and yogurt, lactic acid adds tart flavors to the final product. In muscle cells during vigorous exercise, lactic acid fermentation provides ATP when the circulatory system cannot keep up with the cells' oxygen demands.

Comparing Photosynthesis and Cellular Respiration

Photosynthesis converts sunlight energy to glucose, while cellular respiration converts glucose to energy. The products of photosynthesis are used as the components for cellular respiration and vice versa. Figure 8.12 is a comparison of the two processes.

Item Compared	Cellular Respiration	Photosynthesis
Main purpose	Break down carbon compounds to make ATP	Use light energy to make carbon compounds
Organisms	Almost all organisms, including plants	Some bacteria, protists, and plants
Eukaryotic organelle	Mitochondria	Chloroplasts
Initial energy source	Organic compounds (chemical bond energy)	Light energy
Reducing power	NADH & $FADH_2$	NADPH
Order of steps	Glycolysis Krebs cycle Electron transport Chemiosmosis	Light absorption Electron transport Chemiosmosis Calvin cycle
Processes in common	Electron transport & chemiosmosis (ATP synthase)	
Cyclic processes	Krebs cycle	Calvin cycle
Gas used	O_2 (final electron acceptor)	CO_2 (Calvin cycle)
Gas released	CO_2 (mostly from Krebs)	O_2 (water splitting)

Figure 8.12. Comparison of Cellular Respiration and Photosynthesis

Properties of Water

Water has special properties that make it essential for life on Earth. These include the following.

- **Hydrogen bonding** between water molecules causes **strong cohesion**, which is an attraction between two *like* substances. This cohesion in turn creates a high surface tension. Insects can walk on the surface of water without sinking. The cohesive properties of water also aid in **capillary action**, in which water moves upward in the narrow fibers of a tall tree from its roots to its leaves. For each molecule of water lost by transpiration at the leaf, another molecule is pulled in at the roots.

- Water also has the property of **strong adhesion**, or an attraction between two *unlike* substances. This is why you can pick up a straight pin by first wetting your finger. The water sticks both to your skin and the pin. Adhesion also causes water to cling to the cell walls of vessel elements in plants.

- Water is a **universal solvent** because it is a highly polar molecule and dissolves ionic or polar substances.

- Water has the ability to moderate temperature because of its **high heat capacity**. It cools down and heats up slowly, allowing for stable temperatures in organisms and in the watery environments where many organisms live.

- Water **expands upon freezing**. This makes water less dense as a solid than as a liquid, and allows ice to float. In a pond or lake, floating surface ice serves to insulate the water below, enabling fish and other life forms to survive during winter. In spring, the melting ice turns to denser water, sinks to the lower level of the lake, and ensures circulation of the lake water and its nutrients.

End-of-Chapter Quiz

1. Carbohydrates are excellent energy storage molecules. What is the main reason for this?

   A. The class of carbohydrates called disaccharides transport glucose from place to place in organisms.

   B. Sugars often serve as the building blocks for larger molecules.

   C. Carbohydrates consist of long chains of monomers.

   D. Carbohydrates contain many carbon-hydrogen bonds.

2. Starch has several advantages as a polymer of glucose molecules. For example, it can coil itself into a compact shape, and it is insoluble in water. These factors help it perform its principal function. What is that function?

   A. energy storage in animals

   B. energy storage in plants

   C. transport form of protein in animals

   D. support structure in plants

3. Oils and waxes are formed from which of the following macromolecules?

   A. carbohydrates

   B. lipids

   C. proteins

   D. nucleic acids

4. Which of the following molecules is NOT a polymer?

   A. cellulose

   B. protein

   C. glucose

   D. glycogen

5. An allergic reaction causes the pH level in a person's stomach to rise unexpectedly to between 7 and 9. What effect would this have on pepsinogen, an enzyme that digests proteins in the stomach?

   A. It would become completely inactive.

   B. It would convert proteins into amino acids.

   C. It would work more efficiently.

   D. It would prevent an allergic reaction to food.

6. Which of the following molecules have both hydrophobic and hydrophilic components, causing them to form into double-layer membranes?

   A. lactose

   B. triglycerides

   C. phospholipids

   D. amino acids

7. Hemoglobin, which moves oxygen through the blood, is an example of which of the following?

   A. motion protein

   B. transport protein

   C. messenger protein

   D. storage protein

8. Enzymes are important catalysts that speed up the rate of chemical reactions in cells. How do they accomplish this?

   A. by preventing molecules from colliding

   B. by providing all the proteins required for a metabolic reaction

   C. by raising the required activation energy for the metabolic reaction

   D. by lowering the required activation energy for the metabolic reaction

9. The nucleotide ATP carries its energy in which of the following?

   A. a nitrogen base

   B. pyruvic acid

C. phosphate bonds

D. carbon bonds

10. **Which of the following is the most diverse group of macromolecules in both function and chemical structure?**

   A. proteins

   B. lipids

   C. carbohydrates

   D. nucleic acids

11. **The effectiveness of enzymes as catalysts for metabolic processes is partly due to their structure. Which of the following describes the basic shape of an enzyme?**

   A. primary structure, or chain

   B. secondary structure, or beginning folding pattern

   C. tertiary structure, or three-dimensional globular shape

   D. quaternary structure, or two or more folded chains

12. **Which of the following *best* describes the difference between the functions of carbohydrates and nucleic acids?**

   A. Carbohydrates reinforce the structure of cells, while nucleic acids break down cell membranes.

   B. Carbohydrates store energy efficiently, while nucleic acids store and pass on a cell's genetic information.

   C. Carbohydrates store energy in fats, while nucleic acids donate energy to various biochemical reactions.

   D. Carbohydrates trigger a variety of metabolic processes in cells, while nucleic acids decode and express genetic information as proteins.

13. **Which of the following are the reactants in photosynthesis?**

   A. CO_2 and H

   B. glucose and H_2O

   C. glucose and O_2

   D. CO_2 and H_2O

14. **The waste product generated by the Krebs cycle is which of the following?**

    A. H_2O

    B. CO_2

    C. pyruvic acid

    D. O_2

15. **One product of photosynthesis is oxygen. Which of the following *best* describes the main role that oxygen plays in cellular respiration?**

    A. decomposes glucose to pyruvate

    B. combines with carbon to form carbon dioxide

    C. forms water by acting as an acceptor for electrons and hydrogen

    D. combines with NADH to form glucose

16. **Which statement is true about the interrelationship of photosynthesis and cellular respiration?**

    A. Both photosynthesis and cellular respiration begin with carbon dioxide and water and produce energy in the form of glucose.

    B. Photosynthesis releases energy from unstable molecular bonds to begin the process of cellular respiration.

    C. Photosynthesis produces carbon dioxide and water, which are the chief reactants in cellular respiration.

    D. Cellular respiration releases carbon dioxide and water, which are the reactants in photosynthesis.

17. **Which of the following occurs during the Calvin cycle in the light-independent reactions of photosynthesis?**

    A. Energy from sunlight is absorbed and converted into ATP and NADPH.

    B. Carbon dioxide and released energy from ATP incorporate carbon dioxide into PGAL.

    C. Energy gathered from the light reactions is stored by the formation of ATP.

    D. Pyruvic acid molecules are broken down to release energy for cell activities.

18. Which of the following best describe a result of the hydrogen bonding between water molecules?

    A. Water adheres to narrow tubing or fibers by capillary action.

    B. Water is an excellent solvent of ionic compounds.

    C. Water has a high surface tension, enabling insects to walk on its surface without sinking.

    D. Water has a greater density as a liquid than as a solid.

19. Which of the following outcomes would be *most likely* if water had a low specific heat instead of a high specific heat?

    A. Organisms with the greatest sensitivity to temperature change would die.

    B. All bodies of water on earth would freeze.

    C. Temperature changes between seasons would become more gradual.

    D. Flooding would endanger terrestrial organisms in most parts of the world.

20. Cheese and yogurt are products of which of the following processes?

    A. lactic acid fermentation

    B. aerobic respiration

    C. photosynthesis

    D. alcoholic fermentation

Answers to the Chapter Quiz

1. **D**

    Carbon-hydrogen bonds release energy upon interaction with oxygen molecules. With their numerous carbon-hydrogen bonds, carbohydrates are excellent for storing energy.

2. **B**

    The listed factors help starch perform its function as the principal energy storage molecule in plants.

3. **B**

   Lipids are molecules composed of glycerol and fatty acids, and include animal fat, oils, and waxes.

4. **C**

   Glucose is actually a monomer and consists of a single molecule of glucose. Cellulose and glycogen are polymers that consist of repeating glucose monomers. Protein is a polymer made of amino acids.

5. **A**

   Enzymes such as pepsin become active only at low levels of pH, or very acidic levels. Levels of pH from 7 to 9 are high and would render the enzyme inactive.

6. **C**

   Phospholipids consist of one glycerol molecule with two fatty acid molecules and a phosphate groups attached. Their structure, with a polar "head" that is the phosphate group and two long nonpolar "tails," enable them to form the sandwich-like bilayer of the cell membrane.

7. **B**

   Transport proteins such as hemoglobin move materials into and out of cells.

8. **D**

   Enzymes do not provide energy for a metabolic reaction, but instead lower the amount of energy needed for the reaction to start.

9. **C**

   ATP is an unstable molecule that carries its energy in the bonds between three phosphates that have a negative charge and repel each other. Each time a phosphate bond is broken, energy is released.

10. **A**

    Protein macromolecules vary widely in length, complexity, and function due to the number and various types of amino acids that make up the chain. Proteins are made from different combinations of 20 amino acid monomers.

11. C

The tertiary structure, or three-dimensional globular shape, of enzymes helps them to fit closely around other molecules in order to catalyze metabolic reactions more effectively.

12. B

The main function of carbohydrates, with their many carbon-hydrogen bonds, is energy storage. The main function of nucleic acids is the storage and transmission of genetic information within and between cells.

13. D

In a chemical reaction, the reactants are the chemical compounds that are consumed or transformed to make the products. The reactants in photosynthesis are carbon dioxide and water, which are eventually converted to glucose and oxygen with the aid of light energy.

14. B

The carbon dioxide produced by each full turn of the Krebs cycle is a waste product that is exhaled by the organism performing aerobic respiration.

15. C

Oxygen is the final electron acceptor in the electron transport chain, combining with two protons to form water, which is a waste product of cell respiration.

16. D

An example of the interrelated nature of the two processes is that the reactants in photosynthesis, or the chemical compounds that are acted upon, are carbon dioxide and water. These are the waste products of cellular respiration.

17. B

The Calvin cycle is a cyclical process in which CO_2 is "fixed" into the 3-carbon sugar PGAL. The process is also called carbon fixation.

18. C

The strong cohesive properties of water, including high surface tension, is due to the attraction between like substances resulting from hydrogen bonding.

19. **A**

    Since water has a high specific heat, it absorbs a lot of heat before it gets warm. Thus, it serves to moderate temperature extremes in bodies of water and in the atmosphere. If water had a low specific heat, these temperature extremes would become more pronounced. Lakes and ponds would freeze or become very warm more rapidly and more frequently, causing temperature-sensitive animals to die.

20. **A**

    Lactic acid fermentation is a form of anaerobic respiration in which glycolysis and other reactions generate NAD+ and lactic acid. It is the lactic acid that provides the sharp or tart flavors of products such as certain cheeses and yogurts.

Florida Biology 1 EOC
Practice Test

Also available at the REA Study Center (*www.rea.com/studycenter*)

This practice exam is also available at the REA Study Center. To closely simulate your test-day experience with the computer-based Florida EOC assessment, we suggest that you take the online version of the practice test. When you do, you'll also enjoy these benefits:

- Instant scoring

- Enforced time conditions

- Detailed score report of your strengths and weaknesses

This is a picture of a generic 4-function calculator and its parts.

GENERIC 4-FUNCTION CALCULATOR

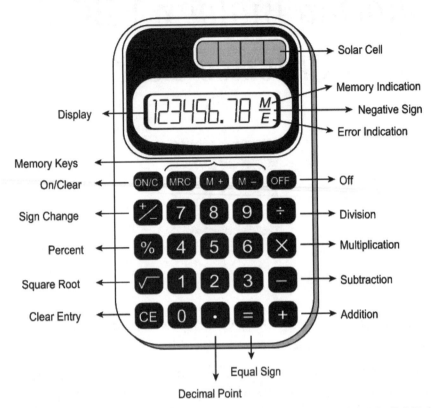

HELPFUL HINTS FOR USING A FOUR-FUNCTION CALCULATOR

1. Read the problem very carefully. Then decide whether or not you need the calculator to help you solve the problem.

2. When starting a new problem, always clear your calculator by pressing the on/clear key.

3. If you see an **E** in the display, clear the error before you begin.

4. If you see an **M** in the display, clear the memory and the calculator before you begin.

5. If the number in the display is not one of the answer choices, check your work.

6. Remember, your calculator will NOT automatically perform the algebraic order of operations.

7. Calculators might display an incorrect answer if you press the keys too quickly. When working with calculators, use careful and deliberate keystrokes, and always remember to check your answer to make sure that it is reasonable.

8. The negative sign may appear either to the left or to the right of the number.

9. When solving items, wait until the final step to round decimal equivalents and/or approximations. Focus on whether the item specifies the decimal place, equivalent fraction, and/or *pi* approximation needed for the answer. In most cases, front-end estimation and truncation are not accurate processes for estimation.

10. Always check your answer to make sure that you have completed all of the necessary steps.

Source: Biology 1 End-of-Course Assessment Sample Questions, Florida Department of Education

PERIODIC TABLE
Atomic Properties of the Elements

NIST
National Institute of
Standards and Technology
U.S. Department of Commerce

Physics Laboratory
physics.nist.gov

Standard Reference Data
www.nist.gov/srd

NIST SP 966 (September 2010)

For a description of the data, visit physics.nist.gov/data

† Based upon ^{12}C. ( ) indicates the mass number of the longest-lived isotope.

Frequently used fundamental physical constants

For the most accurate values of these and other constants, visit physics.nist.gov/constants
1 second = 9 192 631 770 periods of radiation corresponding to the transition between the two hyperfine levels of the ground state of ^{133}Cs

speed of light in vacuum	c	299 792 458 m s^{-1}	(exact)
Planck constant	h	6.6261 × 10^{-34} J s	($\hbar = h/2\pi$)
elementary charge	e	1.6022 × 10^{-19} C	
electron mass	m_e	9.1094 × 10^{-31} kg	
	$m_e c^2$	0.5110 MeV	
proton mass	m_p	1.6726 × 10^{-27} kg	
fine-structure constant	α	1/137.036	
Rydberg constant	R_∞	10 973 732 m^{-1}	
	$R_\infty c$	3.289 842 × 10^{15} Hz	
	$R_\infty hc$	13.6057 eV	
Boltzmann constant	k	1.3807 × 10^{-23} J K^{-1}	

Legend

- Solids
- Liquids
- Gases
- Artificially Prepared

Key

Atomic Number: 58
Symbol: Ce
Name: Cerium
Atomic Weight†: 140.116
Ground-state Configuration: [Xe]4f5d6s^2
Ground-state Level: $^1G_4^\circ$
Ionization Energy (eV): 5.5387

Elements

Group 1 / IA
- 1 H Hydrogen 1.00794 1s $^2S_{1/2}$ 13.5984
- 3 Li Lithium 6.941 1s^{2}2s $^2S_{1/2}$ 5.3917
- 11 Na Sodium 22.98976928 [Ne]3s $^2S_{1/2}$ 5.1391
- 19 K Potassium 39.0983 [Ar]4s $^2S_{1/2}$ 4.3407
- 37 Rb Rubidium 85.4678 [Kr]5s $^2S_{1/2}$ 4.1771
- 55 Cs Cesium 132.9054519 [Xe]6s $^2S_{1/2}$ 3.8939
- 87 Fr Francium (223) [Rn]7s $^2S_{1/2}$ 4.0727

Group 2 / IIA
- 4 Be Beryllium 9.012182 1s^{2}2s^2 $^1S_0$ 9.3227
- 12 Mg Magnesium 24.3050 [Ne]3s^2 $^1S_0$ 7.6462
- 20 Ca Calcium 40.078 [Ar]4s^2 $^1S_0$ 6.1132
- 38 Sr Strontium 87.62 [Kr]5s^2 $^1S_0$ 5.6949
- 56 Ba Barium 137.327 [Xe]6s^2 $^1S_0$ 5.2117
- 88 Ra Radium (226) [Rn]7s^2 $^1S_0$ 5.2784

Group 3 / IIIB
- 21 Sc Scandium 44.955912 [Ar]3d4s^2 $^2D_{3/2}$ 6.5615
- 39 Y Yttrium 88.90585 [Kr]4d5s^2 $^2D_{3/2}$ 6.2173
- 57 La Lanthanum 138.90547 [Xe]5d6s^2 $^2D_{3/2}$ 5.5769
- 89 Ac Actinium (227) [Rn]6d7s^2 $^2D_{3/2}$ 5.3807

Group 4 / IVB
- 22 Ti Titanium 47.867 [Ar]3d^{2}4s^2 $^3F_2$ 6.8281
- 40 Zr Zirconium 91.224 [Kr]4d^{2}5s^2 $^3F_2$ 6.6339
- 72 Hf Hafnium 178.49 [Xe]4f^{14}5d^{2}6s^2 $^3F_2$ 6.8251
- 104 Rf Rutherfordium (265) [Rn]5f^{14}6d^{2}7s^2 6.0?

Group 5 / VB
- 23 V Vanadium 50.9415 [Ar]3d^{3}4s^2 $^4F_{3/2}$ 6.7462
- 41 Nb Niobium 92.90638 [Kr]4d^{4}5s $^6D_{1/2}$ 6.7589
- 73 Ta Tantalum 180.94788 [Xe]4f^{14}5d^{3}6s^2 $^4F_{3/2}$ 7.5496
- 105 Db Dubnium (268)

Group 6 / VIB
- 24 Cr Chromium 51.9961 [Ar]3d^{5}4s $^7S_3$ 6.7665
- 42 Mo Molybdenum 95.96 [Kr]4d^{5}5s $^7S_3$ 7.0924
- 74 W Tungsten 183.84 [Xe]4f^{14}5d^{4}6s^2 $^5D_0$ 7.8640
- 106 Sg Seaborgium (271)

Group 7 / VIIB
- 25 Mn Manganese 54.938045 [Ar]3d^{5}4s^2 $^6S_{5/2}$ 7.4340
- 43 Tc Technetium (98) [Kr]4d^{5}5s^2 $^6S_{5/2}$ 7.28
- 75 Re Rhenium 186.207 [Xe]4f^{14}5d^{5}6s^2 $^6S_{5/2}$ 7.8335
- 107 Bh Bohrium (272)

Group 8 / VIII
- 26 Fe Iron 55.845 [Ar]3d^{6}4s^2 $^5D_4$ 7.9024
- 44 Ru Ruthenium 101.07 [Kr]4d^{7}5s $^5F_5$ 7.3605
- 76 Os Osmium 190.23 [Xe]4f^{14}5d^{6}6s^2 $^5D_4$ 8.4382
- 108 Hs Hassium (277)

Group 9 / VIII
- 27 Co Cobalt 58.933195 [Ar]3d^{7}4s^2 $^4F_{9/2}$ 7.8810
- 45 Rh Rhodium 102.90550 [Kr]4d^{8}5s $^4F_{9/2}$ 7.4589
- 77 Ir Iridium 192.217 [Xe]4f^{14}5d^{7}6s^2 $^4F_{9/2}$ 8.9670
- 109 Mt Meitnerium (276)

Group 10 / VIII
- 28 Ni Nickel 58.6934 [Ar]3d^{8}4s^2 $^3F_4$ 7.6399
- 46 Pd Palladium 106.42 [Kr]4d^{10} $^1S_0$ 8.3369
- 78 Pt Platinum 195.084 [Xe]4f^{14}5d^{9}6s $^3D_3$ 8.9588
- 110 Ds Darmstadtium (281)

Group 11 / IB
- 29 Cu Copper 63.546 [Ar]3d^{10}4s $^2S_{1/2}$ 7.7264
- 47 Ag Silver 107.8682 [Kr]4d^{10}5s $^2S_{1/2}$ 7.5762
- 79 Au Gold 196.966569 [Xe]4f^{14}5d^{10}6s $^2S_{1/2}$ 9.2255
- 111 Rg Roentgenium (280)

Group 12 / IIB
- 30 Zn Zinc 65.38 [Ar]3d^{10}4s^2 $^1S_0$ 9.3942
- 48 Cd Cadmium 112.411 [Kr]4d^{10}5s^2 $^1S_0$ 8.9938
- 80 Hg Mercury 200.59 [Xe]4f^{14}5d^{10}6s^2 $^1S_0$ 10.4375
- 112 Cn Copernicium (285)

Group 13 / IIIA
- 5 B Boron 10.811 1s^{2}2s^{2}2p $^2P_{1/2}^\circ$ 8.2980
- 13 Al Aluminum 26.9815386 [Ne]3s^{2}3p $^2P_{1/2}^\circ$ 5.9858
- 31 Ga Gallium 69.723 [Ar]3d^{10}4s^{2}4p $^2P_{1/2}^\circ$ 5.9993
- 49 In Indium 114.818 [Kr]4d^{10}5s^{2}5p $^2P_{1/2}^\circ$ 5.7864
- 81 Tl Thallium 204.3833 [Hg]6p $^2P_{1/2}^\circ$ 6.1082
- 113 Uut Ununtrium (284)

Group 14 / IVA
- 6 C Carbon 12.0107 1s^{2}2s^{2}2p^2 $^3P_0$ 11.2603
- 14 Si Silicon 28.0855 [Ne]3s^{2}3p^2 $^3P_0$ 8.1517
- 32 Ge Germanium 72.64 [Ar]3d^{10}4s^{2}4p^2 $^3P_0$ 7.8994
- 50 Sn Tin 118.710 [Kr]4d^{10}5s^{2}5p^2 $^3P_0$ 7.3439
- 82 Pb Lead 207.2 [Hg]6p^2 $^3P_0$ 7.4167
- 114 Uuq Ununquadium (289)

Group 15 / VA
- 7 N Nitrogen 14.0067 1s^{2}2s^{2}2p^3 $^4S_{3/2}^\circ$ 14.5341
- 15 P Phosphorus 30.973762 [Ne]3s^{2}3p^3 $^4S_{3/2}^\circ$ 10.4867
- 33 As Arsenic 74.92160 [Ar]3d^{10}4s^{2}4p^3 $^4S_{3/2}^\circ$ 9.7886
- 51 Sb Antimony 121.760 [Kr]4d^{10}5s^{2}5p^3 $^4S_{3/2}^\circ$ 8.6084
- 83 Bi Bismuth 208.98040 [Hg]6p^3 $^4S_{3/2}^\circ$ 7.2855
- 115 Uup Ununpentium (288)

Group 16 / VIA
- 8 O Oxygen 15.9994 1s^{2}2s^{2}2p^4 $^3P_2$ 13.6181
- 16 S Sulfur 32.065 [Ne]3s^{2}3p^4 $^3P_2$ 10.3600
- 34 Se Selenium 78.96 [Ar]3d^{10}4s^{2}4p^4 $^3P_2$ 9.7524
- 52 Te Tellurium 127.60 [Kr]4d^{10}5s^{2}5p^4 $^3P_2$ 9.0096
- 84 Po Polonium (209) [Hg]6p^4 $^3P_2$ 8.414
- 116 Uuh Ununhexium (293)

Group 17 / VIIA
- 9 F Fluorine 18.9984032 1s^{2}2s^{2}2p^5 $^2P_{3/2}^\circ$ 17.4228
- 17 Cl Chlorine 35.453 [Ne]3s^{2}3p^5 $^2P_{3/2}^\circ$ 12.9676
- 35 Br Bromine 79.904 [Ar]3d^{10}4s^{2}4p^5 $^2P_{3/2}^\circ$ 11.8138
- 53 I Iodine 126.90447 [Kr]4d^{10}5s^{2}5p^5 $^2P_{3/2}^\circ$ 10.4513
- 85 At Astatine (210) [Hg]6p^5 $^2P_{3/2}^\circ$
- 117 Uus Ununseptium (294)

Group 18 / VIIIA
- 2 He Helium 4.002602 1s^2 $^1S_0$ 24.5874
- 10 Ne Neon 20.1797 1s^{2}2s^{2}2p^6 $^1S_0$ 21.5645
- 18 Ar Argon 39.948 [Ne]3s^{2}3p^6 $^1S_0$ 15.7596
- 36 Kr Krypton 83.798 [Ar]3d^{10}4s^{2}4p^6 $^1S_0$ 13.9996
- 54 Xe Xenon 131.293 [Kr]4d^{10}5s^{2}5p^6 $^1S_0$ 12.1298
- 86 Rn Radon (222) [Hg]6p^6 $^1S_0$ 10.7485
- 118 Uuo Ununoctium (294)

Lanthanides
- 58 Ce Cerium 140.116 [Xe]4f5d6s^2 $^1G_4^\circ$ 5.5387
- 59 Pr Praseodymium 140.90765 [Xe]4f^{3}6s^2 $^4I_{9/2}^\circ$ 5.473
- 60 Nd Neodymium 144.242 [Xe]4f^{4}6s^2 $^5I_4$ 5.5250
- 61 Pm Promethium (145) [Xe]4f^{5}6s^2 $^6H_{5/2}^\circ$ 5.582
- 62 Sm Samarium 150.36 [Xe]4f^{6}6s^2 $^7F_0$ 5.6437
- 63 Eu Europium 151.964 [Xe]4f^{7}6s^2 $^8S_{7/2}^\circ$ 5.6704
- 64 Gd Gadolinium 157.25 [Xe]4f^{7}5d6s^2 $^9D_2^\circ$ 6.1498
- 65 Tb Terbium 158.92535 [Xe]4f^{9}6s^2 $^6H_{15/2}^\circ$ 5.8638
- 66 Dy Dysprosium 162.500 [Xe]4f^{10}6s^2 $^5I_8$ 5.9389
- 67 Ho Holmium 164.93032 [Xe]4f^{11}6s^2 $^4I_{15/2}^\circ$ 6.0215
- 68 Er Erbium 167.259 [Xe]4f^{12}6s^2 $^3H_6$ 6.1077
- 69 Tm Thulium 168.93421 [Xe]4f^{13}6s^2 $^2F_{7/2}^\circ$ 6.1843
- 70 Yb Ytterbium 173.054 [Xe]4f^{14}6s^2 $^1S_0$ 6.2542
- 71 Lu Lutetium 174.9668 [Xe]4f^{14}5d6s^2 $^2D_{3/2}$ 5.4259

Actinides
- 90 Th Thorium 232.03806 [Rn]6d^{2}7s^2 $^3F_2$ 6.3067
- 91 Pa Protactinium 231.03588 [Rn]5f^{2}6d7s^2 $^4K_{11/2}$ 5.89
- 92 U Uranium 238.02891 [Rn]5f^{3}6d7s^2 $^5L_6^\circ$ 6.1939
- 93 Np Neptunium (237) [Rn]5f^{4}6d7s^2 $^6L_{11/2}$ 6.2657
- 94 Pu Plutonium (244) [Rn]5f^{6}7s^2 $^7F_0$ 6.0260
- 95 Am Americium (243) [Rn]5f^{7}7s^2 $^8S_{7/2}^\circ$ 5.9738
- 96 Cm Curium (247) [Rn]5f^{7}6d7s^2 $^9D_2^\circ$ 5.9914
- 97 Bk Berkelium (247) [Rn]5f^{9}7s^2 $^6H_{15/2}^\circ$ 6.1979
- 98 Cf Californium (251) [Rn]5f^{10}7s^2 $^5I_8$ 6.2817
- 99 Es Einsteinium (252) [Rn]5f^{11}7s^2 $^4I_{15/2}^\circ$ 6.3676
- 100 Fm Fermium (257) [Rn]5f^{12}7s^2 $^3H_6$ 6.50
- 101 Md Mendelevium (258) [Rn]5f^{13}7s^2 $^2F_{7/2}^\circ$ 6.58
- 102 No Nobelium (259) [Rn]5f^{14}7s^2 $^1S_0$ 6.65
- 103 Lr Lawrencium (262) [Rn]5f^{14}7s^{2}7p? $^2P_{1/2}^\circ$? 4.9?

Directions for Taking Biology 1 EOC Practice Test A

Test Questions

This Practice Test contains 60 questions. The exact number of questions on the actual test will vary from 60–65.

- ### Multiple-Choice Questions

  Select the best answer for each question and mark it on the answer sheet on page 267.

Reference Pages

You may refer to the two preceding Reference Pages as often as you like.

Timing

For the actual test you will be given two 80-minute periods to complete the test, with a ten-minute break in between. However, anyone who has not finished will be allowed to continue working.

Checking Your Answers

You will find the correct answers, along with detailed explanations, for this practice test beginning on page 211.

Reviewing Your Work

When finished, turn to the grid on pages 265–266. Circle the number of any questions that you missed in Test A. You will be able to see a pattern that shows which Benchmarks will need your further attention.

1 A student conducts an investigation measuring the rate of water loss in milliliters for three plants. Plant 1 is exposed to high humidity, Plant 2 to high temperature, and Plant 3 to room temperature. Measurements are taken at half-hour intervals for three hours. In planning this investigation, what additional element is needed to ensure that it has an effective control?

A. Plant 1 should also be exposed to high temperature.

B. Plant 2 should be exposed to low humidity.

C. Plant 3 should be exposed to normal humidity.

D. All three plants should be in a well-lit environment.

2 A student places five potato discs in five beakers that contain increasing concentrations of sucrose. The following line graph records the change in mass of the potato discs after one full day in the beakers.

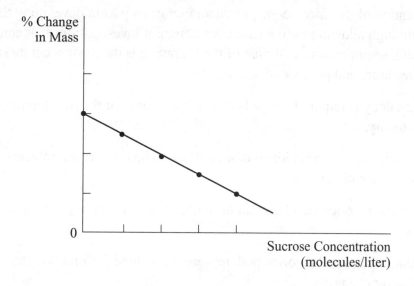

Which is the **best** way to interpret the relationship in the graph between percentage change in mass and sucrose concentration?

A. As the sucrose concentration increases, the % change in mass also increases.

B. As the sucrose concentration increases, the % change in mass decreases.

C. As the sucrose concentration decreases, the % change in mass stays the same.

D. As the sucrose concentration decreases, the % change in mass also decreases.

Go On ▶

3 A company that manufactures sports drinks claims that its products' benefits have been proven scientifically. For this claim to be true, which of the following steps should the company have taken?

   A. The company should have used computer technology to gather and analyze data about its products' effects on athletes.

   B. The company should have consulted with scientists who are experts in sports medicine.

   C. The company should have run advertisements for their sports drinks in popular science magazines.

   D. The company should have had their own test results peer reviewed and repeated to produce the same results.

4 The invention of the microscope played an important part in developing the cell theory through allowing for the extensive design of investigations that confirmed observations with evidence. Which of the following is the most accurate statement about the nature and practice of science?

   A. Technology is required for gathering any data and for the development of a scientific theory.

   B. New scientific information and/or continuous investigations influence the development of scientific theory.

   C. Scientific theories are ideas that have not been tested enough to become scientific laws.

   D. Scientific laws and theories both represent scientific information that is absolute and never changing.

Go On

5 In an osmosis experiment, three cores cut from raw potatoes represent cells with semipermeable membranes. Each core is first weighed and its mass recorded. Then the cores are each soaked in a separate concentration of salt water. The table below presents the results of the experiment.

NaCl Concentration/M	Potato Core Samples	Mass Before Soaking	Mass After Soaking	% Change in Mass
98%	A	1.93	1.42	−26.42
50%	B	2.00	1.77	−11.50
2%	C	1.98	2.17	+9.60

Based on the data in the table, which is the **most likely** inference about osmosis in cells with semipermeable membranes?

A. Water tends to enter the cell when the cell is in an environment of high water concentration.

B. Water tends to enter the cell when the cell is in an environment of medium solute concentration.

C. Water tends to enter the cell when the cell is in an environment of high solute concentration.

D. Water tends to leave the cell when the cell is in an environment of high water concentration.

6 A student investigates the ability of yeast to metabolize two kinds of sugar, glucose and lactose. First, yeast and glucose are added to water. Then the released gas is captured and its volume recorded. Next, yeast and lactose are put through the same steps. For best results in this investigation, which variables should be held constant?

A. the mass of yeast and the volume of gas

B. the water temperature and the volume of gas

C. the mass of yeast and the water temperature

D. the mass of yeast and the mass of glucose and lactose

Go On

7 Water molecules are asymmetrical and highly polar in nature. Which of the following is a result of this property?

   A. Water dissolves a nonpolar substance like vegetable oil.

   B. Water requires a relatively small amount of heat to evaporate.

   C. An ionic substance like salt dissolves easily in water.

   D. Water molecules tend to repel each other.

8 A food is analyzed in a lab and broken down into its base components. It is found to be a mixture of four different compounds. Which of the following provides energy to cells?

   A. $C_6H_{12}O_6$

   B. H2O

   C. NaCl

   D. Fe

9 The following are groups of molecules that produce ATP. Which group has the molecules ranked correctly from greatest to least for their ability to yield ATP?

   A. glucose, NADH, pyruvate

   B. glucose, pyruvate, NADH

   C. pyruvate, NADH, glucose

   D. pyruvate, glucose, NADH

10 Enzymes and nucleic acids have different functions. Which of the following best describes the difference between their functions?

A. Enzymes store the genetic code for protein synthesis, while nucleic acids catalyze metabolic reactions.

B. Enzymes store energy, while nucleic acids release energy.

C. Enzymes make up the bilayer formation of cell membranes, while nucleic acids transport materials between cells.

D. Enzymes are proteins that catalyze metabolic reactions, while nucleic acids store the genetic code for protein synthesis.

11 Water has special properties that make it essential for life on Earth. One of these is the behavior of water in its solid form as ice. Which of the following **best** explains why salt is poured onto icy roads and sidewalks in the winter?

A. The salt raises the freezing point for water.

B. The salt lowers the freezing point for water.

C. Saltwater cannot freeze at any temperature.

D. Fresh water will not mix with saltwater.

12 Which of the following environmental factors does NOT directly affect the rate of photosynthesis?

A. intensity of light

B. temperature

C. oxygen concentration

D. carbon dioxide concentration

Go On ▶

13 Which of the following are the reactants in aerobic cellular respiration?

   A. CO_2 and H_2

   B. $C_6H_{12}O_6$ and H_2O

   C. $C_6H_{12}O_6$ and O_2

   D. CO_2 and H_2O

14 Carbon fixation is a process in which CO_2 and energy from ATP are used to incorporate the carbon dioxide into a 3-carbon sugar. Carbon fixation occurs during which of the following?

   A. the light reactions

   B. the Calvin cycle

   C. the Krebs cycle

   D. glycolysis

15 A student conducts an experiment to determine the effect of temperature on the rate of catalyzed reaction for the stomach enzyme pepsin. Which graph shows the **most likely** result of this experiment?

A.

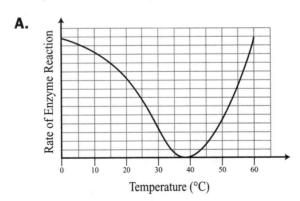

B.

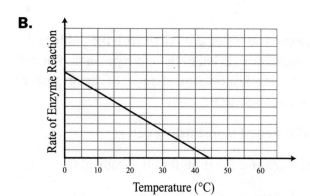

C.

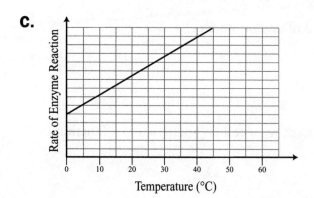

D.

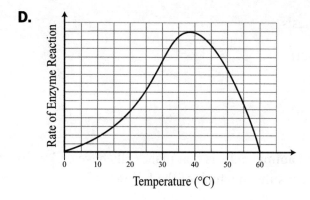

16 The early version of cell theory began to take shape in 1839 with the published work of Schleiden and Schwann. More investigations led to the modern version of cell theory. Which of the following statements describes an element of the original cell theory that was proved incorrect by later research?

A. New cells are formed only by division of a preexisting cell.

B. The cell is the basic unit of structure and function for all organisms.

C. Living cells appear spontaneously from nonliving matter.

D. All living things are composed of one or more cells.

17 Which of the following correctly matches a cell organelle with its function?

A. flagella–movement

B. ribosome–cell regulation

C. Golgi apparatus–protein synthesis

D. mitochondrion–cell wall support

18 A key difference between plant and animal cells is that plant cells have cell walls and animal cells do not. This difference results in which of the following?

A. Plant cells can form themselves into many different shapes in order to perform different functions.

B. Plant cells cannot transport materials among other cells.

C. Animal cells have increased flexibility for advanced cell or tissue specialization.

D. Animals cells depend entirely upon cell membranes for structural support.

Go On

19 Which of the following statements is the **best** comparison of prokaryotes and eukaryotes?

A. Prokaryotes are incapable of movement, while eukaryotes use flagella for movement.

B. Prokaryotes have many internal membranes and compartments, while eukaryotes have a large central vacuole.

C. Prokaryotes have few specialized structures, while eukaryotes contain distinct organelles bound by a membrane.

D. Prokaryotes have a pliable cell membrane, while eukaryotes have a rigid cell wall.

20 Osmosis in animal cells requires the cells to be surrounded by which type of solution?

A. hypotonic

B. hypertonic

C. amphipathic

D. isotonic

21 Unlike passive cellular transport, active cellular transport requires energy to function. Which of the following is an example of active transport?

A. osmosis

B. exocytosis

C. diffusion

D. facilitated diffusion

Go On

22 Which of the following is found in both prokaryotes and eukaryotes?

A. ribosomes

B. lysosomes

C. mitochondria

D. vacuole

23 The structure of a leaf maximizes which physiological process?

A. absorption of water for cell respiration

B. absorption of water for transpiration

C. exchange of gases for photosynthesis

D. manufacture of energy for cell reproduction

24 Dermal tissues in terrestrial plants produce a waxy cuticle that protects the leaf. If this waxy covering were overproduced and the stomata became clogged, which of the following would probably occur?

A. The plant would be unable to absorb oxygen and water from the air, causing the plant to shrivel and its cell functions to cease.

B. The plant's stomata would be unable to open, and it would have a limited ability to perform photosynthesis.

C. The plant's photosynthetic cells would be unable to receive light energy, and the plant would have a limited ability to perform cellular respiration.

D. The plant would be unable to transport glucose to its cells, and the production of energy by cellular respiration would slow down.

25 Guttation is when small droplets of sap form on the tips of leaves in the early morning. Which of the following **best** explains this process?

A. root pressure

B. transpirational pull

C. low rate of transpiration

D. high humidity

26 A plant's vascular tissues are unable to produce phloem. What effect would this have on the physiological processes of the plant?

A. The plant would be unable to transport water and nutrients from the soil to the leaf for photosynthesis to occur.

B. The plant's vascular tissues would no longer be able to move water through the leaf because of air bubbles and other obstructions.

C. The plant's cell walls would not be rigid and the plant would lack structural support.

D. The plant would be unable to transport the glucose produced by photosynthesis throughout the plant, thus preventing cellular respiration from occurring.

27 The amount of water in a plant's tissues is mainly determined by a combination of which of the following natural processes?

A. root absorption and respiration

B. root absorption and transpiration

C. photosynthesis and respiration

D. photosynthesis and root absorption

Go On ▶

28 Which of the following vascular tissue is NOT associated with xylem?

A. meristem

B. tracheids

C. sieve tubes

D. vessels

29 There are three basic kinds of cells that make up ground tissue in plants: parenchyma cells, collenchyma cells, and sclerenchyma cells. What is the main difference among these types of cells?

A. efficiency in respiration

B. ability to store food

C. structure of cell walls

D. ability to move water

30 Look at the illustration below.

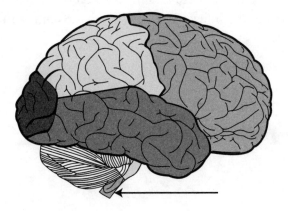

The arrow is pointing to which part of the human brain?

A. occipital lobe

B. medulla oblongata

C. cerebellum

D. temporal lobe

31 Some vaccines improve a person's immunity to a virus for a lifetime, yet people are advised to get a flu shot every year. What is the reason for this?

A. The flu virus weakens the body's immune system.

B. The antibodies for the flu virus lose effectiveness after one year.

C. The flu virus breaks down the vaccine over time.

D. The flu virus changes and mutates.

Go On ▶

32 In an allergic reaction, an allergen such as pollen sets off an inflammatory immune response. A certain agent is released that causes blood vessels to enlarge and rapidly increases blood flow to the infected area. What is the name of this agent?

A. histamine

B. antigen

C. monocytes

D. phagocytes

33 A patient with sneezing, congestion, fever, and a cough visits the doctor and asks for an antibiotic as treatment. Which of the following is a reason why the doctor should agree to prescribe an antibiotic?

A. These symptoms often indicate a virus and an antibiotic can only treat bacteria, not viruses.

B. Antibiotic treatment for mild infections will allow surviving bacteria to become resistant to antibiotics, leading to illnesses that are much more difficult to treat.

C. The patient has already been treated with viral therapy and the infection has persisted for more than a week and spread to include a deep cough.

D. The patient asks for antibiotics each time they get any type of cold or sore throat because she does not want to develop a worse infection.

34 A patient has a suspected case of West Nile virus. What is the **best** way to determine if the patient is infected with the virus?

A. Check for the release of histamines in the patient's blood.

B. Check for signs in the patient of an inflammatory immune response.

C. Check for bacteria in the patient's spinal fluid.

D. Check for antibodies in the patient's blood.

35 A person has large deposits of fatty materials such as cholesterol on arterial walls. This buildup of plaque thickens the arteries, reducing their ability to expand properly and restricting blood flow. What is the name for this condition?

A. Atherosclerosis

B. Arteriosclerosis

C. hypertension

D. diabetes

36 Carcinogens from cigarette smoke can cause somatic mutations in the p53 gene. A longtime worker in a smoke-filled environment develops lung cancer. Which of the following statements **best** describes this situation?

A. Increased levels of carcinogens, caused by the presence of the p53 gene, caused the person to develop lung cancer.

B. Greatly increased levels of the p53 gene, and thus of p53 proteins, leads to certain cancers such as lung cancer.

C. Environmental influence in the form of carcinogens in cigarette smoke caused mutations that weakened the cancer-fighting properties of the p53 gene, enabling the lung cancer to develop.

D. Neither carcinogens from cigarette smoke nor the mutation of the p53 gene ultimately has any verified effect on the development of cancer cells.

Go On ▶

37 A person's temperature rises several degrees above normal during the acute-phase response to invading pathogens. What is the reason for this?

   A. to activate the complement system

   B. to stimulate phagocyte activity

   C. to reduce swelling of tissues

   D. to divide lymphocytes into specialized T cells

38 The io moth, a colorful North American moth, has realistic-looking eyespots hidden on its hindwings. When threatened, the io moth reveals the spots in order to startle the predator and make it retreat. These eyespots are an example of which of the following?

   A. an adaptation

   B. a mutation

   C. an allele

   D. a balanced polymorphism

39 The Saguaro cactus is found in a desert climate. It has a shallow root system, with roots that radiate out to collect the small amounts of available water. The Saguaro's flowers contain sweet nectar that attracts bats, various birds, and other small animals. As they feed, these animals collect Saguaro pollen that they then deliver to other flowering desert plants. This cross-pollination is **most likely** to have which beneficial effect on Saguaro cacti?

   A. increased number of animals that feed on the Saguaro's nectar

   B. increased ability to survive on a small amount of water

   C. variation within the Saguaro species

   D. increased size for the next generation of Saguaro cacti

Go On

40 Male hamsters that have red coats are crossed with female hamsters that have white coats. Both the male and female offspring have coats with a combination of red hairs and white hairs. Which of the following **best** describes the genetics of this situation?

A. The red and white alleles are codominant.

B. The red and white alleles are sex-linked.

C. The red allele is dominant to the white allele.

D. The red allele is recessive to the white allele.

41 At the beginning of the nineteenth century in England, most peppered moths had a pale brown color, with dark peppered moths a rare variation. As the century progressed, smoke from factories killed the lichen on trees and darkened the tree bark. Pale-colored peppered moths became easier for predators to see. What was the **most likely** outcome of this situation for peppered moths in England?

A. Dark-colored peppered moths died out completely.

B. Dark-colored peppered moths became more common.

C. Peppered moths developed a light and dark pattern.

D. Pale-colored peppered moths migrated out of England.

42 A red flower is crossed with a white flower, producing offspring that are all pink. If two pink flowers are then crossed, what percent of the offspring will be red?

A. 0

B. 25%

C. 50%

D. 100%

Go On

43 Paleontologists have compared the skeletal remains of early hominids from 3 million years ago to the modern human skeleton. The hip or pelvis bones of early hominids were shortened and rounded, and thus more like those of modern humans than apes. This arrangement allowed for more stability when walking upright. Which of the following statements **best** describes the importance of this discovery for understanding the process of human evolution?

A. The discovery reveals that the ability to walk upright enabled the ancestors of modern humans to outcompete other hominid species for food.

B. The discovery fails to support the idea that modern humans and apes are related by way of a common ancestor.

C. The discovery supports the idea that the ability to walk upright is not related to the ability to make tools or the instinct to join together in groups.

D. The discovery supports the theory that early hominids were transitional species in the evolution of humans from apelike ancestors.

44 There are about 3,000 inhabitants on the tiny island of Pingelap in the Western Pacific. About 1 in 20 of these people have a genetic disorder that causes color blindness. Researchers trace the condition back to 1775, when a typhoon hit the island. The resulting famine killed all but a few of the islanders. Which of the following **best** explains the fact that color blindness is now so common among the people of Pingelap?

A. The genetic defect was a mutation that appeared spontaneously in the tiny population.

B. A person visiting from outside the island introduced the gene for color blindness and it was passed on by gene flow.

C. At least one of the survivors of the typhoon and famine carried the gene for color blindness and passed it on by the bottleneck effect.

D. All of the survivors of the typhoon and famine were colorblind.

 Go On

45 Which of the following describes why most scientists today have adopted the three-domain system for classifying organisms?

A. Scientists have a better understanding of evolutionary relationships due to genetic research.

B. Scientists have discovered many organisms with characteristics of both plants and animals.

C. Genetic researchers have discovered and are mapping the human genome.

D. Scientists have learned to categorize organisms by the many different methods that they use to get energy.

46 A segment of a DNA strand reads TGA AGA CCG. When the cell replicates its DNA, the mRNA strand built from the old section reads ACU UCU GGC. The next time this DNA replicates, what might be the effect?

A. The new strand that is used as a template will be exactly like the original strand of DNA.

B. The new strand will become progressively shorter as mistakes are eliminated during the transcription.

C. The new strand will be used as a template, assuring that the strand built from it will be different from the original DNA.

D. Cells with the new version of the DNA will operate in a completely different way from cells with the original version.

47 What is the main purpose of tRNA?

A. build ribosomes from various proteins

B. carry amino acids to the correct place on the mRNA template

C. ensure that only expressed genetic information leaves the nucleus

D. provide a template used for sequencing amino acids into a polypeptide

Go On

48 A protein called hemoglobin transports oxygen in red blood cells. Some people have hemoglobin molecules in which a single amino acid differs from the amino acid that belongs in that position in ordinary hemoglobin. Which of the following is the **most likely** cause of this condition?

    A. Enzymes have repaired an error that occurred during the proofreading phase of DNA transcription.

    B. Environmental factors have caused an error in the folding of the hemoglobin molecule.

    C. An extra amino acid has been added to the hemoglobin during translation.

    D. The hemoglobin gene contains a point mutation.

49 Cell mutations that cause skin cancer are not inherited by the next generation. Which of the following explains this?

    A. Skin cancer is caused by the body's failure to produce certain enzymes, which is not a trait that is passed on.

    B. Skin cancer results from a germinal mutation that is not expressed in the carrier's offspring.

    C. Skin cancer is caused by a somatic mutation, which does not occur in cells that give rise to gametes.

    D. Skin cancer results from damaged sex cells that are unable to engage in reproduction.

Go On

50 Look at the diagram below of the human female reproductive system.

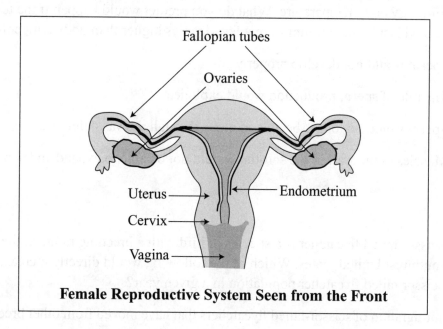

Female Reproductive System Seen from the Front

The female gamete in human reproduction is produced in which of the following?

A. fallopian tube

B. ovary

C. uterus

D. cervix

51 Meiosis and mitosis are processes involved in cell reproduction that differ in certain important ways. Which of the following is characteristic of meiosis but NOT mitosis?

A. proceeds in a single stage of cell division

B. results in daughter cells that are identical to the parent cell

C. results in two diploid daughter cells

D. results in four haploid daughter cells

Go On

52 The scrotum is a sac located outside the body cavity, where the temperature is cooler than ordinary body temperature. What do you predict would happen if the temperature maintained inside the scrotum were a few degrees higher than body temperature?

    A. Sperm would not develop properly.

    B. The rate of sperm production would explode.

    C. Sperm would no longer be able to move through the vas deferens.

    D. Muscles in the wall of the scrotum would not be able to expand and contract.

53 The scissor-tailed flycatcher is a species of bird with a breeding range in the central and southwest United States. Which of the following would directly increase the size of a scissor-tailed flycatcher population in a given year?

    A. immigration of scissor-tailed flycatchers that have moved from other breeding areas

    B. emigration of male scissor-tailed flycatchers that were unable to secure territories

    C. hatching of a smaller percentage of eggs in the scissor-tailed flycatcher population

    D. arrival of a new species that preys on scissor-tailed flycatchers

54 The energy pyramid below is for a desert ecosystem.

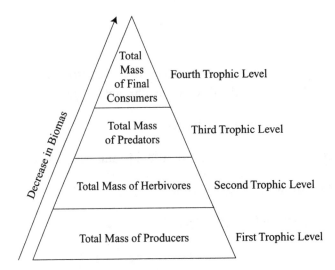

Which of the following **best** explains why there is a decrease in biomass from lower trophic levels to upper trophic levels?

A. Omnivores at the upper trophic levels eat both consumer and producer organisms.

B. More energy is expended by organisms that must hunt for food than by organisms that survive on water and soil nutrients.

C. Only about 10% of the energy available at one trophic level is converted into biomass at the next trophic level.

D. Producer organisms such as shrubs and trees have very little biomass to store energy.

55 Which of the following is NOT one of the ways in which the carbon cycle uses carbon to build organic compounds?

A. plant and animal respiration

B. transpiration

C. photosynthesis

D. combustion

56 *Euglena* is a unicellular freshwater protozoan that is somewhat like a plant and somewhat like an animal. It can act as either a producer or a consumer. In which of the following environments would it consume food like an animal?

A. no-light

B. low-oxygen

C. acidic

D. cold

Use the following information to answers questions 57–58.

Didymo is an invasive freshwater algae found in three rivers in Virginia. It can form massive blooms. According to the Environmental Protection Agency:

"Didymo can smother streambeds and adversely affect freshwater fish, plants and invertebrate populations by depriving them of habitat. It can also impact recreational opportunities but is not considered a human health risk at this time. Didymo develops stalks to attach itself to the streambed. These stalks can form a thick brown mat, effectively covering the entire river channel. . . . It only takes one cell or a fragment of a stalk to contaminate a new waterway."

57 In the lake ecosystem, didymo occupies which position?

   A. decomposer

   B. secondary consumer

   C. primary consumer

   D. producer

58 Which of the following would be the **best** method to prevent the spread of didymo to other rivers and lakes?

   A. Introduce genetically engineered organisms to eat the didymo.

   B. Remove the didymo blooms as soon as they appear and cut the stalks that form.

   C. Encourage all the people who are fishing or boating in the lakes to thoroughly clean all boats, apparel, and fishing equipment after use.

   D. Spray the lakes with powerful chemicals that kill all plant and invertebrate life forms including didymo.

Go On

59 Which of the following is a renewable source of energy for heating a home?

A. heating oil

B. firewood

C. natural gas

D. coal

60 Look at the survivorship curves below.

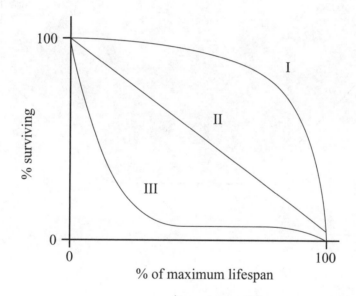

Curve I on the graph **best** describes which of the following situations?

A. a species with low death rates in young and middle age members

B. a species whose members have much the same chance of dying at any age

C. a species that produces large numbers of offspring, most of which die before reaching maturity

D. a species that engages in external fertilization and has no parenting

Go On

This is the end of the Biology Test.

Until time is called, go back and check your work or answer questions
you did not complete. When you have finished, close your
Test Book and Answer Book.

Answers
Practice Test

1   **C**   **SC.912.N.1.1, SC.912.N.1.6   (MC)**

An effective control in an experiment ensures that measured effects are due to the experimental conditions and not to some other factors. In this investigation, Plant 3 is the control, so it should be exposed to normal temperature **and** normal humidity.

2   **B**   **SC.912.N.1.1, SC.912.N.1.6, LA.910.2.2.3, MA.912.S.3.2   (MC)**

The relationship is an inverse one: as the sucrose concentration increases, the percentage change in mass decreases. This is characteristically shown by a line graph that slants down from upper left to lower right.

3   **D**   **SC.912.N.1.1, SC.912.N.1.4, SC.912.N.2.1   (LC)**

A vital element of the scientific method is peer review of experimental results and an attempt to recreate the original experiment's findings. The most respected scientific journals always emphasize the importance of peer review.

4   **B**   **SC.912.N.1.1, SC.912.N.1.6, SC.912.N.3.1, SC.912.L.14.4   (MC)**

A scientific theory such as the cell theory is the culmination of many scientific investigations—some involving new technologies, such as the invention of the microscope, that help with the design of these investigations. Scientific investigations draw together all the available evidence concerning a substantial range of phenomena and represent the most powerful current explanation that scientists have to offer.

5   **A**   **SC.912.N.1.1, SC.912.N.1.6, LA.910.2.2.3, MA.912.S.3.2   (HC)**

The table indicates that core sample C gained mass after soaking in the lowest (2%) concentration of solute, while the other two samples (in higher solute concentrations) lost mass. This leads to the inference that water tends to enter the cell under conditions of high water concentration.

6   **D**   **SC.912.N.1.1, MA.912.S.1.2   (HC)**

The mass of yeast and the mass of each kind of sugar should be constant so that a valid comparison of the metabolic process can be made.

7   **C**   **SC.912.L.18.12   (MC)**

Water is often called a universal solvent because it is highly polar and dissolves all ionic and polar substances quite easily.

8 **A**   **SC.912.L.18.1, SC.912.L.18.10**   **(LC)**

$C_6H_{12}O_6$ is glucose. Glucose provides energy to cells. In animals, glucose is absorbed directly into the bloodstream during digestion. It is one of the main products of photosynthesis in plants.

9 **B**   **SC.912.L.18.1, SC.912.L.18.10**   **(HC)**

A glucose molecule has the potential to produce 36 ATP; a pyruvate molecule, 15 ATP; and a NADH molecule, 2 or 3 ATP. Thus glucose has the greatest potential and NADH the least.

10 **D**   **SC.912.L.18.1, SC.912.L.18.11**   **(MC)**

Enzymes are proteins that activate metabolic reactions and speed them up. Nucleic acids include DNA and RNA, which store and transmit genetic information in the form of proteins.

11 **B**   **SC.912.L.18.12**   **(MC)**

A solution of water and dissolved salt has a lower freezing point than pure water. When salt is added to icy roads or sidewalks, it lowers the freezing point below the temperature of the ice, causing the ice to melt. The salty water in contact with the ice causes more melting, which creates more liquid saltwater, which leads to even more melting, and so forth.

12 **C**   **SC.912.L.18.7**   **(MC)**

Changes in oxygen concentration do not directly influence the rate of photosynthesis. Increases in the other environmental factors listed affect the rate until a limiting factor is reached and then the rate increase levels off.

13 **C**   **SC.912.L.18.8**   **(LC)**

The chemical equation for aerobic cellular respiration is

$$C_6H_{12}O_6 + 6O_2 \rightarrow 6CO_2 + 6H_2O + energy$$

so the reactants, or substances that are acted upon, are glucose and oxygen.

14 **B**   **SC.912.L.18.7, SC.912.L.18.9, SC.912.L.18.10**   **(MC)**

Carbon fixation occurs during the Calvin cycle, which is the main activity of the light-independent reactions in photosynthesis.

15 **D** **SC.912.L.18.1, SC.912.L.18.11 (MC)**

As temperature increases, the reaction rate of an enzyme also increases. However, above an optimal temperature, the reaction rate decreases rapidly. This is because the enzyme molecules become altered as their hydrogen bonds begin to break. The enzyme then becomes "denatured," or incapable of fitting with its substrate and catalyzing the reaction. Graph D shows this situation, with the graph line peaking at $37°$ then falling off.

16 **C** **SC.912.N.1.3, SC.912.N.3.1, SC.912.N.3.4, SC.912.L.14.1, LA.910.4.2 (MC)**

The originators of cell theory believed that living cells could appear from nonliving matter in a process called "spontaneous generation." This idea was disproved by Pasteur's experiments.

17 **A** **SC.912.L.14.2 (LC)**

The flagella (and also the cilia) are hair-like microtubules that control the movement of cells. The ribosome is the site of protein synthesis. The Golgi apparatus modifies and transports proteins. The mitochondrion is the site of aerobic respiration.

18 **C** **SC.912.L.14.3 (MC)**

Animal cells' lack of cell walls enable them to form into various shapes that are better suited to different functions. This is possible because animals have other forms of structural support, such as endo- and exoskeletons.

19 **C** **SC.912.L.14.3 (MC)**

One of the chief differences between prokaryotes and eukaryotes is that prokaryotes have no nucleus, internal membranes, or other organelles, while eukaryotes contain distinct organelles. Thus, eukaryotes have a more complex structure.

20 **D** **SC.912.L.14.2 (HC)**

Since animal cells lack cell walls, osmosis must be controlled. If an animal cell is in a hypotonic solution, too much water enters the cell and it can swell up and burst. If an animal cell is in a hypertonic solution, too much water leaves the cell and the cell shrinks. Therefore, the animal cell must be surrounded by an isotonic solution for equilibrium, with equal levels of solute on both sides of the cell membrane. "Amphipathic" does not refer to solutions but to the hydrophobic and hydrophilic aspects of the bilayer plasma membrane.

21 B SC.912.L.14.2 (MC)

Exocytosis is a form of vesicular transport, which is active transport (fueled by ATP) using vesicles or other organs of the cytoplasm. Exocytosis is the process in which vesicles fuse with the plasma membrane and release their content of newly synthesized proteins to the outside of the cell.

22 A SC.912.L.14.3 (LC)

Prokaryotes are very small and simple cells without organelles such as lysosomes, mitochondria, and vacuoles. Prokaryotes do have small ribosomes where protein synthesis takes place, as opposed to the larger and more complex ribosomes of eukaryotes.

23 C SC.912.L.14.7 (MC)

Structures in the leaf called guard cells open and close the stomata according to the amount of absorbed water, which produces a state of balance for gas exchange. This maximizes the process of photosynthesis and minimizes transpiration.

24 B SC.912.L.14.7 (MC)

If a plant's stomata were clogged due to overproduction of the epidermis and waxy cuticle, the stomata would be unable to open and the plant's ability to perform photosynthesis would be impaired.

25 B SC.912.L.14.7, SC.912.L.18.12 (LC)

Root pressure is created when water moves from the soil to the plant's root and into the xylem. Water is pushed up through the xylem tissue by root pressure. Guttation is a product of root pressure and typically occurs at night when the stomata are closed and transpiration has stopped for the day. The result of guttation is seen in the early morning.

26 D SC.912.L.14.7, SC.912.L.18.7, SC.912.L.18.8, SC.912.L.18.9, SC.912.L.18.10 (MC)

Phloem tissues in the leaf veins move the sugars or glucose produced by photosynthesis to other parts of the plant. These sugars are used as reactants in the process of cellular respiration.

27 **B** **SC.912.L.14.7** **(MC)**

Root absorption determines the amount of water coming into the plant, and transpiration controls the amount of water leaving as water vapor.

28 **C** **SC.912.L.14.7** **(MC)**

Sieve tubes are formed from sieve-tube members in the phloem. Tracheids and vessels are two kinds of xylem cells. The meristem produces both kinds of vascular cells and so is associated with both.

29 **C** **SC.912.L.14.2, SC.912.L.14.7** **(MC)**

These types of ground tissue differ chiefly in the makeup of their cell walls. Parenchyma cells have cell walls that are thin and flexible. Collenchyma cells have thick but flexible cell walls. Sclerenchyma cells have very thick cell walls.

30 **B** **SC.912.L.14.26** **(LC)**

The medulla oblongata is the lower half of the brainstem. It manages involuntary functions such as heart rate, breathing, and blood pressure.

31 **D** **SC.912.L.14.6, SC.912.L.14.52, HE.912.C.1.8** **(MC)**

Since the influenza virus is constantly changing and mutating, old vaccines are not effective at immunization and a new vaccine is required every year before "flu season."

32 **A** **SC.912.L.14.52** **(MC)**

Allergies are the result of an immune response to normally innocuous substances such as pollen or dust, which triggers the release of histamine. This protein contributes to the inflammatory response and also causes constriction of smooth muscle tissues.

33 **A** **SC.912.L.14.6, SC.912.L.14.52, HE.912.C.1.8** **(LC)**

Antibiotics are commonly prescribed medicines that kill bacteria. They are effective against bacterial infections, but not against viruses. Once it has been determined that the patient has a throat infection, such as strep throat, and not a common cold, the doctor should agree to prescribe an antibiotic.

34 D   SC.912.L.14.6, SC.912.L.14.52   (MC)

The presence of antibodies in the patient's blood is the best indicator of infection. With West Nile virus, these antibodies appear very early in the infected person (within 8 days of onset of symptoms) and can be measured in the person's blood or cerebrospinal fluid.

35 A   SC.912.L.14.36   (MC)

Atherosclerosis is a buildup of fatty deposits (or plaque) on arterial walls that reduces the arteries' ability to expand properly and also restricts blood flow. This condition is also called hardening of the arteries. It is similar to but distinct from arteriosclerosis, which is a hardening of the arteries due to any cause, not just plaque buildup.

36 C   SC.912.L.14.6, HE.912.C.1.3, HE.912.C.1.4   (HC)

Breathing cigarette smoke would be an example of an environmental influence. Should carcinogens from the smoke cause somatic mutations in the p53 gene, the gene's ability to fight cancer by repairing damaged cells or destroying cells that are beyond repair would be compromised. This would help cancer cells to spread in the lung.

37 B   SC.912.L.14.52   (MC)

The rise in temperature, or fever, that occurs in early induced innate immunity speeds up the body's metabolism and stimulates the production and activity of phagocytes.

38 A   SC.912.L.15.1   (MC)

The io moth's deceptive and quite realistic-looking eyespots are an example of an adaptation, which is an advantageous trait that has evolved to help an organism escape predators and survive.

39 C   SC.912.L.15.15   (HC)

With cross-pollination, the offspring that is produced has the genes of both parent plants. The resulting offspring is a hybrid that can be heartier than either parent plant and able to withstand harsh conditions. Thus a stronger and more varied gene pool due to genetic recombination enables a species like the Saguaro cacti to adapt to environmental changes.

40 A SC.912.L.16.1, SC.912.L.16.2 (MC)

This is an example of codominance, an inheritance pattern is which both inherited alleles are expressed. In this case, the expressed alleles are for a red coat and a white coat.

41 B SC.912.L.15.13 (MC)

Predators were able to eat the pale-colored peppered moths more frequently because they were easier to see against the background of dark tree bark. The rare dark peppered moths, which had been easy for predators to spot before, survived in much greater numbers because they were now camouflaged. Thus the most likely outcome was a large increase in the relative numbers of dark-colored peppered moths.

42 B SC.912.L.16.1, SC.912.L.16.2 (MC)

The inheritance pattern is codominant. If *RR* is red, *Rw* is pink, and *ww* is white, the cross would look like this:

	R	*w*
R	*RR*	*Rw*
w	*Rw*	*ww*

43 D SC.912.N.1.3, SC.912.N.1.6, SC.912.L.15.1, SC.912.L.15.10 (MC)

The fact that the pelvic bone structure in hominid fossils is similar but not identical to the structure in modern humans is an indication that those hominids were a transitional species in the process of human evolution. The discovery also emphasizes the importance of the evolving bone structure in enabling early hominids to walk upright.

44 C SC.912.L.15.14, SC.912.L.15.15 (MC)

Pingelap is a classic example of the bottleneck effect, in which a natural disaster reduces the size of a population randomly and drastically. A certain allele (such as the gene for color-blindness) may then be overrepresented when compared to the original population.

45 A SC.912.L.15.4, SC.912.L.15.5, SC.912.L.15.6, SC.912.L.15.8 (MC)

Genetic research has led to a more detailed understanding of how organisms are related to each other through the processes of evolution. This research has explored how very small and primitive single-celled organisms living in the oceans evolved over more than a billion years into many different kinds of complex organisms with specialized tissues, body symmetry, cephalization, germ layers, and other developments.

46 **C** **SC.912.L.16.3** **(HC)**

The DNA molecule consists of two strands in a spiral formation called a double helix. In DNA replication, the double helix separates, or "unzips," into a leading strand and a lagging strand. Each of the strands becomes a template, or model, for a new, complementary strand. Therefore two new molecules of DNA are formed, each consisting of one old template strand and one new complement strand. When used as a template in the next DNA replication, the new complement strand will produce a strand that is different from the original strand of DNA.

47 **B** **SC.912.L.16.3, SC.912.L.16.5** **(MC)**

Transfer RNA is a short RNA molecule used for transporting amino acids to their proper place on the mRNA template. Interactions among parts of the tRNA molecule lead to base pairings between nucleotides, causing the tRNA (which in two dimensions resembles a clover leaf) to fold into a three-dimensional molecule that can carry specific amino acids.

48 **D** **SC.912.L.16.3, SC.912.L.16.4** **(MC)**

A point mutation occurs when there is a single nucleotide error in the DNA sequence. In other words, an error has occurred that was *not* repaired during the proofreading phase. The situation described is a substitution, with an incorrect amino acid put in place of the correct one. This can result in a blood disorder such as sickle-cell disease.

49 **C** **SC.912.L.16.4, SC.912.L.16.8** **(MC)**

Skin cells that develop cancer do not give rise to sex cells, so the mutation is not passed on to the next generation by sexual means.

50 **B** **SC.912.L.16.13** **(LC)**

The ovary is the organ where the female gamete, or egg, is produced. Each female has two ovaries.

51 **D** **SC.912.L.16.14, SC.912.L.16.16, SC.912.L.16.17** **(MC)**

Meiosis ends in four haploid daughter cells, each with half the normal number of chromosomes, as opposed to the process of mitosis that results in two diploid daughter cells, each with a complete set of chromosomes. In addition, meiosis takes place in two stages of cell division, while mitosis has only one stage.

52 **A** **SC.912.L.16.13** **(HC)**

Sperm require a temperature cooler than body temperature to develop properly. That is why the scrotum, which holds the testicles where sperm production occurs, is located outside the body cavity. The ability of its walls to expand and contract and therefore move the testicles closer to the body or farther away serves as a "climate control system" for sperm production.

53 **A** **SC.912.L.17.4, SC.912.L.17.5** **(MC)**

The immigration, or arrival, of scissor-tailed flycatchers from other breeding areas is a development that would directly increase the size of a population in a given year. The other choices are developments that would tend to decrease the size of a population.

54 **C** **SC.912.L.17.9, SC.912.E.7.1** **(MC)**

The 10% loss in energy available to convert into biomass at each successive trophic level is due to such factors as the following: heat loss from chemical reactions inside organisms; energy lost as waste; the fact that not all organisms at a lower level are consumed by organisms at the next higher level; and the fact that not all parts of an organism's biomass can be digested by the consuming organism.

55 **B** **SC.912.E.7.1** **(LC)**

Transpiration is part of the water cycle, and is the process by which plants release water vapor into the air.

56 **A** **SC.912.L.17.2, SC.912.L.17.5** **(MC)**

In an environment without light, as at the bottom of a lake, *Euglena* would not be able to perform photosynthesis for food production and would have to consume other organisms for food.

57 **D** **SC.912.L.17.8, SC.912.L.17.9** **(MC)**

Didymo is a producer on the first trophic level of the energy system. Nevertheless, its invasive nature makes it a threat to the other organisms in the ecosystem.

58 **C** **SC.912.L.17.13, SC.912.L.17.20** **(HC)**

According to the EPA message, even a single cell or stalk fragment of didymo can contaminate a new waterway. People who boat or fish in the didymo-contaminated lakes must thoroughly clean their equipment so that no cells of didymo will spread to other bodies of water the people might use. Such precautions would extend to those who fish in waders or use life jackets, etc.

59 **B** **SC.912.L.17.11, SC.912.L.17.20** **(LC)**

Firewood comes from trees that can reproduce, so it is a renewable resource. The other choices are all nonrenewable fossil fuel resources that are ultimately limited in quantity.

60 **A** **SC.912.L.17.5** **(MC)**

Curve I begins horizontally to show the low death rates for young and middle age individuals. Then it bends steeply downward to show high mortality in old age.

Florida Biology 1 EOC Practice Test

Also available at the REA Study Center (www.rea.com/studycenter)

> This practice exam is also available at the REA Study Center. To closely simulate your test-day experience with the computer-based Florida EOC assessment, we suggest that you take the online version of the practice test. When you do, you'll also enjoy these benefits:
>
> • Instant scoring
>
> • Enforced time conditions
>
> • Detailed score report of your strengths and weaknesses

This is a picture of a generic 4-function calculator and its parts.

GENERIC 4-FUNCTION CALCULATOR

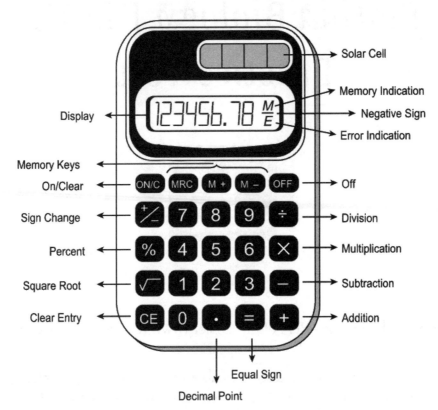

Solar Cell

Memory Indication

Negative Sign

Error Indication

Display

Memory Keys

On/Clear

Sign Change

Percent

Square Root

Clear Entry

Off

Division

Multiplication

Subtraction

Addition

Equal Sign

Decimal Point

HELPFUL HINTS FOR USING A FOUR-FUNCTION CALCULATOR

1. Read the problem very carefully. Then decide whether or not you need the calculator to help you solve the problem.

2. When starting a new problem, always clear your calculator by pressing the on/clear key.

3. If you see an **E** in the display, clear the error before you begin.

4. If you see an **M** in the display, clear the memory and the calculator before you begin.

5. If the number in the display is not one of the answer choices, check your work.

6. Remember, your calculator will NOT automatically perform the algebraic order of operations.

7. Calculators might display an incorrect answer if you press the keys too quickly. When working with calculators, use careful and deliberate keystrokes, and always remember to check your answer to make sure that it is reasonable.

8. The negative sign may appear either to the left or to the right of the number.

9. When solving items, wait until the final step to round decimal equivalents and/or approximations. Focus on whether the item specifies the decimal place, equivalent fraction, and/or *pi* approximation needed for the answer. In most cases, front-end estimation and truncation are not accurate processes for estimation.

10. Always check your answer to make sure that you have completed all of the necessary steps.

Source: Biology 1 End-of-Course Assessment Sample Questions, Florida Department of Education

PERIODIC TABLE
Atomic Properties of the Elements

NIST
National Institute of
Standards and Technology
U.S. Department of Commerce

Physics Laboratory
physics.nist.gov

Standard Reference Data
www.nist.gov/srd

NIST SP 966 (September 2010)

Frequently used fundamental physical constants

For the most accurate values of these and other constants, visit physics.nist.gov/constants
1 second = 9 192 631 770 periods of radiation corresponding to the transition
between the two hyperfine levels of the ground state of ^{133}Cs

speed of light in vacuum	c	299 792 458 m s^{-1}	(exact)
Planck constant	h	6.6261 x 10^{-34} J s	($\hbar = h/2\pi$)
elementary charge	e	1.6022 x 10^{-19} C	
electron mass	m_e	9.1094 x 10^{-31} kg	
	$m_e c^2$	0.5110 MeV	
proton mass	m_p	1.6726 x 10^{-27} kg	
fine-structure constant	α	1/137.036	
Rydberg constant	R_∞	10 973 732 m^{-1}	
	$R_\infty c$	3.289 842 x 10^{15} Hz	
	$R_\infty hc$	13.6057 eV	
Boltzmann constant	k	1.3807 x 10^{-23} J K^{-1}	

Solids
Liquids
Gases
Artificially Prepared

Group
Period

Key example:
Atomic Number 58
Symbol Ce
Name Cerium
Atomic Weight† 140.116
Ground-state Configuration [Xe]4f5d6s^2
Ground-state Level $^1G_4^\circ$
Ionization Energy (eV) 5.5387

For a description of the data, visit physics.nist.gov/data

†Based upon ^{12}C. ( ) indicates the mass number of the longest-lived isotope.

Group 1 / IA
- 1 H Hydrogen 1.00794 1s $^2S_{1/2}$ 13.5984
- 3 Li Lithium 6.941 1s^{2}2s 5.3917 $^2S_{1/2}$
- 11 Na Sodium 22.98976928 [Ne]3s 5.1391 $^2S_{1/2}$
- 19 K Potassium 39.0983 [Ar]4s 4.3407 $^2S_{1/2}$
- 37 Rb Rubidium 85.4678 [Kr]5s 4.1771 $^2S_{1/2}$
- 55 Cs Cesium 132.9054519 [Xe]6s 3.8939 $^2S_{1/2}$
- 87 Fr Francium (223) [Rn]7s 4.0727 $^2S_{1/2}$

Group 2 / IIA
- 4 Be Beryllium 9.012182 1s^{2}2s^2 9.3227 $^1S_0$
- 12 Mg Magnesium 24.3050 [Ne]3s^2 7.6462 $^1S_0$
- 20 Ca Calcium 40.078 [Ar]4s^2 6.1132 $^1S_0$
- 38 Sr Strontium 87.62 [Kr]5s^2 5.6949 $^1S_0$
- 56 Ba Barium 137.327 [Xe]6s^2 5.2117 $^1S_0$
- 88 Ra Radium (226) [Rn]7s^2 5.2784 $^1S_0$

Group 3 / IIIB
- 21 Sc Scandium 44.955912 [Ar]3d4s^2 6.5615 $^2D_{3/2}$
- 39 Y Yttrium 88.90585 [Kr]4d5s^2 6.2173 $^2D_{3/2}$
- 57 La Lanthanum 138.90547 [Xe]5d6s^2 5.5769 $^2D_{3/2}$
- 89 Ac Actinium (227) [Rn]6d7s^2 5.3807 $^2D_{3/2}$

Group 4 / IVB
- 22 Ti Titanium 47.867 [Ar]3d^{2}4s^2 6.8281 $^3F_2$
- 40 Zr Zirconium 91.224 [Kr]4d^{2}5s^2 6.6339 $^3F_2$
- 72 Hf Hafnium 178.49 [Xe]4f^{14}5d^{2}6s^2 6.8251 $^3F_2$
- 104 Rf Rutherfordium (265) [Rn]5f^{14}6d^{2}7s^2? 6.0? $^3F_2$?

Group 5 / VB
- 23 V Vanadium 50.9415 [Ar]3d^{3}4s^2 6.7462 $^4F_{3/2}$
- 41 Nb Niobium 92.90638 [Kr]4d^{4}5s 6.7589 $^6D_{1/2}$
- 73 Ta Tantalum 180.94788 [Xe]4f^{14}5d^{3}6s^2 7.5496 $^4F_{3/2}$
- 105 Db Dubnium (268)

Group 6 / VIB
- 24 Cr Chromium 51.9961 [Ar]3d^{5}4s 6.7665 $^7S_3$
- 42 Mo Molybdenum 95.96 [Kr]4d^{5}5s 7.0924 $^7S_3$
- 74 W Tungsten 183.84 [Xe]4f^{14}5d^{4}6s^2 7.8640 $^5D_0$
- 106 Sg Seaborgium (271)

Group 7 / VIIB
- 25 Mn Manganese 54.938045 [Ar]3d^{5}4s^2 7.4340 $^6S_{5/2}$
- 43 Tc Technetium (98) [Kr]4d^{5}5s^2 7.28 $^6S_{5/2}$
- 75 Re Rhenium 186.207 [Xe]4f^{14}5d^{5}6s^2 7.8335 $^6S_{5/2}$
- 107 Bh Bohrium (272)

Group 8 / VIII
- 26 Fe Iron 55.845 [Ar]3d^{6}4s^2 7.9024 $^5D_4$
- 44 Ru Ruthenium 101.07 [Kr]4d^{7}5s 7.3605 $^5F_5$
- 76 Os Osmium 190.23 [Xe]4f^{14}5d^{6}6s^2 8.4382 $^5D_4$
- 108 Hs Hassium (277)

Group 9 / VIII
- 27 Co Cobalt 58.933195 [Ar]3d^{7}4s^2 7.8810 $^4F_{9/2}$
- 45 Rh Rhodium 102.90550 [Kr]4d^{8}5s 7.4589 $^4F_{9/2}$
- 77 Ir Iridium 192.217 [Xe]4f^{14}5d^{7}6s^2 8.9670 $^4F_{9/2}$
- 109 Mt Meitnerium (276)

Group 10 / VIII
- 28 Ni Nickel 58.6934 [Ar]3d^{8}4s^2 7.6399 $^3F_4$
- 46 Pd Palladium 106.42 [Kr]4d^{10} 8.3369 $^1S_0$
- 78 Pt Platinum 195.084 [Xe]4f^{14}5d^{9}6s 8.9588 $^3D_3$
- 110 Ds Darmstadtium (281)

Group 11 / IB
- 29 Cu Copper 63.546 [Ar]3d^{10}4s 7.7264 $^2S_{1/2}$
- 47 Ag Silver 107.8682 [Kr]4d^{10}5s 7.5762 $^2S_{1/2}$
- 79 Au Gold 196.966569 [Xe]4f^{14}5d^{10}6s 9.2255 $^2S_{1/2}$
- 111 Rg Roentgenium (280)

Group 12 / IIB
- 30 Zn Zinc 65.38 [Ar]3d^{10}4s^2 9.3942 $^1S_0$
- 48 Cd Cadmium 112.411 [Kr]4d^{10}5s^2 8.9938 $^1S_0$
- 80 Hg Mercury 200.59 [Xe]4f^{14}5d^{10}6s^2 10.4375 $^1S_0$
- 112 Cn Copernicium (285)

Group 13 / IIIA
- 5 B Boron 10.811 1s^{2}2s^{2}2p 8.2980 $^2P_{1/2}^\circ$
- 13 Al Aluminum 26.9815386 [Ne]3s^{2}3p 5.9858 $^2P_{1/2}^\circ$
- 31 Ga Gallium 69.723 [Ar]3d^{10}4s^{2}4p 5.9993 $^2P_{1/2}^\circ$
- 49 In Indium 114.818 [Kr]4d^{10}5s^{2}5p 5.7864 $^2P_{1/2}^\circ$
- 81 Tl Thallium 204.3833 [Xe]4f^{14}5d^{10}6s^{2}6p 6.1082 $^2P_{1/2}^\circ$
- 113 Uut Ununtrium (284)

Group 14 / IVA
- 6 C Carbon 12.0107 1s^{2}2s^{2}2p^2 11.2603 $^3P_0$
- 14 Si Silicon 28.0855 [Ne]3s^{2}3p^2 8.1517 $^3P_0$
- 32 Ge Germanium 72.64 [Ar]3d^{10}4s^{2}4p^2 7.8994 $^3P_0$
- 50 Sn Tin 118.710 [Kr]4d^{10}5s^{2}5p^2 7.3439 $^3P_0$
- 82 Pb Lead 207.2 [Hg]6p^2 7.4167 $^3P_0$
- 114 Uuq Ununquadium (289)

Group 15 / VA
- 7 N Nitrogen 14.0067 1s^{2}2s^{2}2p^3 14.5341 $^4S_{3/2}^\circ$
- 15 P Phosphorus 30.973762 [Ne]3s^{2}3p^3 10.4867 $^4S_{3/2}^\circ$
- 33 As Arsenic 74.92160 [Ar]3d^{10}4s^{2}4p^3 9.7886 $^4S_{3/2}^\circ$
- 51 Sb Antimony 121.760 [Kr]4d^{10}5s^{2}5p^3 8.6084 $^4S_{3/2}^\circ$
- 83 Bi Bismuth 208.98040 [Hg]6p^3 7.2855 $^4S_{3/2}^\circ$
- 115 Uup Ununpentium (288)

Group 16 / VIA
- 8 O Oxygen 15.9994 1s^{2}2s^{2}2p^4 13.6181 $^3P_2$
- 16 S Sulfur 32.065 [Ne]3s^{2}3p^4 10.3600 $^3P_2$
- 34 Se Selenium 78.96 [Ar]3d^{10}4s^{2}4p^4 9.7524 $^3P_2$
- 52 Te Tellurium 127.60 [Kr]4d^{10}5s^{2}5p^4 9.0096 $^3P_2$
- 84 Po Polonium (209) [Hg]6p^4 8.414 $^3P_2$
- 116 Uuh Ununhexium (293)

Group 17 / VIIA
- 9 F Fluorine 18.9984032 1s^{2}2s^{2}2p^5 17.4228 $^2P_{3/2}^\circ$
- 17 Cl Chlorine 35.453 [Ne]3s^{2}3p^5 12.9676 $^2P_{3/2}^\circ$
- 35 Br Bromine 79.904 [Ar]3d^{10}4s^{2}4p^5 11.8138 $^2P_{3/2}^\circ$
- 53 I Iodine 126.90447 [Kr]4d^{10}5s^{2}5p^5 10.4513 $^2P_{3/2}^\circ$
- 85 At Astatine (210) [Hg]6p^5 $^2P_{3/2}^\circ$
- 117 Uus Ununseptium (294)

Group 18 / VIIIA
- 2 He Helium 4.002602 1s^2 24.5874 $^1S_0$
- 10 Ne Neon 20.1797 1s^{2}2s^{2}2p^6 21.5645 $^1S_0$
- 18 Ar Argon 39.948 [Ne]3s^{2}3p^6 15.7596 $^1S_0$
- 36 Kr Krypton 83.798 [Ar]3d^{10}4s^{2}4p^6 13.9996 $^1S_0$
- 54 Xe Xenon 131.293 [Kr]4d^{10}5s^{2}5p^6 12.1298 $^1S_0$
- 86 Rn Radon (222) [Hg]6p^6 10.7485 $^1S_0$
- 118 Uuo Ununoctium (294)

Lanthanides
- 58 Ce Cerium 140.116 [Xe]4f5d6s^2 5.5387 $^1G_4^\circ$
- 59 Pr Praseodymium 140.90765 [Xe]4f^{3}6s^2 5.473 $^4I_{9/2}^\circ$
- 60 Nd Neodymium 144.242 [Xe]4f^{4}6s^2 5.5250 $^5I_4$
- 61 Pm Promethium (145) [Xe]4f^{5}6s^2 5.582 $^6H_{5/2}^\circ$
- 62 Sm Samarium 150.36 [Xe]4f^{6}6s^2 5.6437 $^7F_0$
- 63 Eu Europium 151.964 [Xe]4f^{7}6s^2 5.6704 $^8S_{7/2}^\circ$
- 64 Gd Gadolinium 157.25 [Xe]4f^{7}5d6s^2 6.1498 $^9D_2^\circ$
- 65 Tb Terbium 158.92535 [Xe]4f^{9}6s^2 5.8638 $^6H_{15/2}^\circ$
- 66 Dy Dysprosium 162.500 [Xe]4f^{10}6s^2 5.9389 $^5I_8$
- 67 Ho Holmium 164.93032 [Xe]4f^{11}6s^2 6.0215 $^4I_{15/2}^\circ$
- 68 Er Erbium 167.259 [Xe]4f^{12}6s^2 6.1077 $^3H_6$
- 69 Tm Thulium 168.93421 [Xe]4f^{13}6s^2 6.1843 $^2F_{7/2}^\circ$
- 70 Yb Ytterbium 173.054 [Xe]4f^{14}6s^2 6.2542 $^1S_0$
- 71 Lu Lutetium 174.9668 [Xe]4f^{14}5d6s^2 5.4259 $^2D_{3/2}$

Actinides
- 90 Th Thorium 232.03806 [Rn]6d^{2}7s^2 6.3067 $^3F_2$
- 91 Pa Protactinium 231.03588 [Rn]5f^{2}6d7s^2 5.89 $^4K_{11/2}$
- 92 U Uranium 238.02891 [Rn]5f^{3}6d7s^2 6.1939 $^5L_6^\circ$
- 93 Np Neptunium (237) [Rn]5f^{4}6d7s^2 6.2657 $^6L_{11/2}$
- 94 Pu Plutonium (244) [Rn]5f^{6}7s^2 6.0260 $^7F_0$
- 95 Am Americium (243) [Rn]5f^{7}7s^2 5.9738 $^8S_{7/2}^\circ$
- 96 Cm Curium (247) [Rn]5f^{7}6d7s^2 5.9914 $^9D_2^\circ$
- 97 Bk Berkelium (247) [Rn]5f^{9}7s^2 6.1979 $^6H_{15/2}^\circ$
- 98 Cf Californium (251) [Rn]5f^{10}7s^2 6.2817 $^5I_8$
- 99 Es Einsteinium (252) [Rn]5f^{11}7s^2 6.3676 $^4I_{15/2}^\circ$
- 100 Fm Fermium (257) [Rn]5f^{12}7s^2 6.50 $^3H_6$
- 101 Md Mendelevium (258) [Rn]5f^{13}7s^2 6.58 $^2F_{7/2}^\circ$
- 102 No Nobelium (259) [Rn]5f^{14}7s^2 6.65 $^1S_0$
- 103 Lr Lawrencium (262) [Rn]5f^{14}7s^{2}7p? 4.9? $^2P_{1/2}^\circ$?

Directions for Taking Biology 1 EOC
Practice Test B

Test Questions

This Practice Test contains 60 questions. The exact number of questions on the actual test will vary from 60–65.

- ### Multiple-Choice Questions

  Select the best answer for each question and mark it on the answer sheet on page 268.

Reference Pages

You may refer to the two preceding Reference Pages as often as you like.

Timing

For the actual test you will be given two 80-minute periods to complete the test, with a ten-minute break in between. However, anyone who has not finished will be allowed to continue working.

Checking Your Answers

You will find the correct answers, along with detailed explanations, for this practice test beginning on page 253.

Reviewing Your Work

When finished, turn to the grid on pages 265–266. Circle the number of any questions that you missed in Test B. You will be able to see a pattern that shows which Benchmarks will need your further attention.

1 Which of the following resulted from the invention of the microscope?

A. the development of the theory of evolution

B. the development of the cell theory

C. proof that cells can form spontaneously

D. proof that all cells have the same basic structure

2 The potato famine in Ireland (1845–1852) occurred when a fungus *(P. infestans)* escaped by chance out of Mexico and into North America and Europe. The fungus, which caused crop-destroying potato blight, apparently came from a single clonal genotype. The potato population was probably vulnerable to infection by this fungus because of which of the following?

A. lack of genetic drift

B. not enough organisms

C. lack of genetic variation

D. balanced polymorphism

3 Lipid synthesis is carried out in which part of the cell?

A. smooth endoplasmic reticulum

B. rough endoplasmic reticulum

C. ribosomes

D. lysosomes

Go On

4   In hamsters, the gene for short hair (*H*) is dominant to the gene for long hair (*h*). Which is the most likely genotype of the parents if 4 of their 8 offspring have long hair?

   A. *Hh* × *hh*

   B. *Hh* × *Hh*

   C. *HH* × *hh*

   D. *hh* × *hh*

5   Which of the following is a limiting factor that is density-independent?

   A. an outbreak of disease

   B. a forest fire caused by lightning

   C. immigration of new predators

   D. competition for scarce resources

6   Which of the following classifications includes all three of the others?

   A. family

   B. genus

   C. phylum

   D. order

Go On

7 A certain enzyme oxidizes ethanol. If a genetic defect prevents the enzyme from being produced, which outcome do you predict would occur?

A. Ethanol would undergo reduction, which is the opposite process of oxidation.

B. The oxidation of ethanol would proceed only in certain locations in the cell.

C. The cell would employ a different enzyme to oxidize ethanol.

D. The oxidation of ethanol in the cell would happen very slowly or not at all.

8 Which of the following is a key difference between mitosis and meiosis?

A. Mitosis allows for genetic variation, while meiosis results in generations of organisms with stable characteristics.

B. Mitosis produces offspring more slowly, while meiosis has the advantage of producing offspring more quickly and easily.

C. Mitosis produces cells that are almost identical genetically, while meiosis produces cells that differ genetically from each parent or from each other.

D. Mitosis has two cell divisions, while meiosis has only one.

9 Gymnosperms, or conifers, scatter their seeds by which of the following methods?

A. eaten by animals and dropped in feces

B. carried by animals

C. blown by the wind

D. all of the above

Go On ▶

10 Which of the following **best** describes osmosis?

    A. the movement of water molecules out of a cell, resulting in cell shrinkage

    B. the movement of small, uncharged molecules across the lipid bilayer to a state of equilibrium

    C. the movement of charged molecules and larger molecules into and out of the cell

    D. the movement of water molecules across the selectively permeable plasma membrane

11 Look at the marine food web shown below.

Marine Food Web

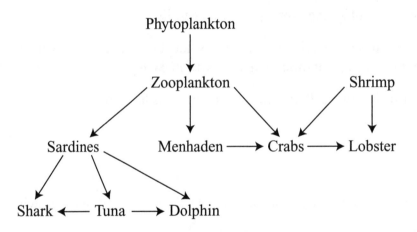

The removal of the lobster from this food web will have which **long-term** effect on the ecosystem?

    A. The zooplankton population will increase.

    B. The crab population will increase.

    C. The shrimp population will decrease.

    D. The phytoplankton population will increase.

Go On

12 A person has a high level of high-density lipoproteins (HDL). Which of the following best describes this situation?

A. HDL is less dangerous to a person's system because it is able to send cholesterol to the liver for elimination.

B. HDL is more dangerous to a person's system because it carries cholesterol to all the cells in the body.

C. HDL levels cannot be treated because they are always the result of family inheritance.

D. HDL levels can be lowered because they are always produced by poor diet and lack of exercise.

13 GAPDH is an enzyme that serves as a catalyst for the sixth step in glycolysis, which is a vital part of cellular respiration. The chart below shows the percentage of similarity between the GAPDH gene in humans and some other species.

Species	Percentage Similarity to Humans for the GAPDH Gene
Chimpanzee	99.6%
Dog	91.3%
Fruit Fly	72.4%
Roundworm	68.2%

Which of the following conclusions can be drawn from this chart?

A. Humans evolved directly from the chimpanzee.

B. The fruit fly and roundworm are not genetically related to humans.

C. Of the species shown, the roundworm has the closest evolutionary relationship to humans.

D. Of the species shown, the chimpanzee has the closest evolutionary relationship to humans.

Go On

14 A ring of bark down to the sapwood is completely removed from the circumference of a tree. This serves to eliminate the phloem at the level of the ring. Which of the following is the most likely effect?

A. an inability to carry on photosynthesis

B. an inability to transport sugars to the roots

C. an inability to transport water to the roots

D. an inability to obtain water from the soil

15 Which of the following describes the process of the light-independent reactions in photosynthesis?

A. the absorption and conversion of light energy to ATP and NADPH

B. the processing of glucose to make pyruvate or pyruvic acid and release ATP

C. the use of ATP and NADPH to convert CO_2 to sugars

D. the breakdown of pyruvic acid molecules to release the energy stored in their molecular bonds

16 Look at the diagram below.

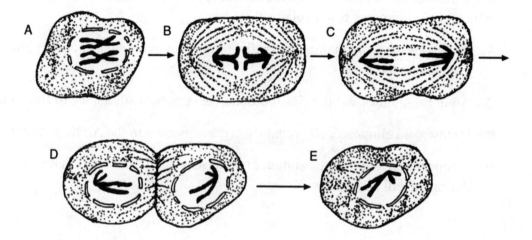

Which phase of cell division is shown in D?

A. anaphase

B. metaphase

C. prophase

D. telophase

17 A plant exposed to high temperatures shows a steady increase in water loss for 90 minutes. Then the rate of water loss **decreases** rapidly. What is the **most likely** cause of this change in the rate of water loss?

A. change in amount of sunlight

B. closing of stomata

C. insufficient CO_2 for photosynthesis

D. insufficient O_2 for photosynthesis

Go On

18 In their early stage of life, insects such as mosquitoes and flies exist as aquatic larvae. Huge numbers of mosquitoes and flies swarm in the Arctic tundra during summer. Which of the following **best** explains this?

    A. Pools of water from melting permafrost in the summer make excellent breeding grounds for the insects.

    B. Adult mosquitoes and flies lay thousands of eggs beneath the ice of frozen lakes.

    C. Intense cold eliminates all predatory organisms even in the Arctic summer.

    D. Frequent rain in the Arctic summer replenishes ponds and lakes that went dry during the fall and winter.

19 Most animals have internal or external skeletons for structure and support. Which of the following parts provide a similar function in plant cells?

    A. cytoplasm

    B. chloroplasts

    C. cell membranes

    D. cell walls

20 Look at the following crosses of plants with green seeds (G) and plants with yellow seeds (g). Which does NOT follow Mendel's law of segregation?

    A. Two green-seed plants ($Gg \times Gg$) produce some green-seed offspring plants.

    B. Two green-seed plants ($Gg \times Gg$) produce some yellow-seed offspring plants.

    C. A green-seed plant and a yellow-seed plant ($GG \times gg$) produce all green-seed plants.

    D. A green-seed plant and a yellow-seed plant ($Gg \times gg$) produce all green-seed plants.

 Go On

21 Look at the illustration below.

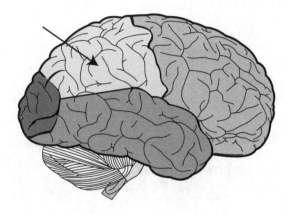

The arrow is pointing to which part of the human brain?

A. frontal lobe

B. occipital lobe

C. parietal lobe

D. temporal lobe

22 A company advertises that their new medication will drastically reduce acid reflux with no side effects. The company's field-testing was conducted on five patients with acid reflux chosen at random from a group of 50 acid-reflux sufferers. Which of the following would be the **best** improvement to the field tests to support the company's claims for this new product?

A. Test the medication on people who do not have acid reflux.

B. Test the medication on a much larger sample size.

C. Compare the results to the claims of rival makers of acid reflux medicine.

D. Have each of the 10 patients write a detailed response to the field test.

23 A root's growth can be broken down into areas based on the activity of its cells. Look at the diagram of a root below.

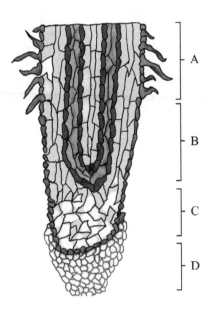

In which area of the root do cells mature and differentiate?

A. part A

B. part B

C. part C

D. part D

24 Which of the following does NOT restrict or decrease blood flow?

A. hardening of the arteries

B. diabetes

C. taking vasodilators

D. very cold temperatures

25 Look at the diagram of an animal cell.

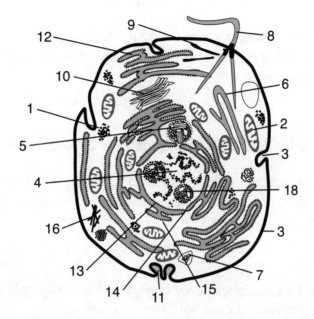

In which part of the cell does aerobic respiration take place?

A. 1

B. 2

C. 3

D. 4

26 Crossing over is a process that occurs during meiosis. Which of the following **best** describes why this results in increased genetic diversity?

A. During prophase I, homologous chromosomes pair up and exchange DNA segments, causing different combinations of alleles.

B. During prophase I, there is independent assortment of homologous chromosomes, creating a variety of genetic outcomes.

Go On

C. During prophase II, each pair of chromatids lines up in the middle of the cell, allowing for the exchange of DNA before the chromatids split and move to either side of the cell.

D. During prophase II, fragments of DNA spontaneously separate from certain chromosomes and attach themselves to the end of other chromosomes, producing new genetic sequences.

Use the following information to answer questions 27–28.

The formation of holes in the Earth's ozone layer due to chemicals used by humans allows more ultraviolet (UV) light to reach the oceans. Increased UV light can kill phytoplankton, marine algae, and other microorganisms.

27 Which statement **best** describes how a large decrease in phytoplankton and marine algae would affect the ocean food web?

A. The effect would not be drastic since the organisms are so small.

B. The number of marine animals would decrease due to the decrease in producers.

C. The number of consumers in the food web would increase as the producers decrease.

D. The number of decomposers would increase as the phytoplankton and marine algae die.

28 Which of the following explains the **most likely** effect of increased UV light on alpine and polar lakes that are very clear?

A. The increase in solar UV radiation would increase the rate of mutation in microorganisms such as phytoplankton and algae, so that they would no longer be a healthy food source for marine animals.

B. The UV light would raise the temperature of the alpine and polar lakes, which would help the microorganisms repair themselves.

Go On

C. The UV light would stimulate photosynthesis, resulting in a more stable ecosystem.

D. The UV light would penetrate to a greater depth in lakes that have clear water, potentially doing greater damage to the ecosystem.

29 Which of the following statements is correct in comparing and contrasting prokaryotes and eukaryotes?

A. Eukaryotes are much larger than prokaryotes, but otherwise they share the same structure.

B. Cytoplasm is found in both prokaryotes and eukaryotes but in a slightly different form in each.

C. Both prokaryotes and eukaryotes are mainly multicellular.

D. Prokaryotes and eukaryotes both have distinct organelles, although prokaryotes have fewer of them.

30 There is evidence that supplying a cup of sugar to certain bacteria could power a 60-watt light bulb for more than 15 hours. Which of the following is the **best** method to affirm this idea?

A. conducting an experiment

B. trading observations

C. formulating a hypothesis

D. researching the scientific literature

Go On ▶

31 A certain breed of sheep has a dominant allele (*W*) that produces white hair and a recessive allele (*w*) that produces black hair. For a white sheep, which of the following could you identify?

   A. the genotypes for both of its parents

   B. the phenotypes for both of its parents

   C. its genotype for hair color

   D. its phenotype for hair color

32 A marathoner's leg muscles often feel heavy and prone to cramping after 20 or more miles. Which of the following is the **best** explanation for this?

   A. A marathoner's muscle cells cannot store glucose for use as energy.

   B. A marathoner's muscle cells contract when glucose reacts with oxygen.

   C. A marathoner's circulatory system cannot take in sufficient oxygen, and the muscle cells must switch to anaerobic respiration for energy.

   D. A marathoner's circulatory system takes in too much oxygen during a race, which causes muscle cramping.

33 Human lifestyle choices affect the environment in many different ways. Which of the following is a personal choice that would benefit the environment and promote sustainability?

   A. Using plastic bags instead of paper bags to preserve more trees.

   B. Using natural gas instead of petroleum as a source for fuel.

   C. Using wind power for electricity generation instead of fossil fuels.

   D. Using a small automobile for transportation instead of a large train or bus.

 Go On

34 One of the three kinds of RNA molecules produced during transcription is mRNA. What is the main purpose of mRNA?

A. build ribosomes from various proteins

B. carry amino acids to the correct place on the genetic template

C. modify the RNA molecules with additions and deletions

D. provide a template used for sequencing amino acids into a polypeptide

35 Which of the following is the **best** description of monocytes and their function?

A. Monocytes are a type of phagocyte that change into macrophages and ingest large numbers of microbes over a long period of time.

B. Monocytes are a type of phagocyte that eat microbes for a very short period of time.

C. Monocytes are a chemical defense made up of 30 different proteins that move freely in the blood plasma and are available during an inflammatory response.

D. Monocytes are a separate class of proteins that come to the body's defense by protecting healthy cells from being infected by neighboring infected cells.

36 A student is conducting an experiment to determine CO_2 levels in four solutions under different conditions. The student prepares four flasks, each containing 75 mL of distilled water. Ten drops of bromothymol blue are then added to each flask. Bromothymol blue is a chemical that indicates increased levels of CO_2 by changing color from blue to green to yellow. At the beginning of the experiment three of the flasks contain blue solutions and one contains a yellow solution. Which of the following should the student do next?

A. use the flask containing a yellow solution as a control

B. pour out the yellow solution and prepare the solution again until it is blue like the others

C. proceed with the experiment using the flasks as they are

D. add CO_2 to the three flasks with blue solution until they all have yellow solutions

Go On

37 Carbohydrates are one of the complex molecules that led to the development of life on Earth. Which of the following **best** explains why carbohydrates are excellent molecules for storing energy?

   A. Carbohydrates consist of three elements—carbon, hydrogen, and oxygen.

   B. Carbohydrates consist of long chains of monomers.

   C. Carbohydrates contain many carbon-hydrogen bonds.

   D. Sugars tend to function as the building blocks for larger molecules.

38 Scientists have found that a mutation that disrupts a single protein they call Sonic Hedge Hog (SHH) is responsible for extra digits in organisms. This mutation has been found in Ernest Hemingway's famous six-toed cats, in certain kinds of mice, and in humans with extra fingers or toes. What does this indicate about evolutionary relationships?

   A. Organisms with mutations all have similar gene patterns.

   B. Genetic patterns in humans, cats, and mice are very similar, showing that they are all closely related organisms.

   C. The mutation in the Sonic Hedge Hog gene shows that natural selection does not work for humans, cats, and mice.

   D. Over time, all humans, cats, and mice will develop extra digits due to stabilizing selection.

39 In the southwestern deserts of the United States, ancient lava flows left black rock formations scattered across light-brown sand. The areas were colonized by black, white, and tan-colored mice. What is the **most likely** outcome of this situation?

   A. The frequency of black mice will increase, while white and tan mice will emigrate to other areas.

   B. The frequency of white mice will increase, while black and tan mice will die off due to predators.

C. The frequency of black mice and tan mice will increase, while white mice will die off due to predators.

D. All the mice will develop protective coloring to survive in the surroundings.

40 When a person hyperventilates, he or she is often given a paper bag to breathe into for relief. Which of the following explains the purpose for this?

A. to increase the acidity of the person's blood

B. to limit the amount of oxygen in the person's lungs

C. to decrease the level of carbon dioxide in the person's blood

D. to increase the level of carbon dioxide in the person's blood

41 The plasma membrane in a eukaryotic cell mainly consists of which of the following?

A. a phospholipid bilayer with proteins embedded in the layers

B. a protein bilayer with phospholipids embedded in the layers

C. a hydrophilic head and a hydrophobic tail

D. a phospholipid layer and a protein layer

42 Which of the following is NOT included in the body's first line of defense against disease-causing agents?

A. stomach acid

B. mucous membranes

C. phagocytes

D. cilia

Go On

43 A food pyramid is shown below.

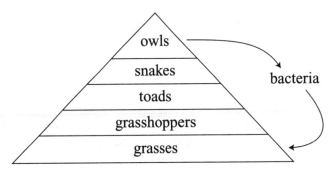

In this food pyramid, toads are which of the following?

A. primary consumers

B. secondary consumers

C. producers

D. tertiary consumers

44 A student conducts an experiment by cutting five small cubes of potato and placing them in five beakers. Each beaker has a different solution consisting of 300 mL of distilled water and 0.2–1.0 M of sucrose. A control beaker contains only a potato cube and distilled water. Which is the **best** method for comparing the changes in the potato cubes?

A. measure the change in mass

B. measure the change in size

C. measure the percent change in mass

D. observe the change in appearance

Go On ▶

45 Which of the following describes the Golgi apparatus?

A. a system of flattened sacs and mazelike channels that crisscross the cytoplasm (Endoplasmic reticulum)

B. the organelle where sacs package proteins and lipids into vesicles

C. vesicles that contain digestive enzymes to break down food, debris, and invading bacteria (lysosomes)

D. a network of protein filaments that give shape to a cell, allow the cell to move, and attach organelles to its plasma membrane (cytoskeleton)

46 Look at the survivorship curves below.

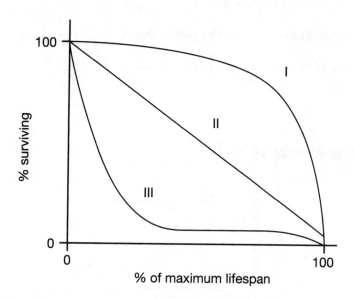

Curve III on the graph **best** describes the survivorship situation of which of the following species?

A. rainbow trout

B. Gila monsters

C. squirrels

D. humans

Go On

47 A student organizes an osmosis experiment in which three cores cut from raw potatoes represent cells with semipermeable membranes. Each potato core is first weighed and its mass recorded. Then the cores are each soaked in a separate concentration of salt water. The table below presents the results of the experiment.

NaCl Concentration/M	Potato Core Samples	Mass Before Soaking	Mass After Soaking	% Change in Mass
98%	A	1.93	1.42	−26.42
50%	B	2.00	1.77	−11.50
2%	C	1.98	2.17	+9.60

Based on the data in the table, which of the statements is true?

A. Sample C is in a hypertonic solution.

B. Sample B is in an isotonic solution.

C. Samples A and B exhibit signs of plasmolysis.

D. Samples A and B exhibit signs of turgor pressure.

48 Look at the population graph below.

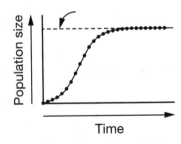

Which of the following population factors does the dotted line represent?

A. lack of competitors

B. carrying capacity

C. migration

D. frequency of reproduction

Go On

49 Which of the following equations describes the process of photosynthesis?

A. $C_6H_{12}O_6 + 6O_2 \rightarrow 6CO_2 + 6H_2O + \text{energy}$

B. $C_6H_{12}O_6 + H_2O \rightarrow 6CO_2 + \text{energy}$.

C. $6CO_2 + 6H_2O + \text{energy} \rightarrow C_6H_{12}O_6 + 6O_2$

D. $CO_2 + H_2O + \text{energy} \rightarrow C_6H_{12}O_6 + O_2$

50 Which of the following uses energy to move substances across the plasma membrane and against their concentration gradient from areas of low concentration to areas of high concentration?

A. osmosis

B. facilitated diffusion

C. exocytosis

D. the sodium-potassium pump

51 The Florida panther once roamed widely in the southeastern United States. The number of Florida panthers was drastically reduced due to loss of habitat, hunting, and even collisions with automobiles. By the 1970s, the estimated number of Florida panthers had shrunk to only six. Which of the following describes the **most likely** next stage in this situation?

A. genetic defects in the population due to inbreeding

B. genetic diversity due to interbreeding with other free-roaming puma species

C. improvement of the Florida panther's gene pool due to inbreeding

D. development of two new breeds of Florida panther

Go On

52 Below is a graphic showing the structure of a leaf.

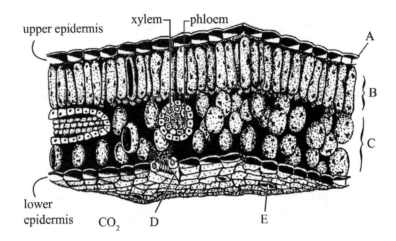

Which of the following kinds of cells are indicated by the labels B and C?

A. guard cells

B. parenchyma cells

C. collenchyma cells

D. bundle sheath cells

53 Which of the following is the end product of translation?

A. DNA

B. RNA

C. amino acids

D. polypeptides

Go On ▶

54 Look at the diagram below of the human female reproductive system.

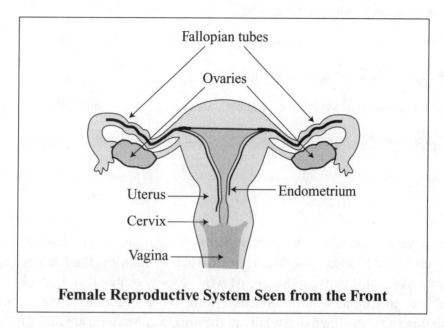

Fallopian tubes

Ovaries

Uterus —

Cervix —

Vagina —

Endometrium

Female Reproductive System Seen from the Front

In human sexual reproduction, the fertilized ovum attaches to which of the following?

A. fallopian tube

B. uterus

C. endometrium

D. vagina

55 A person who contracts chicken pox as an adult lacks which of the following?

A. memory cells

B. memory cells for a specific pathogen

C. plasma cells

D. B lymphocyte cells

Go On ▶

56 The water molecule has many special properties. Which of the following occurs because of water's cohesive behavior?

A. Water is able to cool down and heat up slowly.

B. Water is able to float in solid form.

C. Water is able to dissolve many substances.

D. Water is able to move from the roots to the leaves of plants.

57 In recent years, several exotic species of snakes have caused problems for wildlife managers in the Florida Everglades. One particular culprit is the Burmese python, a huge snake that is native to Southeast Asia yet now is abundant in the Everglades and able to prey on its wildlife. Since its introduction, raccoon, possum, and deer populations have declined drastically in the area. Studies indicate that the Burmese python has trouble eating and digesting food at temperatures below 60 degrees F. Which conclusion can be drawn from this information?

A. The abiotic factors in the Florida Everglades make it an ideal environment for almost any species.

B. The Burmese python will improve the overall ecosystem of the Everglades by eliminating weaker species.

C. Because of abiotic factors, the Burmese python is not a threat to spread to other states in the region.

D. The Burmese python population will soon reach its biotic potential in the Everglades.

Go On

58 Huntington's disease is a disorder caused by a genetic defect. A parent with the abnormal gene for Huntington's disease has a 50% chance of passing on the gene to each of his or her children. Each child's risk is independent of whether a sibling has the disorder. This is an example of which of the following kinds of inheritance?

A. autosomal dominant inheritance

B. autosomal recessive inheritance

C. X-linked inheritance

D. mitochondrial inheritance

59 Which of the following is the beginning step of DNA replication?

A. The enzyme primase starts the complementary strand of DNA with short segments of RNA.

B. The process of elongation adds DNA nucleotides to each complementary strand of DNA.

C. The enzyme DNA polymerase bonds to the RNA primers.

D. The enzyme helicase unzips the DNA double helix.

60 A heterotrophic organism that recycles dead organic matter into nutrients that are useful to plants and other organisms is classified in which of the following kingdoms?

A. Kingdom Protista

B. Kingdom Fungi

C. Kingdom Plantae

D. Kingdom Animalia

Go On

This is the end of the Biology Test.

Until time is called, go back and check your work or answer questions
you did not complete. When you have finished, close your
Test Book and Answer Book.

Answers
Practice Test

1 **B** **SC.912.N.1.3, SC.912.N.2.1, SC.912.N.3.1, SC.912.N.3.4, SC.912.L.14.1, SC.912.L.14.4** **(MC)**

The ability to examine cells with a microscope led directly to the development of the modern cell theory. The theory of evolution developed from observations and deductions by scientists such as Charles Darwin. The idea that cells form spontaneously was an early component of cell theory that was **disproved**. Work with microscopes revealed that cells have a variety of structures.

2 **C** **SC.912.L.15.13, SC.912.L.15.14, SC.912.L.15.15** **(HC)**

Lack of genetic diversity in a population makes it vulnerable to changing factors in the environment, including diseases, pests, and climate change. When the fungus was introduced into Ireland's potato crop, the genetically identical organisms all succumbed. Today, farmers grow crops with diverse genes so that some of the plants will be immune to any new disease. Genetic drift is a random change in the gene pool, which occurred in this case but is not the reason for the crops' vulnerability. There were certainly enough crops to begin with, so B is not correct. Balanced polymorphism is when a population becomes divided into types based on extreme traits.

3 **A** **SC.912.L.14.2, SC.912.L.14.3** **(MC)**

The smooth endoplasmic reticulum, or smooth ER, is the site of lipid and hormone synthesis in the cell, among other functions such as detoxifying the cell.

4 **A** **SC.912.L.16.1, SC.912.L.16.2** **(HC)**

If 4 of the 8 hamster offspring have long hair, then 4 have short hair, and the ratio of long hair to short hair is 1:1. A 1: 1 ratio means that the parents are H/h and h/h. Since half of the offspring have short hair, each of the parents must contribute a recessive *(h)* allele. And one of the parents must have two recessive *(h)* alleles. The cross looks like this:

	h	*h*
H	*Hh*	*Hh*
h	*hh*	*hh*

5 **B** **SC.912.L.17.5, SC.912.L.17.8** **(MC)**

Limiting factors are density-independent when they occur without regard to population size and have effects that are not worsened as population increases. Natural disasters such as fires, floods, and tornadoes are density-independent factors. The other answer choices are all density-dependent.

6 **C** **SC.912.L.15.4, SC.912.L.15.6** **(LC)**

Phylum includes all the other three classifications. The classifications in order from general to specific are domain, kingdom, phylum, class, order, family, genus, species.

7 **D** **SC.912.L.18.1, SC.912.L.18.11** **(MC)**

An enzyme accelerates the rate of a biochemical reaction by lowering its required activation energy. Should the enzyme not be produced due to genetic mutation, the biochemical reaction (in this case, the oxidation of ethanol) either would proceed at a much slower rate or not occur at all.

8 **C** **SC.912.L.16.14, SC.912.L.16.16, SC.912.L.16.17** **(MC)**

Mitosis decreases genetic diversity because the cells produced by this process are almost identical genetically. This is a key difference from meiosis, which allows for genetic change and improvement through the mixing of parental genetic material. This key difference is mistakenly reversed in answer A. Answers B and D also mistakenly reverse mitosis and meiosis in describing their rates of producing offspring and the number of cell divisions in each process.

9 **C** **SC.912.L.14.7** **(MC)**

For pollination, gymnosperms rely on their seeds being carried by the wind. Angiosperms can pollinate by methods A, B, or C.

10 **D** **SC.912.L.14.2** **(LC)**

The movement of water molecules across the plasma membrane from a hypotonic solution to a hypertonic solution is called osmosis. Vesicular transport moves large molecules and food particles across the plasma membrane using vesicles or other organs. Active transport is the movement of molecules against a concentration gradient. Facilitated diffusion is the movement of charged molecules such as potassium ions and larger molecules such as glucose across the cell membrane.

11 **B** **SC.912.L.17.9, SC.912.E.7.1** **(HC)**

In this food web, the lobster is a secondary consumer that eats the crab, which is a primary consumer. If the lobster were eliminated from the food web, more crabs would survive, thus increasing the crab population.

12 **A** **SC.912.L.14.6, SC.912.L.14.36, HE.912.C.1.4, HE.912.C.1.8** **(MC)**

HDL is often called "good cholesterol" because of its ability to carry cholesterol to the liver for elimination. It is LDL that is more harmful because it carries cholesterol to all the body's cells. High levels of serum cholesterol are not solely the result of either genetics or poor diet and lack of exercise. The condition is often caused by either one or the other.

13 **D** **SC.912.N.1.3, SC.912.N.1.6, SC.912.N.3.1,**
SC.912.L.15.1, SC.912.L.15.4, LA.910.2.2.3 **(MC)**

The chart shows that the percentage similarity for the GAPDH gene is closest between humans and the chimpanzee. This indicates that humans have a much closer evolutionary relationship to chimpanzees than to the other species shown. The chart does not indicate that humans evolved from chimpanzees. The chart does show that the fruit fly and the roundworm are genetically related to humans, although more distantly than the dog and the chimpanzee. The roundworm has the most distant relationship of the species in the chart.

14 **B** **SC.912.L.14.7** **(MC)**

Phloem moves carbohydrates by active transport to other parts of the plant. With the phloem tissue gone at the level of the ring, the tree would not be able to transport sugars down to the roots. Since the xylem (the sapwood) is left untouched, water transport would not be affected.

15 **C** **SC.912.L.18.7, SC.912.L.18.8, SC.912.L.18.9, SC.912.L.18.10** **(LC)**

The light-independent reactions in photosynthesis combine ATP and NADPH with CO_2 to produce sugar, which can then be used to make various other carbohydrates. Answer A describes the light-dependent reactions in photosynthesis. Answers B and D describe stages in the process of cellular respiration.

16 **D** **SC.912.L.16.14, SC.912.L.16.17** **(MC)**

Part D of the diagram shows telophase, the last stage of mitosis. In this stage, the mitotic spindle disassembles and the chromosomes unwind from their highly compacted state. A new nuclear membrane forms and surrounds each new complete set of chromosomes.

17 B SC.912.L.14.7 (MC)

When a plant in a hot environment cannot sufficiently replace the water lost to transpiration by water gained from the root, the stomata close to prevent the plant from wilting.

18 A SC.912.L.17.2, SC.912.L.17.4, SC.912.L.17.5 (MC)

The aquatic larvae breed easily in the pools of melting water during the Arctic summer. This is an example of an abiotic factor improving the conditions necessary for a population to grow.

19 D SC.912.L.14.2, SC.912.L.14.3, SC.912.L.14.7 (LC)

Rigid cell walls made of cellulose serve the same function of structure and support in plant cells as skeletons do in animals.

20 D SC.912.L.16.1, SC.912.L.16.2 (HC)

The situation in answer D would produce some yellow-seed plants (*gg*). The cross is here:

	g	*g*
G	*Gg*	*Gg*
g	*gg*	*gg*

21 C SC.912.L.14.26 (LC)

The parietal lobe, which receives and controls sensory input, is located directly behind the frontal lobe in the human brain.

22 B SC.912.N.1.1, SC.912.N.1.4, SC.912.N.1.6 (MC)

To get dependable results in its product field-testing, the company should gather a much larger sample size of patients with acid reflux—perhaps using the entire original group of 50, or even recruiting 500. A sample size that is too small can produce misleading results.

23 **A** **SC.912.L.14.2, SC.912.L.14.7** **(MC)**

Cells in the zone of maturation (A) mature and differentiate into xylem, phloem, parenchyma, or epidermis cells. The other areas shown are the zone of elongation (B), the zone of cell division or meristematic zone (C), and root cap (D).

24 **C** **SC.912.L.14.36** **(MC)**

Persons with high blood pressure take vasodilators to open blood vessels by relaxing muscles in vessel walls. Thus, vasodilators are medications that increase blood flow.

25 **B** **SC.912.L.14.2, SC.912.L.14.3, SC.912.L.18.8** **(MC)**

Cellular respiration is carried out in the mitochondria. Label 2 (B) is a single mitochondrium. An active cell may contain more than 2,000 mitochondria. Aerobic cellular respiration is how the cell obtains energy (as ATP) from carbohydrates. Label 1 (A) is ribosomes. Label 3 (C) is the plasma membrane. Label 4 (D) is the nucleolus.

26 **A** **SC.912.L.16.16, SC.912.L.16.17** **(MC)**

It is the exchange of DNA between homologous chromosomes during prophase I that results in the mixing of maternal and paternal DNA and greater genetic diversity. Independent assortment occurs during metaphase I and anaphase I, so answer B is incorrect. Answers C and D incorrectly describe how genetic information is exchanged during meiosis.

27 **B** **SC.912.L.17.2, SC.912.L.17.4, SC.912.L.17.5, SC.912.L.17.8** **(MC)**

The numbers of marine animals that are primary consumers in the ocean food web would decrease because of the decrease in phytoplankton and marine algae that they depend on. The small size of the organisms does not affect their importance to the ecosystem (A). The number of consumers would decrease, not increase, with the loss of microorganisms. Decomposers would also decrease due to the overall effect on the ocean food web.

28 **D** **SC.912.L.17.2, SC.912.L.17.4, SC.912.L.17.5, SC.912.L.17.8** **(HC)**

The most likely effect is that clear waters in alpine (mountain) and polar lakes would allow UV radiation to penetrate to a greater depth, which would increase the potential damage to the organisms in the lakes and thus to the entire ecosystem. By affecting rates of photosynthesis and reproduction, this abiotic factor would probably decrease biodiversity and limit the carrying capacity of each lake.

29 **B**   **SC.912.L.14.2, SC.912.L.14.3, HE.912.C.1.3   (MC)**

Both prokaryotic cells and eukaryotic cells have cytoplasm. However, the cytoplasm in the prokaryote is granular and viscous and the nuclear material floats freely without a nuclear membrane. Eukaryotes are indeed much larger than prokaryotes, but the latter has a much more primitive structure. Prokaryotes are unicellular and do not have distinct organelles.

30 **A**   **SC.912.N.1.1, SC.912.N.1.6   (MC)**

The best method for affirming a scientific idea like the one proposed is to design and conduct an experiment and see if the results support or refute the idea.

31 **D**   **SC.912.L.16.1, SC.912.L.16.2   (MC)**

The information given in the question establishes that white hair is the sheep's phenotype, or how the gene is expressed in physical appearance. From the information given, you cannot determine the genotype of the white sheep (answer C), since it could be either *WW* or *Ww*. You also cannot determine the genotypes of the parents (answer A) since they could be *WW* × *WW*, *WW* × *Ww*, *WW* × *ww*, or *Ww* × *Ww*. It is also not possible to determine the phenotypes for both parents; while one must be white the other could be white or black.

32 **C**   **SC.912.L.18.8   (MC)**

A person's body cannot store oxygen as it can glucose, and a marathoner cannot take in sufficient oxygen to keep up with energy needs for a long race. Thus, the marathoner's muscle cells must switch to anaerobic respiration for energy. Instead of reacting with oxygen, the glucose in the muscles forms lactic acid for energy. This lactic acid builds up in the muscles, leading to feelings of heaviness and cramping.

33 **C**   **SC.912.L.17.11, SC.912.L.17.13, SC.912.L.17.20, HE.912.C.1.3   (LC)**

Wind power is a sustainable source of energy that many feel is a desirable alternative to fossil fuels for generating electricity.

34 **D** **SC.912.L.16.3, SC.912.L.16.5** **(MC)**

The Messenger RNA, or mRNA, sets up the template for the sequencing of amino acids that are then assembled into a polypeptide in translation.

35 **A** **SC.912.L.14.6, SC.912.L.14.52** **(MC)**

The description in answer choice A is the best description of monocytes and their function. The other type of phagocyte is neutrophils, which are described in Answer B. Answer C describes the complement system. Answer D describes interferons.

36 **B** **SC.912.N.1.1, SC.912.N.1.4, SC.912.N.1.6** **(HC)**

For the experiment to be valid, all the solutions should be the same color at the beginning, indicating identical levels of CO_2. Once the yellow solution in the fourth flask has been replaced with blue solution, that flask or one of the others could be used as a control for the experiment.

37 **C** **SC.912.L.18.1, SC.912.L.18.7, SC.912.L.18.8, SC.912.L.18.9, SC.912.L.18.10** **(LC)**

Carbohydrates have numerous carbon-hydrogen bonds, which release energy upon interaction with oxygen molecules. This makes carbohydrates an excellent means of storing energy that the body can access quickly.

38 **B** **SC.912.N.1.3, SC.912.N.1.6, SC.912.L.15.1, SC.912.L.15.4, SC.912.L.15.5, SC.912.L.15.15, SC.912.L.16.9, SC.912.L.16.10** **(MC)**

The fact that the mutation that disrupts the SHH gene results in extra digits in humans, cats, and mice shows that these species are all closely related on the evolutionary scale. In fact, mice are often used to test the effects of new medicines because their biochemical makeup is so similar to humans'.

39 **C** **SC.912.L.15.13, SC.912.L.15.15** **(HC)**

The black mice have protective coloration for living among the black rocks, while the tan-colored mice have protective coloration for living on the light-brown sand. These two groups would increase in frequency because predators would not see them as often. The white mice, however, would stand out against the black rocks or the light-brown sand and would succumb to predators in much greater numbers.

40 D SC.912.L.14.36 (MC)

When a person breathes too fast, as in hyperventilation, he or she loses carbon dioxide from the blood too quickly. This makes the blood too alkaline (reduced acidity) and causes the person to feel faint and dizzy. Breathing into a paper bag forces the person to inhale some of the carbon dioxide that is exhaled into the bag, thus increasing levels of carbon dioxide in the blood and relieving the symptoms.

41 A SC.912.L.14.2, SC.912.L.14.3 (MC)

The plasma membrane consists mainly of a phospholipid bilayer with proteins dispersed throughout the layers. The hydrophobic tail and hydrophilic head is part of a phospholipid.

42 C SC.912.L.14.52 (LC)

Phagocytes are special cells that ingest invasive microbes as part of the body's nonspecific immune response in the second line of defense against disease. The other answer choices are all part of the first line of defense.

43 B SC.912.L.17.9, SC.912.E.7.1 (MC)

In this food pyramid, toads are secondary consumers that feed on the herbivore grasshoppers, which are primary consumers.

44 C SC.912.N.1.1, SC.912.N.1.4, SC.912.N.1.6, MA.912.S.1.2 (MC)

Since the potato cubes did not all have the exact same mass at the beginning of the experiment, the best way to control for the variation is to find the percentage change in mass.

45 B SC.912.L.14.2, SC.912.L.14.3 (LC)

The Golgi apparatus packages substances produced in the rough endoplasmic reticulum and moves them to other parts of the cell or to the cell's surface. Answer A describes the endoplasmic reticulum. Answer C describes lysosomes. Answer D describes the cytoskeleton.

46 **A** **SC.912.L.17.5** **(HC)**

Curve III on the graph shows a very high death rate among young offspring followed by a declining death rate for the few individuals who survive to maturity. This describes the situation of fish such as rainbow trout, which produce 400–3,000 eggs depending on the size of the female. Gila monsters and squirrels have a fairly constant death rate over their life span, which is consistent with Curve II. Humans, whose offspring are protected by parenting and have very low death rates through middle age, are represented by Curve I.

47 **C** **SC.912.N.1.1, SC.912.N.1.4, SC.912.N.1.6,**
SC.912.L.14.2, SC.912.L.14.3 LA.910.2.2.3, MA.912.S.3.2 **(MC)**

Plasmolysis, or cell shrinkage, occurs when water flows out of a cell from a higher concentration of water to a lower concentration, as with samples A and B. Notice that their masses **decrease** after soaking in the saltwater solution. Sample C is in a hypotonic solution (low concentration of solute) so answer A is incorrect. If sample B were in an isotonic solution, its mass would be almost exactly the same after soaking in the solution as before. Answer B is incorrect. Samples A and B would have to gain mass to exhibit signs of turgor pressure, so answer D is incorrect.

48 **B** **SC.912.L.17.4, SC.912.L.17.5** **(MC)**

The dotted line in the graph represents the point at which the habitat's carrying capacity is reached and population growth therefore levels out. Factors such as lack of competitors and frequency of reproduction would affect the carrying capacity of a habitat but are not specifically represented by the dotted line. Limiting factors (disease, predators, toxic environment, natural disasters, etc.) are those that prevent a population from growing to its biotic potential.

49 **C** **SC.912.L.18.7, SC.912.L.18.8, SC.912.L.18.9** **(MC)**

The formula describes the photosynthetic process in which carbon dioxide, water, and energy from the sun are combined to produce glucose and oxygen in a plant cell. Answer choice A is the formula for cellular respiration, which is the reverse of the equation for photosynthesis.

50 **D** **SC.912.L.14.2** **(LC)**

The sodium-potassium pump (also called the cell membrane pump) uses energy to move sodium ions and potassium ions across the cell membrane and against the concentration gradient. It is also important in maintaining a difference in charge across the plasma membrane.

51 **A   SC.912.L.15.13, SC.912.L.15.14, SC.912.L.15.15   (HC)**

The Florida panther, with its drastically reduced numbers, was subject to the bottleneck effect, in which a reduced population must survive by inbreeding and is consequently much more vulnerable to the effects of certain alleles than usual. This frequently results in genetic defects in the population. This is in fact what happened to the Florida panther. While it has avoided extinction, its population now has certain genetic defects including a hole in the heart.

52 **B   SC.912.L.14.2, SC.912.L.14.3, SC.912.L.14.7, SC.912.L.18.7   (MC)**

The cells indicated by the labels B and C form the parts of the inner leaf called the palisade mesophyll (B) and the spongy mesophyll (C), both of which are made of parenchyma cells that are specialized for photosynthesis. These cells are tightly packed in the upper part of the palisade layer and more loosely packed in the lower spongy layer.

53 **D   SC.912.L.16.3, SC.912.L.16.5   (MC)**

In translation, RNA is translated into the language of amino acids, which are the building blocks of proteins. Using the mRNA transcript, ribosomes synthesize the proteins to produce an amino acid chain, or polypeptide. Thus polypeptides are the final product of translation. Altogether, this process allows for gene expression in organisms.

54 **C   SC.912.L.16.13   (LC)**

The fertilized ovum attaches to the endometrium, which is the inside wall of the uterus.

55 **B   SC.912.L.14.6, SC.912.L.14.52, HE.912.C.1.8   (MC)**

Memory cells are a kind of T cells that are created when an antigen such as the chicken pox virus appears. Unlike plasma cells, which fight an antigen for about two weeks, memory cells remain in a person's system for a very long time, ready to reactivate immediately should the same antigen reappear. Memory cells are always specific to a pathogen, so that an adult person who has never had a certain virus will not have memory cells in his or her system to attack that antigen. That person may, however, have memory cells keyed to another antigen.

56 **D** **SC.912.L.17.2** **(MC)**

The cohesive properties of water are due to the hydrogen bonding between water molecules. This aids in capillary action, in which water moves upward in the narrow fibers of a plant or tree from the roots to the leaves. The ability of water to cool down and heat up slowly (A) is due to its high heat capacity, not its strong cohesion. Water floats as a solid (B) because it expands upon freezing. It is a universal solvent (C) because it is a highly polar molecule.

57 **C** **SC.912.L.17.5, SC.912.L.17.8, LA.910,4.2.2** **(HC)**

Since the Burmese python has difficulty eating and digesting food at cooler temperatures than those found in the Everglades, it almost certainly will not spread to other states in the region, which all lie to the north and have relatively cooler climates. This means that the abiotic factor of temperature will limit its biotic potential in the region.

58 **A** **SC.912.L.14.6, HE.912.C.1.4** **(MC)**

In autosomal dominant inheritance, only a single copy of the abnormal gene needs to be passed on to a child for the disorder to appear. A single abnormal gene on one of the first two nonsex chromosomes from either parent can result in an autosomal disorder. In Huntington's disease, a section of DNA is repeated more times than it is supposed to. As the gene is passed down through a family, the number of repetitions of this gene tends to grow. This increases a person's chances of developing symptoms at an early age.

59 **D** **SC.912.L.16.3** **(MC)**

The process of DNA replication begins when helicase separates, or "unzips," the DNA molecule into two strands, each of which serves as a template to assemble a new strand that is complementary. The enzyme helicase acts to form the Y-shaped replication fork.

60 **B** **SC.912.L.15.6** **(MC)**

Kingdom Fungi consists of organisms such as mushrooms, truffles, bread mold, mildews, yeast, and other common fungi. Fungi, which grow as threadlike filaments, support the ecosystem as decomposers of dead organic matter that absorb and pass on beneficial nutrients.

Practice Test Benchmark Assessment

Circle **those** specific numbers for those questions you answered incorrectly. Use this chart to determine which areas need **additional work**. You will find a description of these benchmarks in the Introduction to this book. Each chapter lists and then reviews the individual benchmarks.

Benchmarks Classification	Benchmark Assessed in Practice Test A Problems	Benchmark Assessed in Practice Test B Problems
SC.912.N.1.1	1, 2, 3, 4, 5, 6	22, 30, 36, 44, 47
SC.912.N.1.3	16, 43	1, 13
SC.912.N.1.4	3	22, 36, 44, 47
SC.912.N.1.6	1, 2, 4, 5, 43	13, 22, 30, 36, 44, 47
SC.912.N.2.1	3	1
SC.912.N.3.1	4, 16	1, 13
SC.912.N.3.4	16	1
SC.912.L.14.4	4	1
LA.910.2.2.3	2, 5	47
LA.910.4.2.2	16	
MA.912.S.1.2	6	44
MA.912.S.3.2	2, 5	13, 29, 47
SC.912.L.14.1	16	57
SC.912.L.14.2	17, 20, 21, 29	3, 10, 19, 23, 25, 29, 41, 45, 47, 50, 52
SC.912.L.14.3	18, 19, 22	3, 19, 25, 29, 41, 45, 47, 52
SC.912.L.16.3	46, 47, 48	34, 50, 53
SC.912.L.16.4	48, 49	
SC.912.L.16.5	47	34, 53
SC.912.L.16.8	49	
SC.912.L.16.9		38
SC.912.L.16.14	51	8, 16
SC.912.L.16.16	51	8, 26
SC.912.L.16.17	51	8, 16, 26
SC.912.L.18.1	8, 9, 10, 15, 33	7, 37
SC.912.L.18.7	12, 14, 26	15, 49, 37, 52
SC.912.L.18.8	13, 26	15, 25, 32, 37, 49
SC.912.L.18.9	14, 26	15, 37, 49
SC.912.L.18.10	8, 9, 14, 26	15, 37

Benchmarks Classification	Benchmark Assessed in Practice Test A Problems	Benchmark Assessed in Practice Test B Problems
SC.912.L.18.11	10, 15	7, 15
SC.912.L.18.12	7, 11, 25	
SC.912.E.7.1	54, 55	11, 43
SC.912.L.14.7	23, 24, 25, 26, 27, 28, 29	9, 14, 17, 23, 52
SC.912.L.14.26	30	21
SC.912.L.14.36	35	12, 24, 40
SC.912.L.14.52	31, 32, 34, 37, 37, 38	35, 42, 55
SC.912.L.14.6	31, 33, 34, 36	12, 35, 55
SC.912.L.16.10		38
SC.912.L.16.13	50, 52	54
SC.912.L.17.2	56	18, 27, 28, 56
SC.912.L.17.4	53	18, 27, 28, 48
SC.912.L.17.5	53, 56	5, 18, 19, 27, 28, 46, 48, 57
SC.912.L.17.8	57	5, 27, 28, 57
SC.912.L.17.9	54, 57	11, 43
SC.912.L.17.11	59, 60	33
SC.912.L.17.13	58	33
SC.912.L.17.20	58, 59	33
HE.912.C.1.3	36	33
HE.912.C.1.4	36	12, 58
HE.912.C.1.8	31, 33	12, 55
SC.912.L.15.1	38, 43	13
SC.912.L.15.4	45	6, 13, 38
SC.912-L.15.5	45	38
SC.912.L.15.6	45	6, 60
SC.912.L.15.8	45	37
SC.912.L.15.10	43	
SC.912.L.15.13	41, 42	2, 39, 51
SC.912.L.15.14	44	2, 51
Sc.912.L.15.15	39, 44	2, 38, 39, 51
SC.912.L.16.1	40, 42	4, 20, 31
SC.912.L.16.2	40, 42	4, 20, 31

Biology Practice Test A

Answer Sheet

1.	Ⓐ	Ⓑ	Ⓒ	Ⓓ	21.	Ⓐ	Ⓑ	Ⓒ	Ⓓ	41.	Ⓐ Ⓑ Ⓒ Ⓓ
2.	Ⓐ	Ⓑ	Ⓒ	Ⓓ	22.	Ⓐ	Ⓑ	Ⓒ	Ⓓ	42.	Ⓐ Ⓑ Ⓒ Ⓓ
3.	Ⓐ	Ⓑ	Ⓒ	Ⓓ	23.	Ⓐ	Ⓑ	Ⓒ	Ⓓ	43.	Ⓐ Ⓑ Ⓒ Ⓓ
4.	Ⓐ	Ⓑ	Ⓒ	Ⓓ	24.	Ⓐ	Ⓑ	Ⓒ	Ⓓ	44.	Ⓐ Ⓑ Ⓒ Ⓓ
5.	Ⓐ	Ⓑ	Ⓒ	Ⓓ	25.	Ⓐ	Ⓑ	Ⓒ	Ⓓ	45.	Ⓐ Ⓑ Ⓒ Ⓓ
6.	Ⓐ	Ⓑ	Ⓒ	Ⓓ	26.	Ⓐ	Ⓑ	Ⓒ	Ⓓ	46.	Ⓐ Ⓑ Ⓒ Ⓓ
7.	Ⓐ	Ⓑ	Ⓒ	Ⓓ	27.	Ⓐ	Ⓑ	Ⓒ	Ⓓ	47.	Ⓐ Ⓑ Ⓒ Ⓓ
8.	Ⓐ	Ⓑ	Ⓒ	Ⓓ	28.	Ⓐ	Ⓑ	Ⓒ	Ⓓ	48.	Ⓐ Ⓑ Ⓒ Ⓓ
9.	Ⓐ	Ⓑ	Ⓒ	Ⓓ	29.	Ⓐ	Ⓑ	Ⓒ	Ⓓ	49.	Ⓐ Ⓑ Ⓒ Ⓓ
10.	Ⓐ	Ⓑ	Ⓒ	Ⓓ	30.	Ⓐ	Ⓑ	Ⓒ	Ⓓ	50.	Ⓐ Ⓑ Ⓒ Ⓓ
11.	Ⓐ	Ⓑ	Ⓒ	Ⓓ	31.	Ⓐ	Ⓑ	Ⓒ	Ⓓ	51.	Ⓐ Ⓑ Ⓒ Ⓓ
12.	Ⓐ	Ⓑ	Ⓒ	Ⓓ	32.	Ⓐ	Ⓑ	Ⓒ	Ⓓ	52.	Ⓐ Ⓑ Ⓒ Ⓓ
13.	Ⓐ	Ⓑ	Ⓒ	Ⓓ	33.	Ⓐ	Ⓑ	Ⓒ	Ⓓ	53.	Ⓐ Ⓑ Ⓒ Ⓓ
14.	Ⓐ	Ⓑ	Ⓒ	Ⓓ	34.	Ⓐ	Ⓑ	Ⓒ	Ⓓ	54.	Ⓐ Ⓑ Ⓒ Ⓓ
15.	Ⓐ	Ⓑ	Ⓒ	Ⓓ	35.	Ⓐ	Ⓑ	Ⓒ	Ⓓ	55.	Ⓐ Ⓑ Ⓒ Ⓓ
16.	Ⓐ	Ⓑ	Ⓒ	Ⓓ	36.	Ⓐ	Ⓑ	Ⓒ	Ⓓ	56.	Ⓐ Ⓑ Ⓒ Ⓓ
17.	Ⓐ	Ⓑ	Ⓒ	Ⓓ	37.	Ⓐ	Ⓑ	Ⓒ	Ⓓ	57.	Ⓐ Ⓑ Ⓒ Ⓓ
18.	Ⓕ	Ⓖ	Ⓗ	Ⓘ	38.	Ⓐ	Ⓑ	Ⓒ	Ⓓ	58.	Ⓐ Ⓑ Ⓒ Ⓓ
19.	Ⓐ	Ⓑ	Ⓒ	Ⓓ	39.	Ⓐ	Ⓑ	Ⓒ	Ⓓ	59.	Ⓐ Ⓑ Ⓒ Ⓓ
20.	Ⓐ	Ⓑ	Ⓒ	Ⓓ	40.	Ⓐ	Ⓑ	Ⓒ	Ⓓ	60.	Ⓐ Ⓑ Ⓒ Ⓓ

Biology Practice Test B

Answer Sheet

1. Ⓐ Ⓑ Ⓒ Ⓓ
2. Ⓐ Ⓑ Ⓒ Ⓓ
3. Ⓐ Ⓑ Ⓒ Ⓓ
4. Ⓐ Ⓑ Ⓒ Ⓓ
5. Ⓐ Ⓑ Ⓒ Ⓓ
6. Ⓐ Ⓑ Ⓒ Ⓓ
7. Ⓐ Ⓑ Ⓒ Ⓓ
8. Ⓐ Ⓑ Ⓒ Ⓓ
9. Ⓐ Ⓑ Ⓒ Ⓓ
10. Ⓐ Ⓑ Ⓒ Ⓓ
11. Ⓐ Ⓑ Ⓒ Ⓓ
12. Ⓐ Ⓑ Ⓒ Ⓓ
13. Ⓐ Ⓑ Ⓒ Ⓓ
14. Ⓐ Ⓑ Ⓒ Ⓓ
15. Ⓐ Ⓑ Ⓒ Ⓓ
16. Ⓐ Ⓑ Ⓒ Ⓓ
17. Ⓐ Ⓑ Ⓒ Ⓓ
18. Ⓕ Ⓖ Ⓗ Ⓘ
19. Ⓐ Ⓑ Ⓒ Ⓓ
20. Ⓐ Ⓑ Ⓒ Ⓓ

21. Ⓐ Ⓑ Ⓒ Ⓓ
22. Ⓐ Ⓑ Ⓒ Ⓓ
23. Ⓐ Ⓑ Ⓒ Ⓓ
24. Ⓐ Ⓑ Ⓒ Ⓓ
25. Ⓐ Ⓑ Ⓒ Ⓓ
26. Ⓐ Ⓑ Ⓒ Ⓓ
27. Ⓐ Ⓑ Ⓒ Ⓓ
28. Ⓐ Ⓑ Ⓒ Ⓓ
29. Ⓐ Ⓑ Ⓒ Ⓓ
30. Ⓐ Ⓑ Ⓒ Ⓓ
31. Ⓐ Ⓑ Ⓒ Ⓓ
32. Ⓐ Ⓑ Ⓒ Ⓓ
33. Ⓐ Ⓑ Ⓒ Ⓓ
34. Ⓐ Ⓑ Ⓒ Ⓓ
35. Ⓐ Ⓑ Ⓒ Ⓓ
36. Ⓐ Ⓑ Ⓒ Ⓓ
37. Ⓐ Ⓑ Ⓒ Ⓓ
38. Ⓐ Ⓑ Ⓒ Ⓓ
39. Ⓐ Ⓑ Ⓒ Ⓓ
40. Ⓐ Ⓑ Ⓒ Ⓓ

41. Ⓐ Ⓑ Ⓒ Ⓓ
42. Ⓐ Ⓑ Ⓒ Ⓓ
43. Ⓐ Ⓑ Ⓒ Ⓓ
44. Ⓐ Ⓑ Ⓒ Ⓓ
45. Ⓐ Ⓑ Ⓒ Ⓓ
46. Ⓐ Ⓑ Ⓒ Ⓓ
47. Ⓐ Ⓑ Ⓒ Ⓓ
48. Ⓐ Ⓑ Ⓒ Ⓓ
49. Ⓐ Ⓑ Ⓒ Ⓓ
50. Ⓐ Ⓑ Ⓒ Ⓓ
51. Ⓐ Ⓑ Ⓒ Ⓓ
52. Ⓐ Ⓑ Ⓒ Ⓓ
53. Ⓐ Ⓑ Ⓒ Ⓓ
54. Ⓐ Ⓑ Ⓒ Ⓓ
55. Ⓐ Ⓑ Ⓒ Ⓓ
56. Ⓐ Ⓑ Ⓒ Ⓓ
57. Ⓐ Ⓑ Ⓒ Ⓓ
58. Ⓐ Ⓑ Ⓒ Ⓓ
59. Ⓐ Ⓑ Ⓒ Ⓓ
60. Ⓐ Ⓑ Ⓒ Ⓓ

Notes

Notes

Notes

Notes

Notes

Notes

Notes

Notes

Notes

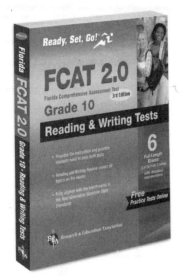
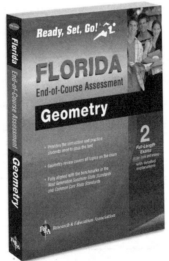
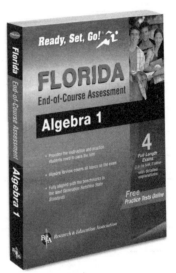